Four Homeless Millionaires

How one family found riches
by leaving everything behind

RIK LEAF

PROMONTORY
PRESS

Cover design by Marla Thompson of Edge of Water Designs

Published by Promontory Press
www.promontorypress.com

Second Edition-April 2015

ISBN 978-1-927559-90-1

Printed in Canada

0 9 8 7 6 5 4 3 2 1

Preface

I inherited a love of telling stories from my Mom. I spent my childhood watching her and her friends dress up and perform skits and silly songs on stage. I loved watching her make people howl with laughter.

When I was really young and money was tight, she sold Tupperware. Five nights a week she'd pull out of the driveway, her car packed to the gills with plastic products that she'd sell at house parties. Through her crazy antics and hilarious sense of humour, she could have a house full of ladies claiming her Tupperware party was the best night out they'd had all year.

This is something I often think of when I'm on tour, filling my car to the gills with instruments and CDs, and the thrill I feel taking the stage to share my stories and songs with rooms full of people.

This book is a celebration of my Mom's encouragement to take risks and live the most exciting life possible, and the joy that comes from sharing it with others.

To avoid any confusion (or maternal retribution), the filthy language and irreverent sense of humour are mine. My mother's hands are clean ... she spent the first eighteen years of my life scrubbing my mouth out with soap.

I am deeply thankful for all the talented, passionate individuals at Promontory Press that helped me craft this story.

Zara, Zion, Riel, and I want to thank all the incredibly generous people that opened their homes and gave us a place to stay throughout the year. My Mom, Paul & Corey, Bruce & Kathy, Curtis & Andrea, Doug & Sharon, Marie-Josee & Johanna, Ian

& Ros, John & Judith, David & Lisa, RoseAnna, Darin & Erika, Kevin & Heather, Sean & Alice, Peter & Christine, Dom & Emma, Anthony & Bernadette, Graeme & Margie, Ben & Liz, Kevin & Louise, John & Marie, Don & Judy, John & Jean, Gray & Ngaire, Howard & Pauline, Paulo & Gillian, Amanda, Franco & Katherine, Peder & Tina, Christer & Lena, Hakan & Margaretta, Arno & Dani, Richard & Lorna, Paul & Sarah, Bob & Claire, Christopher & Katherine, Rob & Nikki, Ryan & Anna, Johnny and Juliet, Nadine, Shane & Catharine. We would never have been able to afford our homelessness without you!

Live Deep, Travel Light

Table of Contents

Four Homeless Millionaires

CANADA

A Whirlwind of Epic Nose-Plowing Proportions

Stars explode behind my eyes as a wave of darkness and nausea blurs my vision. I've never been punched in the face before and it is every bit as awful as I imagined it would be. I reel across the lawn holding my face in my hands, expecting to see and feel a hot sticky bloodbath gushing between my fingers as I open my eyes.

When I'm finally able to focus, I see Zara and the kids are tracking my stumbling gait as we lurch across the lawn like a migrating flock of birds. Gathering in concert, their concern forces me to try to turn the NC-17 tirade bubbling to my lips into something more PG-13.

"HOLY … SON OF A … MOTHER … FUGGER!" I sputter lamely.

Riel is a sweet, sensitive nine-year-old girl as startled as she is concerned and firing questions in all directions trying to make sense of what just happened to her Dad. I want to comfort her and tell her it's all going to be OK, but I've got my figurative hands full trying to turn my 'f#%s' into 'fuggs' and 's#%s' into 'shizas'. To make matters worse, I'm the ass that just punched me in the face.

I've been loading what remains of our worldly possessions into our mini van that is now bulging like a pregnant walrus. It's not even 9:00 a.m. and I've spent the last two hours sweating and swearing like a teamster trying to pack an ungodly amount of crap.

Instead of a hard shell roof rack, we bought a giant roof bag, which seemed to be working great as I was stuffing all manner of things in it. The problem started when I tried to close it. This is how I ended up standing half in half out of the van, with my body suspended at a 45-degree angle, pulling on the zipper towards myself with all my might when my sweaty hands slipped and I plowed myself in the nose. If the truly courageous in this life are the ones willing to face a humble beginning, I am Richard the Brave.

Twelve months ago my wife Zara and I started making plans to sell our house in Winnipeg, Manitoba, so we could spend a year traveling around the world with our son Zion (13) and our daughter Riel (9). After a year of dreaming and scheming, it has all come crashing down to a whirlwind of epic nose-plowing proportions. At this stage, we only know one thing; we are not coming back to Winnipeg. We plan to spend the first three months traveling from coast to coast in Canada in an attempt to find out where we might like to land when all the travel is done. In November, right about the time winter comes to Canada we will head to Hawaii, Malaysia, Australia and New Zealand, before spending our last three months touring across Europe.

For weeks now we've been packing, selling off furniture, giving things away to friends, renting storage bays, arranging moving trucks, racing all over the city from one end to the other signing papers at lawyers and banks, getting final readings for utility companies, canceling accounts and buying travel insurance. Now that it's crunch time I'm worried I've got a soft, creamy centre.

As the exploding stars and nausea fade, the good news is there is no blood; the bad news is, any vestige of positive vibes and happy laid-back Dad are gone. Zara mutters something about me being a menace to society as she heads back in the house.

At midnight, the new owners officially took possession of our house and we are still not entirely out. They arrive twenty minutes later with two trailers full of stuff and a happy crew of Christians from their church to help them move in.

This makes the sewer spewing from my lips less vulgar and more profane. I just can't believe how much stuff we still have kicking around underfoot. The four of us start scrambling around the house grabbing anything and everything and throwing it willy-nilly onto the veranda: blankets and pillows, the coffee maker, a loaf of bread, peanut butter and jam, some odd clothes, a broom, a bottle of gin and some tonic. Pretty soon it looks like a thrift store took a dump on our porch. I apologize profusely to the new owners who, thank God, are prayerfully focused on God blessing their new home and don't seem particularly concerned with my pagan presence.

In the past forty-eight hours, we have realized there is such a thing as too many good ideas in one place at one time. Our plan was for Zara and the kids to leave first thing in the morning and drive fourteen hours from Winnipeg, Manitoba to my mom's place outside Calgary, Alberta. My band, Tribe of One, is performing at the Brandon Folk Festival in a few hours, which is why I'm not going with them. I'll play tonight in Brandon, drive back to Winnipeg in the morning, jump on a plane and meet up with Zara and the kids in Calgary tomorrow night for a wedding rehearsal. My niece Brianne is getting married on Sunday and Riel is the flower girl, Zion is an usher, and I'm playing the bridal party down the aisle. They are all great ideas, but trying to combine them in twenty-four hours is not so good.

Even though we've been paring down to the bare necessities for months, every square inch of the van is packed, under, around, beside, and behind every seat from top to bottom. In exasperation with yet another tub of plastic pieces, I ask Zion why he has to have so much Lego.

"I've horcruxed my soul so no one will be able to kill me," he replies, unfazed by my frazzled state.

Eventually I just run out of space and declare that the van is officially loaded. In a frenzied flurry of sweaty hugs and kisses and "see-you-soons", Zara, Zion and Riel take off. No sooner have they disappeared around the corner than my friend Marie-Josée shows up. I'd thrown all our stuff from the porch onto the lawn, which made it seem as if I wasn't moving as much as migrating. We fill MJ's car to the roof and start across the city to her house where I lug the remainder of my worldly possessions, which I'm starting to feel is actually just a bunch of stupid crap, down into her basement. I totally believe this year is going to be the experience of a lifetime; it's just getting out the door that's the trick.

Four hours later I'm in the backseat of another van that is also packed to the roof, this time with instruments, costumes, and regalia. We haven't even hit the city limits and I'm feeling like a Conquistador embroiled in a head-on cultural collision.

I founded Tribe of One twelve years ago with a group of musicians, painters, and dancers, combining our different disciplines into each performance. Over the years, the vision has evolved into a fusion of indigenous cultures and modern forms of artistic expression. Buffy, our Anishinabe First Nations dancer, is driving as we speed through a prairie landscape so empty it's profound. I'm pretty sure just off to the left I can see the middle of nowhere. Tom, our Brazilian capoeira dancer, is in the passenger seat and Marie-Josée, a French Metis, is in the back with me. On stage we are a force to be reckoned with; off stage we are a collision of accents running headlong into a language barrier. Looking around I feel like Sid the Sloth in Ice Age; this is my herd.

Tribe of One is the most exciting job I've ever had. The fusion of Native pow-wow dancing, live performance painting, new world music, and slam poetry combines the creative energy of the most creative people I've known. A couple of weeks earlier we performed at the Great Northern Arts Festival in Inuvik, located a hundred miles north of the Arctic Circle. Last night I performed at a house concert the Member of Parliament hosted to honour my time in the neighbourhood and our work together in the city. A couple of hours from now as I'm tuning my guitar between songs, my mouth will kick into autopilot and I' ll hear myself say, "I just sold my house today."

Which is when it will dawn on me, we actually did it; we sold our house. I'm homeless and our world tour has started.

While I'm on stage in Brandon, Zara, Zion, and Riel pulled into the city of Regina, Saskatchewan. Zara decided to get a hotel with a pool and waterslide so the kids could burn off some steam. Stopping in Regina meant they would need to get up at 5:00 a.m. to drive the remaining eight hours to my mom's place on Saturday. When they arrived, the kids jumped into the shower and my mom hemmed up Riel's dress for the wedding as Zara unloaded the vehicle. That is when she discovered the 'ungodly amount of s#%' (her words not mine) that I had packed, and started referring to our Ford Windstar as the Horn of Plenty. Most guys would love to conjure images of Greek mythology in their partner's eyes. Personally I'd have liked something more along the lines of Dionysus, the god of wine-fueled drunkenness and orgasmic sex, rather than a mythological packer. Cleaned up and sorted out, they all piled back into the van and drove into Calgary for the rehearsal dinner.

That same morning, Tribe of One drove back to Winnipeg, swinging by the airport to dump me off at the curb. With a friendly pat on the back and a goodnatured knuckle bump, they were gone. I'm a poet and a songwriter, so I'd always pictured some deeply profound, teary-eyed moment as I left Winnipeg, my home of twelve years. I envisioned a romantic scenario where I'd write a song about the city shrinking in the rearview mirror as we drove away from the city limits, but that it was closer than it appeared, you know, because of all the memories. I thought maybe we'd pull over on the side of the road, spread a checkered blanket in the grass beside Highway #1 and evoke an ancient blessing ceremony that involved Slurpees and Timbits. Maybe even erect an altar, or at the very least, a monument, that the kids could visit annually. Instead, it felt as profound as someone flushing the toilet. I was just a little turd swirling my way into the great beyond and this was only day two.

As we pulled into my mom's place on Sunday night, we breathed a deep sigh of relief. In the first forty-eight hours of our world tour, we'd sold our house, headlined a folk festival, traveled 1500 kilometres and played, ushered, and sprinkled flowers at a wedding.

I wrote in our day timer: Monday – Chill-the-#@%! Out

The Sacrilegious Spirit In The Embryonic Soup

We're in Three Hills, Alberta, the incredibly small town I grew up in. In many ways, Three Hills is a very typical small prairie town. Downtown is three blocks long; there is one Main Street with a postage stamp post office, one grocery store, two gas stations, and a tavern. A couple of grain elevators and an ancient water tower are the only structures that rise above the prairie fields. What makes Three Hills a wild and crazy place is the religious institution known since its inception in the 1920s as Prairie Bible Institute.

The road that runs in from Highway #21 splits the little town perfectly down the middle. To the south is a sleepy little prairie town. To the north is Prairie Bible Institute, the brain child of L.E. Maxwell, the Orwellian despot and founding father of the faithful flock. Growing up on the south side of the tracks, my friends and I abbreviated P.B.I. to 'Peebs,' a tonal designation we used to describe staff and students from the institute.

My family straddled the divide so to speak. My Grandparents taught at Prairie, both my parents attended high school and Bible school there and the pastor of our small community church was a professor at the Institute.

I had a sneaking suspicion growing up that I was actually part of a Nurture vs. Nature sociology experiment like Eddie Murphy and Dan Akroyd in *Trading Places* meet Stanley Milgram ... in Roswell, New Mexico. One thing is certain, Three Hills was a fertile field for my irreverent imagination and I can honestly say I would not be the man I am today without the experience. It's why I think the Great Stork in the Sky inseminated my sacrilegious spirit into the embryonic soup.

I spent all of my formative years in Three Hills. For most people high school seems to have been a hellish experience with all the stuffing of bodies in lockers, the snapping of bra straps, the potty humour and sexual ambiguity, but for me those were the things that made each day so special.

When I was in grade twelve, my friends and I pitched in $50.00 each and purchased a 1956 International school bus. It had faded purple flames on the hood and a giant smokestack running up the driver's side. And to forestall the obvious question as to why we would want to buy a 1956 International school bus, we needed a vehicle big enough so that we could all cruise together.

A reclusive missionary family of Peebs living in the northern reaches of the province had converted the bus into a post-apocalyptic motor home. The interior was a rickety mish-mash of bunks and beds and there was a big overhang off the back for hauling camping gear and firewood. We gutted the interior, laid some gold wall-to-wall shag, moved in a couple of couches and a beanbag chair. Then we converted the back overhang into a patio, perfect for those hot summer nights when you'd like to grab some lawn chairs and sit out on the back of your vehicle while you and your friends drive up and down the fourteen-and-a-half streets in your small town.

At Christmas time, some oil companies hired us to be their drivehome service. Suddenly our buffoonery was transformed into a vehicle for the noble aspirations of a concerned citizenry. Almost overnight, we were seen as socially responsible crusaders cleaning up the mean streets of Three Hills, as national TV crews and reporters came calling for interviews. I got letters from the Minister of Youth and our MLA praising our virtues and thanking us for being such an inspiration for Canadian youth. My Dad was not impressed with the level of investigative journalism to say the least, knowing that I commonly credited 'The Bus' with being the best opening line I'd ever had with the ladies.

Monday morning I woke up in my old room in my parents' house in Three Hills, and as I lay in bed, it really hit me that our year of travel and adventure has started: so now what? We don't have to get back to work; we don't really have a schedule per se. It feels as if we're in the process of shifting gears; we're going to have to learn how to look at ourselves, our days and schedules in a different way.

I got up, and for the first time in years, started asking what there was to see and do in Three Hills. My mom had just read a story in the paper about an equestrian ranch that had started up just a couple of miles from her farm, so we took Riel for her first riding experience. The couple who owned it were awesome and not only gave us a tour of their farm and their horses, but also gave us a quick history lesson on the styles and backgrounds of horse riding. While Riel donned her little jockey helmet and rode around the arena, Zion spent his time playing with a brood of newborn kittens.

I had a friend from high school also named Rick. These days he is a successful businessman with his own company who still lives in town, but hasn't entirely shed his own unique brand of madness. Rick purchased a vast array of paintball guns for a 'team building' exercise with his employees. Zion has been jonesing for some paintball action ever since I took him and his friends to a range in Winnipeg for his 11th birthday. I made the call and asked Rick if there was any chance we could do some team building of our own. Two days later there we were, following the kind of directions you get from people who live in the country, "pass such-and-such an intersection, go over the hill and past the farm with lots of junk in the yard, turn left down a gravel road until you see a sign hanging on a barbed wire fence that says "No Trespassing".

We pull off the road and start navigating a couple of parallel goat trails that lead me to believe vehicles have come this way before. I'm just starting to think I'm not in the right farmer's pasture when one of Rick's sons comes flying over the hill on a quad. His face is hidden behind an impressive grill on his wrap-around helmet, but he flashes some military-type hand signals that seem to communicate that we, in Charlie Company, should keep our eyes open, our heads down, and follow him. There's some other stuff I don't understand, an eagle might be in the air or maybe a knock list is in the open. It's either that or he's telling us we're pussies who can kiss his ass. It's kind of hard to tell with all the bouncing around going on.

We follow him to a camp hidden deep in a clearing of trees that I can only describe as what I envision a group of Afghani freedom fighters would set up if they were converted by Peeb missionaries and moved to Three Hills. There are army jeeps and tanks and huge metal storage containers hidden back under the thick foliage, presumably to avoid detection from NORAD satellites and black ops reconnaissance drones. Army guys have always kind of freaked me out, and I start scanning the tree line for sentries or anyone wearing a keffiyeh. Just then, Rick comes barreling through the trees on a tractor and waves us over. I discover Rick is a passionate WWII collector and travels to auctions all over North America, buying whatever he can get his hands on. One of his latest and greatest acquisitions is a 4-ton Bedford REME (Royal Electrical & Mechanical Engineers) personnel carrier used by the British Army in WWII. Rick has two boys who jump up into the carrier on the back along with Zion and his cousin Remond, as I clamber up into the passenger seat. Rick takes off through the pasture with an evil grin and gleam in his eye, heading straight for the steepest hill he can find. Without a word of warning to the boys in the back, he starts climbing up the hill, bouncing over logs and debris. I barely keep my seat enough to turn around to see how the boys are doing. I hear an awful commotion of crashing and screaming as the kids get nutted in the crotch with pieces of corrugated plastic pipe and other garbage while they hold on for dear life to seventy-year-old leather safety straps. After a rousing display of all-terrain driving, we get down to the serious business of sneaking through the woods and shooting each other with paintballs. The kids play a few rounds and then we do a few more rounds mixing up the teams. Then just as the sun is starting to set, Rick looks around the circle and says, "Hey, maybe for the last round it should be my boys and me against the rest of you."

I'm not the only one who feels a sudden chill in the air and a sense of foreboding that the stakes have suddenly gotten a lot higher. Of course, we agree. As we skirt the depths of the dark forest on our way back to our starting point, we made sure to ask God for forgiveness and mercy as we prepare to enter a world of pain.

Moments later, Zion and I are moving with speed under the cover of stealth. I'm fully expecting booby traps and pits with sharpened stakes at the bottom, or the old tree-trunk-swinging-down-through-the-branches-at-chest-height trick. Zion raises his left hand in a fist, signalling an immediate stop. Following his gaze, I see one of Rick's sons, crouched down beside a tree. As Zion takes careful aim, Christian, perhaps sensing his imminent demise yells out, "Just a second; my gun is jammed."

Neither Zion nor I make a move or a sound. Seconds later, before the K, of OK, is fully out of Christian's mouth, Zion squeezes the trigger, sniping Christian in the face guard. He follows up his kill shot with an excited blast meant to humiliate his opponent before Christian can yell hit.

Just as I'm congratulating Zion on a great shot I hear a fire fight explode over on the left. I start moving in that direction when our teammate Jason yells, "Rik, move in, I've got him pinned down!"

I stand and run, crashing through branches and brambles as gunfire and screams fill the woods. My heart is thumping as I crest the rise and see the lay of the land. Rick has wedged himself in a shallow hollow, ringed with thin brush that perfectly disguises his location. Jason is on a rise above him on the other side of the clearing, firing down on his position. The entire length of Rick's body is exposed from my vantage point. I waste no time in flicking off my safety and jumping out from behind a tree firing. Everyone who plays paintball knows that when you get hit you're supposed to yell "hit" and raise your gun and walk off the field. I unload a dozen bullets into Rick's torso. But he never says "hit", so I unload a couple of dozen more, moving my barrel ever so slightly up and down and side to side, just to make sure I'm covering every square inch. Still, he never says "hit", though he does turn and start returning fire in my direction. I duck behind the tree and rest my back against the trunk as it absorbs Rick's return fire while Jason rains hell and damnation from the ridge. As Rick turns back to return fire with Jason, I pop out once again, this time emptying dozens and dozens of paintballs into Rick's body. Finally, he yells, "OK. OK, I'm hit. Bloody hell, I'm hit."

He's covered in leaves and underbrush, with bright splashes of paint masking most of his body as blood pours freely down his face where numerous paint balls have hit his head, opening up his scalp. Our return trek to camp is a loud raucous affair as everyone tells his version of hits and near misses. Zion claims it was the best homeschooling Phys. Ed. class ever.

The Most Realistic People On the Planet

We continued our westward migration by heading to Canmore. Nestled in the bosom of the Rocky Mountains just down the road from Banff National Park, Canmore has a funky small town, wilderness vibe. With seventy kilometres of trails within the town limits, Canmore is an active, nature-based community. We arranged to stay with Paul and Corey, some friends I'd met over the years through touring. They have four kids; their youngest two, Logan (13) and Mack (12), are mirror images of Zion, which means our son was in heaven. He threw his pillow and blanket in a heap in the corner, grabbed an X-box controller and emotionally, at least, moved in. The family also has a pug named Quigley, which meant Riel was in a heaven of her own, playing, petting, and taking Quigley for walks. I'd stayed with Paul and Corey at their B&B a few times when I was touring, but this was the first time I'd been there with Zara. It was an awesome few days. Logan and Mack both had part time jobs at a local coffee shop, providing them with disposable income to fuel their burgeoning social lives. It was the first time we'd ever seen Zion strolling around town like a gadabout, sipping $6 mocha frappuccinos.

Much to Zion's incredulity, we hadn't come to Canmore to play X-Box 24/7 and he was extremely put out when we insisted he join the rest of the family as we headed up to Johnston Canyon where rushing glacial water has carved a deep path through the limestone terrain. It was a spectacular five-and-a-half kilometre hike beside waterfalls and deep pools of crystal-clear mountain-fed water. Some sections of the trail were carved into the side of the canyon and others hung suspended over the river. It was late July and the peak of the tourist season. The trail had heavy foot traffic going both ways.

Zion clung to his pissy mood in retaliation for removing him from his heavenly experience playing X-Box with Logan and Mack, complaining incessantly about the strenuous nature of our leisurely stroll. I responded in kind by continually pointing out senior citizens and toddlers who were passing us, in an effort to shame him. But a teen wallowing in the throes of self-pity cannot be rescued through pedestrian observation. Somewhere along the way, I changed my tactical approach from encouragement to mocking, derision, and public humiliation.

Banff National Park draws tourists from all over the world and at times it felt as if we were on a path leading to the tower of Babel. It seemed as if every group passing us was speaking another language. I tried to employ the ancient parental art of embarrassing your child into a malleable state of subservience through public humiliation. I would wait until we were about to pass a group of tourists and then I'd start talking excitedly to Zion in fake languages. "Un Vicodin, Fluevog, a Guggenheim et Zion?" I said in faux German gesticulating wildly. Not even a smirk.

"Bienvenue, a je ne sais quoi, Louis Vuitton, L'Oréal et Peugeot and Citroën," I exclaimed in animated pretend French, suggestively miming large bosoms and curvaceous bottoms with my hands as I spoke.

His only response was to increase his speed and power ahead of us down the trail before I could rock some Klingon and Uruk-hai.

Riel was happily nibbling away on an apple, throwing little pieces to squirrels along the path. I had just stopped filming and put the Flip back in my pocket, when an ambitious little squirrel jumped up and grabbed the whole apple out of her hand. It turned to dart back into the forest with its gigantic prize that weighed more than it did. The last we saw, it was barrel-assing its way down the mountain with all four paws dug in and hanging on for dear life.

We had a great supper back at the B&B, and as Zion and the boys disappeared and Riel ran off to spend some quality time with Quigley, we sat down with Paul and Corey and started talking about the actual day-to-day grind of investing in dreams. Zara and I had just had a conversation with someone who had oohed and aahed about what we are doing, exclaiming that this was exactly what they wanted to do. But it was one of those conversations where we got the distinct impression that what they really meant was, if everything in their life could stay the same and there was absolutely no risk involved, then they would love to risk everything and do something wildly adventurous too. Of course, then they wouldn't be doing anything like what we're doing.

Somewhere in the conversation, Paul gave me a timely piece of advice, though in the moment I had no idea how soon I would need it.

"When you're a creative person, you get ideas all the time, and it's easy to think that that's how it is for everyone, but it isn't. You need to recognize that your ideas have creative and monetary value, and are integral to establishing an innovative career in a competitive market. But for that to happen, you have to invest in your ideas, you have to take risks to turn those creative ideas into action."

We savoured many moments of that long conversation, poured over numerous glasses of Cabernet and Shiraz.

Personally, I think dreamers are the most realistic people on the planet. For a dreamer, hope is not tied to probabilities, but possibilities; to what could be, as opposed to just what is. As we were dreaming and scheming on how to make this year a reality, the world had entered an economic recession. Politicians and policy makers, economists and market advisers were counseling the global community to batten down the hatches with fierce fiscal restraint and weather the storm of the century. But if we believed them, we'd never do anything. I guess ultimately as artists, this is where Zara and I have an incredible advantage. Our 'job' is creating something out of nothing, whether it's a song, a painting, or a tattoo. We work with the palette of possibility every day to create something we've never said, sung, or seen before.

Some of the choices we've made over the years have allowed us to do what we're doing this year. Zara and I have never bought furniture, appliances, electronics, or a vehicle on a payment plan, we hardly ever eat out in restaurants, and we carry no outstanding monthly balance on our credit cards. When we sold our house and no longer had a mortgage payment or monthly utilities, we were left with one monthly bill to pay: $168.00 for the 10' x 10' storage bay where we put our worldly possessions.

It seems like most people end up working harder at jobs they hate so they can buy things they don't need to fill the house they can't afford. But what do I know … the saner I feel, the crazier the world and everyone in it seems.

A few years ago, I switched our high speed Internet from DSL to cable. The cable company offered a better rate for phone and long distance so we switched that at the same time. Then they offered us the full cable TV package. We'd never had cable TV before, in part because we just watch lots of movies, but also because my attention span does not exist to be interrupted every six minutes for commercials. But the offer sounded like a novelty, so I agreed to the two-month free trial. Cable TV was exciting for about five minutes. Then it just pissed me off.

The thing that struck me as the most insidious was the constant barrage of highly manipulative, overly rendered marketing messages bombarding my kids. Our home had always been a place, maybe the only place, free from all that crap. But I didn't want to make some patriarchal pronouncement about canceling it, so at supper we sat around the table and talked about it. Zion was probably nine at the time, so Riel would have been five. My argument was that for some people cable TV is understandable, but that I felt that we were too talented, artistic, and gifted to waste our time with it. In the end, the four of us agreed we'd cancel the cable. I don't think we even had it two weeks.

Zion is a great cheerleader, and for weeks after our decision, he would walk through the house loudly proclaiming that he just more creative now that we'd canceled the cable. "I've noticed that

I'm playing with Lego more and drawing more," he would pontificate. Not wanting to leave Riel out of the effusive praise, he would loudly applaud her creative genius every time he'd see her playing with her stuffies or Polly Pockets.

Holy S#*! Babe! That's Messed Up

From Canmore we continued west over the Rocky Mountains and across the Strait of Georgia to Vancouver Island. Some incredibly generous friends offered to let us use their cabin for a week.

After the initial madness of getting out of Winnipeg, it was awesome to be staying somewhere where the worst that could happen in a given day was too much peace and quiet. The cabin sits on six acres of farmland just minutes from the beach. There was a little creepy forest beside the cabin with an abandoned shack that looked like the type of place they show on the news as the anchor says: "forensic teams have been working around the clock trying to identify the remains."

Riel and I decided to make a horror movie. She did her own wardrobe and makeup, making it look like she had a little black eye. I filmed her running around being chased by someone or something. That's when we hit a snag. What exactly was she running from? Kids these days have pretty much seen everything, so Riel's initial suggestions were fantastical and amazing, but each would require the full processing power of Weta Workshop, and the combined efforts of a dozen green screens and stunt teams.

I was embarrassed to admit I was thinking more along the lines of a bed sheet with eyeholes. I ended up taking a thin black headscarf and wrapping it tight around my face and pulling up a black hoodie. Then we found an axe by the woodpile, which seemed menacing and horror movieish. Which is how I found myself standing in the shadows inside the creepy shack, hoping a skunk or raccoon wasn't about to charge me, as Riel ran the camera from the doorway and said "action!"

I loomed up from the dirt floor raising the axe above my head rushing at the camera simulating a killing blow. Riel and I thought we were really onto something and were congratulating ourselves on our gritty indie realism. It was all great until Zara caught me editing the film hours later and muttered something under her breath that sounded like, "Holy s#% babe! That's seriously messed up!"

Apparently a psychotic crazy man swinging an axe at a little nine year-old girl in a forest was going too far, which is something I told Riel artists need to do from time to time to determine their boundaries.

So the next day we shot pickups for a different ending; Riel dutifully changed back into her outfit and applied her eye make up and we created a different ending. By this point Zion had become involved on a creative level and suggested that perhaps the forest was haunted and the trees were trying to kill the little girl. Zion doubled as our special effects unit, tying a fishing line to tree branches and tugging them as Riel walked underneath. During the filming, a bunch of Zara's siblings arrived. That night we all sat around on the back deck sipping wine and hot chocolate around the fire while Riel did voice-overs.

"Quiet on the set," I'd say, and a hush would fall as we all listened to Riel project various degrees of scaredness and fear into her voice, as she'd say, "hello … is anyone there?"

The next day, with siblings in tow, we all piled into the van and drove up to Elk Falls Provincial Park located west of Campbell River. It was an amazing hobbit-like hike down the trail that brought us to this gorgeous twenty-five metre waterfall where the Campbell River cascades over a rocky precipice into a canyon below. We hiked around for a while before deciding to head up the trail above the falls where we discovered a serene pool. The water was intoxicatingly blue and the trees and moss were electric green. It was one of those moments when you just know you have to immerse yourself because it may never come around again. Before Zion and Riel knew what was happening, and long before they had emotionally prepared themselves, their parents and aunties had all shimmied out of their clothes and were swimming in their underwear.

Zion would later describe the experience to his uncle Nick, "I will never forget the day my eyes were burned out of their sockets when my Dad took his pants off."

Our hosts had left us with a little list of local spots to find while we were there. One of them was a place called Stokum Falls. The Puntledge River runs from the Forbidden Plateau down to the town of Courtenay where it empties into the ocean. At Stokum Falls waters runs, often only inches deep, over soft limestone. Over the years, the water has carved incredible pothole Jacuzzis. We discovered several tiered waterfalls that cascaded down into swimming pools where we took turns jumping off rocks into cool water or lying out on sunwarmed stones. We spent hours down there, and thanks to uncle Nick and his waterproof camera, got some spectacular footage.

Before we left Winnipeg, I had decided to create a series of videos throughout the year called *Where in the World Are Zion and Riel?*, We bought a Flip, a pocket-size digital video camera with a USB connector that 'flips' up, allowing the camera to be directly connected to a laptop. Using iMovie on my Mac, I was able to create short films combining photographs and video segments. I used songs from CDs I've released over the years as the template and soundtrack. I created a YouTube channel specifically for these videos and let friends and fans know they could go to YouTube.com/zionriel to keep up with our adventures along the way. From a purely practical point of view, it could not have been better. The Flip has sixty minutes of digital memory, which meant I had to keep dumping it into my computer if I wanted to keep the footage. This was so much better than arriving back home after a year of traveling, with a shoebox full of video tapes that no one would ever look through. The fact that the cameras could fit in our pockets also meant we had them with us everywhere we went. With no camera bags, tapes, batteries, or tripods necessary, we had our cameras with us for everything from mountain hikes to surfing in the ocean. *Zion & Riel – Stokum Falls* was the first video we posted, followed closely by *Haunted Forest*.

When we got back to the cabin, I wandered around the pasture at the end of the driveway holding up my laptop as I slowly turned in circles. One of the neighbours must have Wi-Fi, but the signal kept coming and going. I finally caught a couple of bars and managed to download my emails, including one from Marie-Josée, my music partner from Tribe of One.

Back in March, MJ and I had met with a director of a musical association. We had been working on a grant proposal. It was a collaborative project between indigenous artists from Canada, Australia, and New Zealand. While I am on tour this year, I am hoping to connect with some artists from these countries. MJ and I had approached the director with an invitation for him to be part of our proposal. We thought his involvement might open some doors with similar music associations in these countries.

MJ's startling email informed me that this same director had just approached her, inviting her to be part of a project he was submitting to the same funding agency, for a proposed collaboration between indigenous artists from Canada, Australia, and New Zealand. It was a direct rip off: the plan, the schedule, the countries, and artists. The email felt like a giant vacuum that threatened to suck up all the beauty of the day, the tranquility of the cabin, and the excitement of our adventure. If I had not just had my conversation in Canmore with Paul about the monetary and creative value of my ideas, and their role in allowing me to establish an innovative career in a highly competitive market, I probably would not have reacted the way I did. But I'd been starting to realize that the "starving artist" category might exist because people keep stealing ideas from artists and because the artists don't recognize the value of who they are and what they bring to the table.

We had only been touring for a month, but even in that short amount of time the lights were starting to come on. I was able to view the world of possibilities without looking through the lens of the industry. Gatekeepers usually only have power if we are convinced we need to go through their gate. Turn a few degrees left or right and all of a sudden, you see a great big world just waiting to be discovered. I was freer than I'd ever appreciated. I was touring the world, on my own dime, with my family. We were going where we wanted, doing whatever we wanted when we got there, and it wasn't anyone's business but ours. It was an awesome revelation. So far, the adventure and discovery I'd hoped to experience during the whole year was far exceeding my expectation.

After an awesome week at the cabin, we packed up and traveled down Vancouver Island's interior highway to spend the afternoon along Victoria's waterfront taking in the expansive personalities of street performers.

Dragon boats raced in the harbour, a guy on a unicycle was juggling machetes as a group of African percussionists busking outside Starbucks drew a crowd so big people were spilling out into traffic, clogging the downtown corridor. We ate sushi on a grassy bank down by the water where we watched hippie-wannabes smoke an impressive amount of weed. From Victoria we made our way to Swartz Bay to catch the ferry back to the mainland where we were going to head up and over the Coquihalla Highway to Kelowna.

There had been a few emotional hiccups along the way. Riel inflicted an ill-tempered mood born out of hunger and thirst upon the rest of us. Once we scored her an obscenely-priced fruit smoothie and some veggies, we managed to equalize her dietary ballast and crawl out from the emotional shelters where we go to weather her storms.

As the ferry set sail, I strolled along the decks enjoying the West Coast scenery as it slowly slid by. Though I've learned to embrace my unique blend of creative chaos, I've never been able to figure out why everyone else's photographs are cooler than mine. I go to great lengths trying to take cool photos, practically turning the process into an extreme sport.

On this sunny August day, I wandered around the deck hanging my ass over the edge of the ferry to shoot exterior shots of the bow. I crawled around on all fours snapping shots through sheer undergarments and over toupees. I spent ten minutes panting hot, heavy sex breaths on the lens trying to create a faux mist and still my pictures lacked a certain joie de vivre.

In the midst of my full-blown psycho-photographic episode,

I noticed a middle-aged Asian man lurking suspiciously in the shadows. It wasn't really his Asian-ness or middle-agedness that caught my eye … it was his shadowiness.

He's wearing a nondescript tan windbreaker, white running shoes, blue jeans and a dark blue fisherman's cap. He has large framed glasses that are almost touching the brim of his hat. His overall unassuming demeanor is brought into sharp contrast with what he's holding in his hands; it doesn't look like a camera as much as it does the nose off a space shuttle. His prodigious photographic girth dangles between his legs like a gargantuan phallic lens that leaves me feeling completely inadequate, not just as a photographer, but as a man. Standing there with my puny digital camera with its little retractable nubbins, I'm filled with shame and deep-seated body issues. This little emotional cocktail transports me back to grade seven when raging hormones and track pants would betray my pre-pubescent stiffy morning after morning as I tried desperately to walk unobtrusively through the high school halls to my locker. All of this triggered what my therapist calls an incapacitating neurotic episode, and in the blink of an eye, I recognize that this innocuous-looking traveler is in fact almost certainly an international spy with nefarious ties to the Asian triads.

I search the deck for The Mark. Within moments, I've sussed out the entire situation. I'm pretty sure there's a knock list involved and this character wants to get the list into the open. Money laundering is not only possible, but probable, which means unscrupulous international bankers are involved, whom everyone knows are in bed with Columbian drug cartels. I wipe my sweaty palms on my shorts, amazed at how quickly our innocent day trip has turned into such a frigging nightmare.

"How is it," I mutter under my breath, "that innocent people always get caught up in this kind of drama."

Our situation aboard the ferry puts us in a vulnerable position and I assume before we reach the Tsawwassen terminal we can expect a highjacking on the high seas. I scan the horizon, expecting to see a Norwegian whaling ship bearing down on our port side. I can actually *feel* the satellite orbiting thousands of feet above us broadcasting our images to a secret NORAD facility where army brass move us around like pawns on an international chessboard, casually referring to us as acceptable collateral damage. Instinctively, I pull the brim of my own cap down a bit lower and make sure I don't look up. Mrs. Leaf didn't raise no fool.

Every once in a while, Agent X raises his protuberance to his eye and snaps away. Then he goes back to trying not to be noticed.

"What an amateur!" I guffaw aloud, startling an elderly couple who quickly move away from me.

A lack of inter-agency cooperation allowed us to arrive without incident. With my own limited resources, I was never able to get an ID on the perp. I watched the news for the next couple of days waiting to see officers escorting Agent X into a squad car. I never saw him on the news, but that doesn't mean anything. These cabals are able to whitewash the news. Hell, most of them own their own media corporation to control the spin. I'm just saying, I know what I saw.

Please visit our YouTube channel where all of the videos from our world tour are available.

Stokum Falls is the first video in the series and celebrates the amazing, natural beauty of Vancouver Island as we play in some spectacular waterfalls.

Haunted Forest was a fun way to spend a couple days running around the woods together letting our imaginations run wild.

Reduced to a Puddle of Blubbering Tears

We grabbed some food while the kids fired up movies in the back of the van, and headed over the Coquihalla Highway for Kelowna. Zion in particular was beside himself with excitement as he anticipated his reunion with his old friends Mik and Cai: apparently the most awesomest friends a kid could ever have. As we came down the connector highway and hit the outskirts of the city, Zion's positivity was firing on all cylinders.

"Oh my God! Look at that McDonalds," he exclaimed. "That is the best-looking McDonalds I've ever seen ... and that's saying something!"

The spirit of Cai and Mik was sprinkled like fairy dust over everything. Zion oohed and aahed over the glass architecture of a Staples storefront, professed amazement with the Dairy Queen on the highway, and claimed the city lights reflecting on the surface of Lake Okanagan looked liked a host of angels dancing on a mirror.

Zara, Riel, and I were starting to believe we were going to find Mik and Cai in swaddling clothes lying in a manger at the peak of Dilworth Mountain. We pulled into the yard under the cloak of darkness and all enjoyed a grand reunion with some of our best friends: Bruce and Kath and family. We sat out under the stars eating late-season cherries, spitting the pits off the deck while sipping gin and tonic; it was hard to believe life could get any better.

In 1998, we'd moved from Kelowna to Winnipeg with Bruce and Kath. For three years, we'd lived in the same house, founding Tribe of One together and forging a friendship that would last a lifetime. Their daughter Alexa and Riel were born weeks apart, and are as close as Zion is with Mik and Cai.

They moved back to Kelowna in 2003 and now live on an orchard. In addition to an amazing amount of food production, they've also developed an RV park on the property. Basically, that means there's more work to do than there are hours in the day.

On the first morning, I make an important decision. Rather than getting involved in some meaningful way in an activity that resembles manual labor, I decide to borrow a mountain bike and go for a ride. Kelowna is a resort destination located on Lake Okanagan. In summer, it's an arid desert with suffocating temperatures, and it's at high noon that I make my asinine decision to go riding.

As an active biker back in Winnipeg, I think nothing of charging off down the gravel road that eventually peters out into a path that runs along an ancient aqueduct used decades earlier for irrigating orchards. The path eventually pops out into a suburb and as I continue to ride, it eventually deposits me on Summit Drive. A ride along a summit sounds absolutely delightful. In my mind's eye, I envision breathtaking vistas accompanied by gusts of refreshing breezes blowing in off the lake. As I head through the intersection and turn to go up the mountain, I notice a group of bikers coming up the road behind me. Being passed on a bike by someone else on a bike, especially on a hill, is just embarrassing. You're usually both going so slowly that it seems to take forever. And the one being passed is forced to suffer the additional humiliation of staring straight into the oscillating ass of the passer, as his butt cheeks wiggle insultingly. I haven't been on a bike in a month and as I climb the mountain I am immediately aware of the fact that I have spent the last 12 years biking in one of the flattest cities in North America. Now here I am, wheezing my way up a mountain cliff in the stifling mid-day heat in a desert, painfully aware that there is a pack of undulating ass cheeks coming up behind me.

I pour on the coals and give it everything I have, mustering a lukewarm effort at best. My vision blurs from the heat waves rising off the searing asphalt as stinging sweat pours into my eyes. The desert climate seems to be setting my lungs on fire as each gasp tears new holes in the membranes. The muscle tissue in my quads turns to Very Berry Jello. I'm in the easiest gear the bike has, imperceptibly creeping up stupid Summit Drive, which at this point doesn't sound idyllic at all; it sounds dangerous as shit. I'm sure each twist in the road is going to be the last and I'm going to find myself at the top, but it just keeps going and going and going.

As I make my wobbly way onward, I realize no one has passed me, and I find additional motivation in the thought that there are bikers who are at that moment starring at MY undulating ass. I picture what I must look like through their eyes, my calves and quads moving like exquisitely sculptured pistons, moving up and down in powerful strokes. As my inner eye takes over, I realize what an intimidating physical presence I am on the mountain. I look for all the world like a conquering hero that tackles mountain passes before breakfast. "Oh my god, I look magnificent!" I gasp.

When I finally reach the top, I coast along as if it was no big deal. I glance behind me in an imperial manner with a clever non sequitur poised on my lips ready to deliver a word of encouragement to the bikers who were unable to keep up with my blistering pace.

The road is empty, which is when I realize they must have turned off onto the road I'd come from at the base of the mountain.

"What a bunch of pussies," I mutter, shaking my head ruefully at the lack of mental and physical fortitude of the younger generation.

On Friday, it's a guys-only road trip. Bruce and Kathy's oldest son Cai has been away at teen camp for the week, so Bruce and I throw Zion and Mik into the van and head up to get him. I've been to camp a couple of times in my life. The first was when I was six years old. I was officially too young to be there, but my mom was working in the kitchen and they assumed that by having my Mommy on site I should be able to handle it.

It was a Christian camp, which meant a lot of fun was tainted with sermonizing and moral diatribes. God bless the genius that forced zealous 18-year-old Bible school students to demand that six-year-old Ricky Leaf memorize scripture during the summer holidays.

I have two prevailing memories from Camp Silverside. One

was a nine-year-old chubby bully that made me his camp bitch. He used to slam his fat ass into my face every morning in the yard as we lined up to sing a stupid ditty about Alice the stupid Camel and her stupid humps.

My other memory is of the evening ritual where campers had to successfully recite Bible verses from memory to their counselor after supper. If you couldn't recite the passage you couldn't leave. The end of each day followed the same ritual. I would be unable to recite the verse, and seriously with all the Thees and Thous and in so much as it pleaseth the Lords, it's hardly surprising. My inquisitor would make me stay, while the rest of the kids ran outside playing and squealing with glee. Left alone in that cold, concrete bunker, my drill sergeant would go all Godly-Gestapo on my six-year-old heathen ass, until I was reduced to a puddle of blubbering tears crying for my mommy. Thankfully, my mommy was actually in the kitchen, and would console me.

This is why you'll never hear me say, "Hey kids: who wants to go to camp?"

I'm reliving some of these salient memories as we pull into the camp and see Cai walking across the yard, surrounded by his teenage peers. I'm curious to see what reception he'll give Mik and Zion as they run up. The three of them instantly fall into an excited chatter, swapping stories, silly songs, and hilarious anecdotes that usually involved someone eating something gross and farting, or both.

Bruce is particularly inspired this evening, and puts together the perfect boys' night out. We stop at a store and load up with beef jerky, bags of chips, pop, and a couple of beers for the supervisors before heading over to a drive-in theatre to watch the new G.I. Joe movie.

Drive-in theatres attract a fascinating breed of humanity. People show up with RVs and vans full of lawn chairs and BBQs. Soon they start throwing footballs and Frisbees around as cigarette smoke and laughter fill the air. When Mother Nature finally dims the lights, we sit back and enjoy a movie ideally suited for twelve to fourteen-year-old boys. This movie doesn't waste any time with character development, dialogue, or a discernible story line: nothing is allowed to get in the way of balls-to-the-wall action and explosions. On the way back to Kelowna, the boys come up with a game in which they exchange the first part of a person's name with dick, and then add the last part of the name. Mikale becomes Dick-ale, Zion is Dick-on, but Cailas gets the biggest laugh of the ride for Dick-las. I have more camp-related fun that night than at any other time of my life.

Kelowna is nestled in the Okanagan Valley in the interior of British Columbia. Zara and I met, got married, and Zion was born in Kelowna before we moved to Winnipeg. In the twelve years since we left, development in the city has exploded as gated communities and sprawling suburbs have crept up the valley's thighs like cellulite on steroids.

The area is known for its orchards and vineyards that sprawl along the shores of Lake Okanagan, where the myth of a lake demon known as Ogopogo lurks. Slightly less famous than the Loch Ness monster, sightings of a forty to fifty-foot-long water serpent have been reported since the 19th century.

We spent many hours and many days soaking up the sun and the sand as Zion and Riel played and swam with Cai, Mik, and Alexa. Perhaps tuning into the spirit of the haunted waters, Zion came screaming up the beach one afternoon chattering excitedly, "I saw a fish fly by my face 20 feet down in the water. I was crawling my way along the bottom when it just flew by all wiggly!" He shuddered.

"What did you do?" I asked with the camera rolling.

"I came up and started screaming trout! I mean, I knew there'd be fish, but not in the swimming area. They've got to learn their boundaries," he pronounced seriously.

Moments later, he was back, "we were out swimming for fish, cause I realized that they're not scary when they're not swimming right in front of your face; we probably saw a million!" This was the ultimate tag line for *Zion & Riel in British Columbia*.

British Columbia starts aboard the B.C. Ferries as we explore the city of Victoria, waterfalls, marine life, adventure swimming, and underwater encounters of the 'Trout'kind.

God, Guns & Glory

After a glorious week in Kelowna filled with nothing more strenuous than carrying a blanket and picnic basket from the car to the beach, it was time to head out. As we said our goodbyes and pulled out of the orchard, we realized we will have travelled around the world before we see our friends again.

From Kelowna, we headed north to Fort St. John, just a fourteen-hour hop, skip, and a jump away. Zion was deep in the throes of despair having to leave Mik and Cai and made us stop at every Dairy Queen we saw so he could order an Iced Cap. This suited Riel just fine because she got various ice creams every time we stopped too. I'd booked an economy hotel in Prince George, actually parking right under the humongous banner advertising rooms for $69.00 a night. I walked into the lobby where a group of swarthy men of unknown origins stopped talking and sat staring at me. I waited for someone to say, "Are you eyeballing me, princess?"

I was consciously trying to avoid eyeballing anyone, as Swarthy Boss Guy told me to cough up $129.00 for the room we'd reserved for $69.00. Just as I was about to tuck my fuchsia tail between my legs and crabwalk my candy ass out of there, Zara walked in. She sussed the situation and started giving the guy hell for quoting $69.00 on the phone and then doubling the rate.

Badda-bing-badda-bang and my little rock and roll queen snagged the room for a very economical $69.00. When we opened the door, the full frontal assault on our sense of smell was vicious and unmerciful. A high-powered combination of cleaning agents had spent the afternoon reacting on a molecular level. They began buffeting us about the nose and throat. At this point of the trip, I was teaching the kids the first steps of hotel occupation according to my germaphobic playbook.

"The first thing you do is make sure no one has left the remnants of a session in the toilet," I instructed. "The second thing you need to do is pull the bedspread off the bed and chuck it on the floor. God knows when those things are washed."

As I said this, I was thinking of the pipeliners I used to work with who would lounge around the hotel room letting their back and ass hair dry naturally. One guy used to walk straight out of the shower and actually crawl into his bed and roll around in the sheets to dry off. Anyway, even after ten minutes with the door and windows wide open, my eyes were still watering. Either the cleaning staff had absolutely no sense of smell, or Febreze was using a cheap hotel in northern B.C. to conduct testing on human subjects. We stuffed the bedspreads into the closet and sealed the door, opened all the windows as wide as they'd go and headed into town to buy some groceries and see what Prince George had to offer. Twenty minutes later we were back in the room having seen everything there was to see, digging into our supper of snacks as we watched movies on the laptops.

Fort St. John is a northern Canadian city established in 1794 as a trading post. It still has a wilderness vibe that attracts people interested in the hunting and fishing type of lifestyle. It's the kind of town that inspires Jeff Foxworthy's jokes.

Our friends Doug and Sharon regularly have deer and moose wander into their backyard. In one action-packed tale, their sixteen-year-old daughter was getting out of the shower when she noticed a pack of coyotes in the back yard moving in on their dogs. Without a moment's hesitation, she grabbed a rifle, ran out onto the deck and started firing pot shots at the pack, still wrapped in her towel.

Doug and Sharon are another couple I'd met through touring. They have five incredible teenagers and a house filled with lots of laughter and music. When we visited they were dog-sitting some little fluff ball with an underbite named Griffin. Riel wanted to put him in her pocket and take him with her everywhere.

I've never felt that owning or operating guns would be in my best interest, or in the interest of the people around me. I don't think accident-prone and gunowner should go on the same resume. My one and only hands-on experience with a gun happened when I was twelve years old. Walking back to the house with my older brother, I watched with rapt fascination as he pushed a little button on the bottom of his shotgun and ejected all the shells from the chamber with one spectacular 'chuck-chuck' after another. I waited until Sunday afternoon when my whole family lay down for an afternoon nap before I snuck into his room. I loaded up all the shells, pushed the little button, grabbed the fore stock, and did an awesome 'chuck-chuck' and then KABOOM! I blew a gigantic frigging hole in the wall, perforating the curtains, as the concussive retort rendered me deaf and dumb. Ever since that day, the smell of gunpowder still reminds me of my brother's room. But in Fort St. John it seems that everyone owns a gun and Zion is fascinated with guns. So it was an incredible adventure when Doug took Zion and me down the road to the shooting range. I made a point of keeping my sordid past to myself as we stepped out of the car to the sound of shots thundering off behind the trees.

"Sounds like a 12-gauge," Zion said immediately.

I expressed my skepticism, falling for that age-old parental prejudice where you can't imagine your kid knowing something about a subject you don't know anything about at all. But when we peeked around the hedge, sure enough, the guy was reloading all 12-gauges. That afternoon was Zion's first opportunity to try out his sniping skills with real bullets and a real gun and a real target, and he was having a really great time. Then he noticed the shell casings littering the ground around his feet. When Doug told him some of them were Uzi shells, Zion started scrambling around, filling his pockets until they bulged like squirrel cheeks.

That night Doug regaled us with a story about the annual men's retreat organized by a local church, called "God, Guns & Glory" – an event that sounds like something that could only happen in Fort St John … or maybe Texas. Even the title was horrifying and hilarious. Apparently, it all started innocently enough when a couple of guys brought out some small-power rifles to the men's retreat and took turns firing at cans and targets after the prayer session one night. The next year more guys brought more guns, and the highlight of the retreat was when someone shot a little portable propane tank causing a small explosion. Soon the situation escalated, as these types of things have a habit of doing, and the men's retreat began to drift toward an ammunitions depot just shy of surface-to-air missiles and amour-piercing bullets. Eventually someone brought a big BBQ tank that exploded in a blaze of "glory" sending jagged shards of shrapnel whizzing past people's heads amidst open-throated howls of ecstasy. I was never clear where God fit with all the guns and glory.

On the weekend, Doug and Sharon hosted a backyard concert where I played for their friends and neighbours. They set up a gazebo tent and strung party lights around the yard creating a magical ambiance as guests arrived with platters of food and bottles of wine. We had a fabulous evening in the garden under the bright northern lights. Zion and Riel were flying under the radar, and were stoked to discover a platter of sushi. With the childlike belief that the sun, moon, and sushi platters revolve around them, they ignored the little cocktail plates and filled the enormous lids from their Lego bins with heaping mounds of sushi in a total disregard for anyone else. Sharon managed to snap a picture of them at that moment. Riel looked like a frightened deer in the headlights, probably concerned someone was going to make her put some sushi back, while Zion looked on with an "are you eyeballing me, princess?" superiority.

As we were leaving their house, Doug and Sharon gave us a number of gifts. There were some books, some food and drinks for the trip, and an envelope we didn't open until we were driving down the road. Inside the envelope was a wad of cash and a note that said that their family also had dreams of traveling together and that they believed that sometimes the best way to keep your dreams alive was to share and invest in the dreams of others. The note said that they were giving us this money for our trip for a moment somewhere along the way when there was something we'd really like to do, but couldn't really afford to. That's when they wanted us to pull their gift out and use it.

An hour down the road Zion took off his headphones and with the mother of all delayed reactions said, "Wait! Who gave us money again?"

"Wow," he said thoughtfully, after we repeated the events. "I've never met anyone who gives us a gazillion dollars before."

He had just put his headphones on and was about to press play when he stopped and said, "Wait, why did they do that again?"

Anti-Social Middle Aged Basement Dwellers

After Fort St. John, it was time to start our journey across Canada heading for the east coast. More than almost anything else, Canada is filled with a lot of empty space. Lots of prairie people love the endless wide-open spaces. Zara and I aren't those people. We typically drive through the night so we can avoid looking at all the nothing, which is what we did as we headed back to Winnipeg. This inadvertently produced some stunning early morning footage for our next video *Zion & Riel – Crossing Central Canada*, as the sunrise illuminated vibrant green prairie fields frosted with misty clouds of fog.

Marie-Josée and her partner were out of town and offered us their place. Maybe MJ was hoping I'd move all my stupid crap out of her basement, but as our storage bay was packed to the gills that really wasn't an option. For one night, we transformed MJ's living room into a tattoo studio so Zara could sling some ink on our friend Craig and his girlfriend Anna. Zion had just gotten a demo version of World of Warcraft and was fully enamoured by it all. I'm no gamer, but W.O.W. sounds like an amazing gig … for its creators. I think there are over 10 million subscribers who pay $15.00 a month.

Zara and I were not interested in our son joining the ranks of antisocial, middle aged basement dwellers who scurry about in the shadows wiggling their fingers and thumbs at a computer screen. Craig is a gamer and, God bless his heart, was trying to persuade Zion not to venture down the slippery W.O.W. slope with his own cautionary tale.

"Dude, one night I spent forty-five minutes just RUNNING."

Craig did not mean that he had literally spent forty-five minutes physically running gaining valuable exercise, he was talking about holding the toggle of his controller in a constant position for forty-five minutes as his animated self ran.

Zion would repeat this story reverentially for weeks as if it displayed fortitude of character and a persistence of will that he himself aspired to one day attain.

From Winnipeg we continued on to Thunder Bay. Fort St. John to Thunder Bay is about 2700 kilometres, which would be the equivalent of driving from Stockholm to Bucharest. You pass a couple of trees in Saskatchewan and there's a cool barn in southern Manitoba, but really, not a lot else.

Just outside Thunder Bay, we stopped at Kakabeka Falls. Known as the Niagara of the North, the Kaministiquia River plunges forty metres over sheer cliffs and some of the oldest fossils in the world. It was late afternoon on a gorgeous summer day as we hiked around the falls taking pictures and video. Riel had spent the last couple of days rolling around in the back of the van and her hair looked like it was slowly drifting toward one giant dreadlock. I dubbed her Mowgli as she started wielding a giant stick in the forest. Zara and Zion were walking up ahead of us engaged in some animated debate. I caught Zion's last volley as he headed off into the woods and yelled, "You're not yanking my crank are you, Mom?"

Zara's reply drifted through the trees, "I'm not going anywhere near your crank, Zi."

There is a cool Ojibwa Legend surrounding Kakabeka Falls about an Indian princess named Green Mantle. Her father, White Bear, was the chief, and learned that a Sioux war party was on its way to destroy his tribe. To save her people, the princess paddled her canoe up the Kaministiquia, where she entered the camp of her enemies. Pretending to be scared and lost, she bargained with them to spare her life if she led them to her father's camp. The next morning the Sioux put Green Mantle in the lead canoe and she led them all over the falls. She gave her life to spare her tribe and it is said that the Great Manitou looked kindly upon her bravery and even now, you can see her figure in the mist as a monument to her memory. We didn't, but not for lack of trying.

From the falls, we headed into Thunder Bay to look for a hotel. We drove down the strip as I tried time and again to find a great deal. We finally ended up at the Victoria Inn where a little flirtatious banter with a couple of young ladies at the front desk procured a bargain basement price for a family suite. Zion and Riel were beside themselves as they explored the separate kid's room with a Play Station and balcony that looked out on the pool and waterslide. It was definitely money well spent.

The next morning we went to the Hoito Restaurant, where world-famous Finnish pancakes have been served since 1918. Thunder Bay has a lot of Finns; some boast it is the largest Finnish population outside of Scandinavia. The boasters include some friends I've made over my years of touring. Steven, our good friend, and consummate guide for all things Finnish, met us for breakfast and we had a great time catching up. (Just for your information, Steven recommends that if you make it to the Hoito, you want to order the Finnish pancakes with crispy edges.)

From Thunder Bay, we continued east, up and over Lake Superior, one of the five Great Lakes. It was a nine-hour drive from Thunder Bay to Sault St. Marie, through some of the most rugged, isolated terrain in the country. Riel had been missing her best friend Kayla since we left Winnipeg. Whenever she starts feeling homesick or lonely she asks for one of two songs she and Kays sang together. The first is *Bring Me To Life*, by Evanescence, and the second is *Living on a Prayer* by Bon Jovi.

Zion for one was sick of it. As soon as he heard the piano intro for *Bring Me To Life*, he groaned loud and long and concluded with an admonishing "Riel!" as if missing home is a crime.

I'll admit that song is firmly embedded in my memory as the sound track for traveling across Canada and I hope I never hear it again … but I understand.

The following day we arrived in North Bay where I had a concert scheduled. North Bay is about a three-and-a-half-hour drive straight north of Toronto and is a city I'd toured to almost every year for the past ten years. Our friends, Ian and Ros, had bought a new place since the last time I was there, an incredible lake-front property. A short stroll down the garden path led us out onto the deck beside the lake where we swam, paddled and played with their three big dogs, Mocha, Tummy, and Chummy, and one little shit-disturber named Sammy. I had wrongly assumed, before we started traveling, that high-speed WiFi would be readily available everywhere we went. It was a preconceived notion I quickly learned to regret as I spent most of the year driving through neighbourhoods and side streets searching for unprotected signal so I could check emails. Ian and Ros had a great connection so we actually hung around an extra day just so we could book our tickets from Hawaii to Malaysia and Malaysia to Australia.

Zara and I have completely different personalities, which is something I usually give thanks for. I provide the high maintenance personality and all the emotional outbursts, breakdowns, and full-on freak-outs our marriage requires. This frees Zara up to provide the cool, calm analytical observations and research that grounds us all.

This includes online research, which led her to CheapOAir, an online company where we discovered incredible deals on airline tickets. That sunny Sunday afternoon we were able to book tickets on Air China and Air Malaysia for less than half of the next lowest airfare. Everyone knows that if it seems too good to be true, it probably is. But as we hemmed and hawed and debated, we came to the conclusion that it wasn't too good ... it was just incredibly good. With my fingers crossed, I clicked Buy Now, and hoped everything would turn out OK. From North Bay, we drove on to Old Quebec where we immersed ourselves in French culture. We strolled along the boardwalk outside the Chateau Frontenac, looked out over the Seaway, took the tram down to the windy streets where we drank cappuccinos and ate sorbet and chocolate. We took the guided tour of the Quebec Citadel, also known as the Gibraltar of the Americas. The Citadel is a national historic monument and an official residence of the Governor General.

The Citadel dates from the early 1800s and is one of Québec City's most distinctive features. On the heights of Cap Diamant, the star-shaped twenty-five-building fortress was built on the edge of the Plains of Abraham, the site of Canada's most famous battle between Britain and France.

The Citadel still serves as a base for the Royal 22nd Regiment. I am oblivious by nature, not willful intent, and inadvertently walked through the armed gate. This forced the sentry-on-duty to snap to attention and chase me down to issue a stern reprimand. My family tried to distance themselves from me by joining a Japanese tour group.

The tour guide wanted two volunteers to hold either end of a giant scroll that depicted a timeline of the history of the city. I'm sure if there were no kids present he'd have had some respectful way of conscripting adults, but many adults seem to feel they have the right to subject children to demeaning public activities.

Zion and Riel were plucked unceremoniously out of the crowd and forced to don silly hats while they held either end of the banner. This was more humiliating, at least for Zion, than hanging around with me. Instead of rescuing them, I decided to film their humiliation and use the footage for our next YouTube video *Zion & Riel in Quebec City*.

The tour took us up on the walls that overlook the Plains of Abraham, the site of the final battle in the 1759 conquest of New France by Britain where both the French General Montcalm and the British General Wolfe were killed in the battle. We came down off the ramparts and into the Royal 22nd Regiment Museum, which has a military collection spanning more than 300 years. At one point, Zion seemed really interested in the display so I sidled up to find what point of national history was engaging his imagination.

"It reminds me of Assassin's Creed," he said, referring to one of his video games as he pointed at a period military uniform.

"Yeah, would you wear something like that?" Zara asked.

"If I was an assassin."

We caught the changing of the guard while the Governor General handed out awards inside her official residence. We disagreed on how to get back down into the heart of the old city when the tour was over and ended up taking the long way around the Citadel. Zion chose his own path high up along the wall. When he saw us through the trees, he thought he'd run down the hill and surprise us. He totally misjudged the steepness of the hill and was completely out of control with arms and legs pin wheeling as he tried his damndest to stay upright. He managed to pull off an epic ass-heel slide just before launching off a retaining wall into oncoming traffic.

At that point, we decided our homeschooling should move from military history to culinary exploration. We stopped at the information centre to ask where we could find the best poutine in the city. Poutine is essentially French fries topped with fresh cheese curds, covered with brown gravy ... so basically a fatty, cholesterol-induced heart attack served in a bowl that you eat with a fork. The name came about when someone exclaimed: "ça va faire une maudite poutine". (It will make a damn mess!)

The information centre directed us to Chez Ashton, which brazenly claims to be the birthplace of poutine. The dish originated in Quebec, Canada, in the late 1950s. There are many Québécois communities that claim to be the birthplace, but as we were sitting at Chez Ashton, we decided to believe the authenticity of their claim.

Crossing Central Canada involved many days and nights driving in the van listening to loud rock music. Along the way we hiked around Kakabeka Falls, ate Finnish pancakes, and explored some of the Great Lakes.

Quebec City is the heart of Francophone culture in Canada, and the site of historical battles, fascinating architecture, and the home of poutine. A heart attack served in a bowl.

Candy-Coated Duvet Covers and Kool-Aid Waterslides

I've been having strange dreams for weeks now, crazy dreams that usually involve being chased and hunted by packs of rabid predators. Too much media stimulus as a child has empowered my overly active mind to construct nightmares complete with multiple camera angles and rapid editorial cutting.

Last night's nightmare opened with a close up of running feet, then cut to a wide shot that just captured a blur of dark gray fur streaking through the foliage. A wide-angle crane shot showed me tripping and falling, dirt and forest debris sticking to my tear-stained cheeks as the camera moved in to reveal my pupils dilated with frenzied fear. A startling close up of overly developed incisors flecked with foam rose to a crescendo as a devilish creature tipped back its head and delivered a blood-curdling howl. For what seemed like an eternity, I narrowly avoided being devoured by teeth and talons. When I startled awake, I thought I could smell burning toast.

"Oh great," I mumbled. "I've woken up just in time for a stroke."

As I drifted in and out of consciousness, my two psychotic episodes merged and I spent the rest of the night stumbling through a dream forest pursued by snapping branches and canines, dragging my useless leg and swinging my numb arm like a pendulum screaming, "Zzzzara! Halb! I' b habbing a stoke!"

We're back in the van, listening to *Bring Me To Life* again as we continue our eastern drift from Quebec City to the Maritimes, following Highway #20 along the banks of the St. Lawrence River under cobalt skies and periodic showers. It's a great day to be snuggled up inside a vehicle. The kids spin nests out of fuzzy blankets and Stuffies. They are watching movies in the back as Zara and I talk about our experiences so far. We've been on the road for almost two months and have a new appreciation for how crazy sane people can be.

I'm amazed at the tenuous grasp many people seem to have on life and how many survive through the extensive use of pharmaceuticals, caffeine, and installment buying. Like the upstanding, middle-class Christian family we stayed with one night. They were friends of friends who lived in a city we were passing through. The offer of a free night's accommodation seemed serendipitous, at least until we arrived and sat down to the evening meal. The family screamed everything at each other, from "pass the butter!" to "you're such a stupid, fat cow. I hate you!"

The teenage son came to the table with a swastika shaved in his hair as the parents told "humorous" stories of needing to shut the windows in the summer when they started fighting because the neighbours kept calling the cops.

Or the night we sat out on a deck sipping wine under the setting sun and I innocently asked our hosts how they were doing. "Well, not very good," the wife replied. "We've been married for five years and I still don't even know if he wants to be, so I think at this point it's either shit or get off the pot!"

"Can't argue with that," the husband commented as he downed another beer. The fact that we're just passing through seems to make us a pressure release valve for people to get things off their chests knowing that we're pulling out in a couple of hours and will take their confessions with us.

It's mid-September, and we've finally made it to the Atlantic coast. It's over 6000 kilometres from Vancouver Island to Charlottetown, Prince Edward Island. In the two months since leaving Winnipeg, we've driven over 10,000 kilometres, which represents a lot of hours the four of us have spent together in a very confined space.

Yesterday was a pretty, magic day on Prince Edward Island. We slept in, had a relaxing morning as Zara and I took care of email business while the kids played with Lego. We headed out around noon and made our way up to the Cavendish area where we explored beaches ringed with red sandstone cliffs. Zion and Riel took turns jumping from the tops of pillowy sand dunes. Zara got one photo of Zion in mid-air that has already become a featured pic in our latest video *Zion & Riel – PEI.*

As we tootled around the area, we took the "Road to Avonlea", also the name of a TV series about a young girl in the early 1900s sent to live with relatives on PEI. We stopped in for a photo op at Anne of Green Gables House and swung by the homestead where Lucy Maude Montgomery lived. Eventually we headed down to Summerside where we savoured seafood chowder and mussels at the Lobster House as the sun set over the water. After supper, we made our way to the Harbourfront Theatre where we enjoyed our first musical as a family, called Anne & Gilbert. PEI is synonymous with Anne of Green Gables, so it was a fitting end to our day to sip raspberry cordial as we wound our way back up to Charlottetown with Maritime show tunes running through our heads.

In the morning we choked back the complimentary breakfast of Rice Krispies and Wonder Bread and left the 60s porcelain shower behind as we headed toward downtown Charlottetown. Charlottetown is the capital city of PEI and calls itself the "Birthplace of Confederation" after a landmark meeting in 1864 that led to Canadian Confederation. It was a beautiful sunny day perfect for strolling along the cobblestone streets and boardwalk by the bay. Zara and I sipped lattes while the kids tested the validity of Cows, a Cavendish ice cream manufacturer that brazenly boasts the best ice cream in the world. According to Zion and Riel, their taste experiment was inconclusive and would need further investigation at upcoming ice cream parlours before they could submit a decision.

Leaving Charlottetown we had one of our rare meltdowns. I was driving and Riel was in the backseat crying because Zion was doing something nefarious. I bellowed and blustered from my Captain's chair on the bridge, demanding an immediate cessation of hostilities. But the crying continued and my commands were met with mockery and derision. Soon emotions were erupting as I pulled over on the side of the road, opened the back door and started screaming at my son.

His incredibly long eyelashes suddenly seemed insolent and condescending. Everything I yelled was turned away with such acerbic wit and sarcasm that I soon felt as if I was standing on the side of the road with my pants around my ankles. I started looking mournfully at passing cars, hoping that someone with an even quicker and more sarcastic wit would come to my rescue. When that did not happen, I was forced to close the door and do the walk of shame back to the Captain's chair, which seemed a hollow symbol of authority.

I cranked the music and started driving, glancing over at Zara who muttered under her breath, "Well, that went well."

"He kicked my ass," I replied, still reeling from the indignity.

I admit, I was secretly proud of what a formidable foe my son is at only thirteen years old, but if Zion decides to use his powers for evil ... we're screwed.

From Charlottetown, we headed back over the Confederation Bridge and down toward Halifax, Nova Scotia. Halifax is a beautiful harbour city with a rich and colourful history. In December 1917, it was also the site of the biggest man-made explosion in the world before the atomic bomb. A French munitions ship about to cross the Atlantic to join the war collided with a Norwegian ship heading to New York to pick up relief supplies. The collision detonated a blast that leveled most of the city.

The meltdown has been long forgotten, fences have been mended, and serenity reigns once again. We are facing bigger problems, namely Zion's expectations regarding accommodations. Zion is not afraid to share his feelings, at great length, and has spent a good part of the day slagging the Prince Edward Island accommodations we just checked out of. Apparently, I'm only as good as my last hotel.

There are always a few hiccups when you're making up your life as you go. We are still trying to figure out the best way to do things. In Quebec City, we chose the hotel based on the posted price on the sign, which turned out to be the old "Bait & Switch" routine. Lesson learned.

For PEI, we'd done some research online and picked what seemed to be a reasonably priced room with a kitchenette. But as we drove through the city, we saw a whole row of hotels that looked better and were priced lower. Heading to Halifax, we didn't book in advance, thinking it would be best to just figure it out when we got there.

That is why we are now driving in circles through a residential neighbourhood trying unsuccessfully to find a wireless connection so we can search for a room. A single bar of signal from somewhere keeps coming and going. It's taunting me with the hope that I can figure out our accoms from the comfort of the passenger seat. Tired of idling and listening to a constant stream of profanity passing not so quietly under my breath, Zara makes the arbitrary decision to start driving in circles again. Exasperated, we eventually pull into an Esso station where I proceed to ask advice and directions from the woman behind the counter.

A hotel? Sure, just turn at the next light go under the overpass and turn at the white building; there was an inexpensive hotel right there.

"Great," I say, armed with a name and a napkin map, ready to head for the hills.

"Are you sending him to the hotel on Main St?" the woman waiting in line behind me asks incredulously. As I turned around I suddenly became aware of a great line of customers snaking behind me as their voices rose like the dawn.

Apparently, the helpful attendant is sending me to an inexpensive crack house that rents rooms by the hour. The woman in line shuffles me out the door and gives me directions to the Hampton Inn & Suites. Just driving up to the exterior of the hotel stretches our shoestring budget taut and I feel a sinking sensation in my stomach. As Zion and Riel catch sight of this glorious mansion, they start dreaming of candy-coated duvet covers and waterslides with fast moving rivers of kool-aid and soda pop.

That is how I find myself swaggering through the sliding doors with a grin a mile wide and my vocal chords raised two semitones to accompany the effervescent persona I hope will commandeer a reduced rate. Damn if that shtick doesn't work almost every time. Walking back to the van after successfully negotiating a reduced rate for a night in regal surroundings, I remind myself never to underestimate the seductive power of the slightly effeminate, clearly enunciated vocal styling of the sexually ambiguous male.

Zion is over the moon, and professes his love and admiration for me more than once. Riel is swept off her feet by her brother's emotional gusts and is standing beside the van quivering with anticipation. I give the kids one of the key cards and tell them to go open the door for us. By the time Zara and I lug the bags around the corner, the kids are actually bouncing in the hallway talking at the same time describing the beds, the covers, and the flat screen TV. Zion goes so far as to draw our attention to the contoured bathroom vanity, which he claims is the nicest he's ever seen.

Zion & Riel – PEI follows our exploration along the red cliffs of Cavendish as we jump into pillowy soft sand dunes and the enjoy the world of Anne of Green Gables with our first musical of the trip.

Sounds from Deep Within an Esophagus

The Maritimes is an amazing place to be in late September, as autumn leaves turn various shades of amber, ochre and rosewood. I could be just about anywhere doing just about anything; what I am actually doing is driving in a van through this panoramic kaleidoscope as my thirteen-year-old son sits behind me trying desperately to make himself puke. When Zion is sick and tired of being in a vehicle, as he is this morning, he tries really, really hard to make himself throw up. He has always been lured by the seductive validation puking gives to a claim of being sick. I think he believes regurgitation will be irrefutable proof to the validity of his position. Thankfully, in all the years of retching and gagging, he has almost zero percent success. Not that that ever keeps him from trying.

So as we drive down the highway through this beautiful New Brunswick countryside, the rest of the family has to listen to Zion hack and wheeze as he guzzles his water bottle to induce his gag reflexes. All he's managed so far is a couple of soggy burps and gurgles amid Riel's exclamations of "gross, sick", and "oh, yuck!"

I feel bad for her, having to share the second row of seating beside her brother when he's hell-bent on inflicting the rest of us with himself.

I secretly admire his tenacity, though like most parents I wish it were focused toward an activity I could support. I bellow and bluster from the front seat, aware that for reasons beyond my comprehension, I have adopted the southern drawl of a Pentecostal preacher as I scowl into the rearview mirror.

"I command you in Jay-sus name, to repent of all vomit-related activities!" But Zion knows I'm just full of hot air and, as a product of the school of parenting where belts are only used to hold up pants and wooden spoons are only used for cooking, no shadow of fear or doubt inhibits him.

It's at times like these reality starts to feel like a TV show. "Urgh! Gurgle, burp," he sighs.

"Oh, SICK!" Riel exclaims.

"Zion, in the name of all that is holy I command you to stop that!" I quiver forcefully. Watery retching sounds emanate from deep within his esophagus.

"Ohhh, that's so gross," Riel shivers in disgust.

"I'm serious, cut that out!" I bellow, channeling Bill O'Reilly into my vocal chords.

This goes on for far too long, definitely longer than I want to write or you want to read about it.

At one point Zara dumps out a bag of Jelly Bellies and passes it back, but the sides of the bag are see through, which means Riel has to watch spittle and phlegm slither down the inside.

We manage to arrive at King's Landing Historical Settlement without significant spewage. Located in the St. John River valley, King's Landing depicts the area of New Brunswick in the 1800s. Over seventy historic buildings have been moved onto the property and restored, complete with furniture, tools and equipment. Staff are dressed in period costume and trained to provide 19th century stories to visitors.

We wander into the print shop where the print maker is running the press by foot power. The whole presentation is incredibly well done and it's a great day for all four of us, with lots of hands-on interactive information.

It is mid-September, which means school is back in session and the season is winding down, so the grounds are nearly empty letting us explore at our own pace. One of the highlights is the wood mill where a giant waterwheel powers a giant band saw. The actor hired to play the mill foreman is a wonderfully eccentric French guy with an accent so strong it takes a couple of seconds from the time the words hit your ears before your brain realizes you knew what he said. It makes for a very humorous, lurching conversation. The actor has an expansive personality and sweeps us up with his historical tales of life in the mill. Apparently, in addition to their hourly wage, the workers were also paid 20 ounces of rum per day. He says that if you were building a house, you'd want to pick up your lumber first thing in the morning, because the boards would be straighter before the guys started drinking. And it was also important for the workers to have horses or donkeys that could find their own way home, because after twenty ounces of rum most people weren't in the best shape to find their own way.

The community of Quispamsis is twenty-five minutes down the road from St. John, NB, located along the Kennebecasis and Hammond rivers. We have just arrived for a week at our good friends David and Lisa's place.

For years they've been the pastors of a Vineyard church in town. Pastoring isn't the kind of thing I'd wish on anyone, well OK, maybe on a Peeb. But that was how we met David and Lisa back in 2000. Zara was pregnant with Riel; Zion was three years old; and we were in the middle of a three-month tour across Canada and the U.K. It was my first tour to the Maritimes so I was hitting up every contact of every musical friend I could find. David agreed to have me come and play music Sunday morning with his worship team. Church worship teams are often the most eager, energetic individuals who produce some of the most God-awful musical swill on the planet. If you're a traveling musician who agrees to play with a church worship band, I've learned it's best to keep your expectations so low they are almost non-existent. Even then, you're likely going to be disappointed.

When I walked in the door for the first time, I discovered the drummer had a twenty-piece drum kit, platinum blond hair, black leather pants and a billowy white shirt open to his navel. The bass player and lead guitarist both had incredible gear, beautiful tone, and kicked serious musical ass. During one of the songs, the drummer laid out the most ferocious, double-kick, syncopated two-and-a-half-bar drum fill I've ever heard. It was so unexpected and beautiful I burst out laughing in the middle of the song. I had to channel the Grateful Dead and pull a twenty-eight-bar jam out of my butt before I could get myself back together.

We really hit it off with David and Lisa and their three kids Josh, Jesse, and Casile who are now all grown up. I've been back a few times over the ten years, but not nearly as often as I'd wish. Their home is right on the banks of the Kennebecasis River. The close proximity to the Bay of Fundy causes the river to actually change direction depending on whether the tide is coming in or going out. The Maritime region has a rich indigenous history and is one of the first areas populated by European immigrants. The influences are never more obvious than in the town names, most of which you'd have to be a local to pronounce properly. You pass Cascumpeque, Nauwigewauk, Tatamagouche, Tabusintac, Antigonish, Kouchibouguac, and Passamaquoddy. I did a concert once in Shubenacadie, so I know it means 'the place of the potato'.

Then there is the rich heritage of European immigrants unable to think outside the box. After leaving behind hearth and home and crossing the Atlantic in what was likely a harrowing journey surrounded by nothing but a world of possibilities, these people dreamed up New Glasgow, New Perth, New Edinburgh, New Salem and New Waterford. I can imagine a meeting where someone's arguing "Let's call it NEW Edinburgh like where we just came from only it's NEW !"

We took up residence in David and Lisa's basement and spent a week drinking copious quantities of wine and single malt scotch.

Today we're exploring the Bay of Fundy, specifically St. Martins Sea Caves. In typical East Coast fashion, the original name was the unpronounceable Goolwagagek, a Mi`kmaq word meaning haunt of the hooded seal.

Zion says that makes it sound like a slightly racist underground aquatic society.

The Bay of Fundy has some of the highest tides in the world, so we time our visit with low tide so we can explore the gigantic caves.

We hike in the red clay, and as part of a descriptive home-schooling lesson, ask the kids to stand barefoot in the mud, close their eyes, and describe the sensation.

"It feels squishy and cold," Riel says.

"It feels like stepping in slimy poo," Zion adds.

We hike up and around the corner into a narrow basin with 40'-60' cliff walls. The differing layers of rock, sand, and dirt make it look like the spines of giant books stacked flat on a huge shelf. We know we need to keep a watchful eye on the tide. The water comes in fast and furious when the tide turns. At the far end, we discover an escape rope tied off to a tree high up and over the edge. Nice to know there's some sort of escape hatch in place, but I wouldn't want to have to use it, especially with my nine-year-old daughter. Even with our watchfulness, we almost get caught; one minute there's nothing and the next the water's up to our knees as we scramble for higher ground and made our way back around the point.

There were some people interested in getting tattoos while we were in the area, so Zara set up a temporary shop in Lisa's office. She borrowed some high-powered yellow construction lights from the basement. Not only were the lights as bright as a nuclear blast, the heat generated in the room was staggering. In spite of the mercurial conditions, David and Lisa's daughter Casile got a beautiful flower on her back, just below her neck. Darin, the bass player we had first met in 2000, got a cover up of a huge cross, and Christina, Jesse's girlfriend at the time, got an amazing floral back tattoo.

On Saturday night, David and Lisa threw a party. It was an awesome night filled with lots of great food and wine and an opportunity to reconnect with people I'd met over the years. It was also a chance for the newly-inked in the community to pull up and down their shirts to reveal their new tattoos.

The next morning David had asked me to be the guest speaker and musician for his church service. His son Jesse is a great drummer and volunteered to play with me, along with Darin and his newly minted tattoo. Jesse crashed on the living room floor for the night. Five minutes before we were supposed to leave, he stood up, grabbed his shoes and walked out the door to the car.

As we drove to church, he sniffed dramatically a couple of times and commented, "Oh man, I stink."

"Yeah," David commented, "you still smell like White Russians." He paused before adding, "If you have a smoke when you get to church it will probably mask the smell."

I laughed till I cried, once again feeling like Sid the Sloth. My herd is awesome!

Cujo-Meets-The-Blair-Witch

After a week in New Brunswick, it was time to start the long trek back across the country. As we pulled out it was overcast and grey, which made it a perfect day for traveling. The kids once again made a nest of fuzzy blankets, pillows, and stuffies in the very back of the van. From St. John, we were heading to Toronto. Google says it's just over 1500 kilometres and should take 17 hours driving. As soon as we started driving, Zion and Riel started playing a game that seemed to involve wrestling and tickling, a lot of laughing, and quite a bit of shrieking. As any parent knows these sounds are much preferred to whining, crying, tantruming, and "are-we-almost-thereing."

When we got to Fredericton, an hour down the road, they were still happily squealing and laughing in the back. For over three hours, they kept it up. Zara and I were up front cranking the stereo to ear-bleeding levels and somehow the miles just flew by the windows.

The world was officially in the throes of a global economic recession, and it seemed all levels of government had decided to single-handedly revitalize our economy by green-lighting every road project on the books. I think we spent 15 out of the 17 hours driving through construction.

When we finally pulled into the yard at our friend RoseAnna's outside Toronto, we were all happy to get out of the van. We had met RoseAnna in the late 90s when we played at a Toronto festival. She was in charge of the green room where artists hung out when they weren't performing. We'd just come off stage and I was dripping with sweat. When RoseAnna left the room, I thought it was just our band in the room. I took off my pants and kicked back in all my silkboxered glory and started cracking dumbass innuendos about penis pythons, elephant trunks and warning everyone to stand back cause I wasn't sure how big this thing was going to get. That was right about the time I realized there was a blonde girl sitting so quietly and motionless in the corner that I hadn't even registered her presence. Feeling like an ass for talking about a penis, namely my own, I put my pants back on and starting apologizing to the rest of the band for my callous disregard for boundaries. That quiet blonde girl was RoseAnna's daughter Tina, an incredible painter who became one of our best friends and a founding member of Tribe of One. Since that illustrious beginning, Tina had met her DJing partner, Andrew, and together they have a son named Nigel.

Hanging out on RoseAnna's acreage seemed like the perfect place to shoot another horror movie. Riel and I enlisted Nigel and his dog Simon, who brought enthusiastic canine energy to the production. At first, I wasn't sure how well we were going to gel creatively. When I asked for their ideas for a storyline, Nigel launched into an impassioned description of a spaceship that beamed aliens down, and there were monsters with ray guns. In the end, we settled on a Cujo-meets-the-Blair-Witch storyline.

Riel and Nigel start off the film kicking a soccer ball back and forth, inter cut with flashes of a ferocious, snarling animal running through the grass. An errant kick sends the ball off into the tall grass. When Nigel heads off to retrieve the ball, he disappears. As Riel starts calling his name and searching for him, we see Nigel's body being dragged off into the grass. To film the scene, I got Nigel to lie on his back with his hands up over his head. As I tugged him jerkily into the tall grass, I just remember him giggling hysterically. After muting the live sound and replacing Nigel's giggling with horrid badger squealing and sinister minor synth chords, his belly laughing seems positively creepy, as if he's already in spasms. We follow Riel into the grass and watch her discover something disgusting, holding up what looks like a bloody clump of hair. She screams and starts running. A rapid succession of shots follows as Riel runs and hides from Cujo/Simon. More flashes of fur and an overdubbed audio of wolverine growling climax with a rabid creature crashing through the foliage and devouring Riel in screaming, writhing horror. That night back at Tina and Andrew's place, I recorded a little horror piano piece and a radio announcer reading a news story about police investigating a military genetics lab and rescue crews searching for a couple of children who went missing.

Military conspiracy, genetic modification, and a media cover up ... not only did we all feel like we'd spent a great afternoon together, we congratulated ourselves for making an important work of art with a serious social commentary. There was a lot of laughter as we uploaded *Horror Attack* to Zion and Riel's YouTube channel.

After a few days in southern Ontario we were heading west, back up and over the great lakes. I'm not sure what happened to the communities along the northern edge of Lake Superior. It seems like a vast, end-of-the-world movie set, where all the settlements are emptied and residents have either been transported to heaven by the second coming of Christ, or more likely, at least according to Zion, were caught in the zombie apocalypse, which he says everyone knows is inevitable.

When we were heading east, it was still summer holidays in North America, so the roads were filled with RVs and travelers. But now it's September, school is back in session, and we have the road and every motel to ourselves. We are starting to get the hang of embracing the season we're in. On most trips, you're actually trying to get somewhere and usually in a hurry. We, of course, have nowhere we need to be and nothing else we need to be doing. So we take our time getting up in the morning. We spend hilarious amounts of time searching for a great cup of coffee, bottles of wine, and sushi.

One of the few scheduled activities left on the calendar is a Tribe of One tour at the end of September. We arrive in Winnipeg the day before I'm scheduled to fly out with the band. The plan is for Zara to head back to my Mom's place with the kids.

The next morning we woke to a horrific scene ... snow was starting to fall. In Winnipeg you don't screw around with winter 'cause it will kill you and then cryogenically freeze your ass for nine months. Winnipeggers learn to read the snow the way surfers read waves or climbers read a cliff face. We could tell this wasn't going to be a light, fluffy dusting, this was a full frontal assault. There weren't any sirens or megaphones instructing people to their stations, but we hit the ground running. Bags were packed, the roof rack was secured, the kids were hustled into the van with their blankets and in a flurry of hugs and kisses, they were off. They barely managed to stay ahead of Old Man Winter as the snowstorm chased them for over 600 kilometres. They finally managed to outrun it on the other side of Regina, Saskatchewan.

We hit November and with just a few weeks left before the family adventure are went international, expectations are high. So are parental insecurities and fears.

The absence of Wi-Fi sucks. Zara and I are trying to arrange international flights, research hostels, hotels, and vehicle rentals. Then I discover the farm half-a-mile down the road has an unprotected Wi-Fi. I start spending a couple of hours a day parked behind the hedges working on this stuff. We've also been paring down our portable empire. The initial move from a two-story house into a van was a challenge. We bought big duffle bags for each of us and still had a ton of loose stuff kicking around. After a couple of months, we realized we were just using the top five inches of our bags and pared down even further. Today we went to Mountain Equipment Co-op and bought new backpacks, ones that were perfectly suited and the right size for each of us. We are not a family of campers or hikers. Riding my bike to Starbucks for a mocha frappuccino is about as extreme outdoors as I've ever been. I've been having night terrors, imagining us collapsing under the weight of our backpacks at a train station in Europe.

Homeschooling isn't going well. Riel's Grade Four lessons make me feel like a dork. I can't even understand the directions in chapter one. The first page of Zion's Grade Eight English book uses words I've never even seen before. I keep looking at the cover, hoping I'm reading the French version.

As Zara tries to decipher the school material, I have been organizing dry land training sessions with the kids. We load up our packs with a bunch of random crap and walk around in the cow pasture feeling like goofballs. Tired of feeling like a failure I spend the night creating a kick-ass lesson-plan for tomorrow's class field trip.

"Run!" I yell over my shoulder as a surge of adrenalin launches my body into a spasmodic windmilling gallop as I stumble over railway ties and loose shale. The long mournful train whistle is just starting to fade as I glance over my shoulder to see if Zion and Riel are still with me. My explosive admonishment startled them into motion and I'm thrilled to see that the three of us are scuttling over the uneven terrain in unison, even if it is in a ragged, single-file zombieesque kind of way.

I dragged them out into the middle of an eighty-acre canola field as part of a homeschooling project. Today we're exploring descriptive writing. I brought them to a train trestle where I pictured them writing with such interpretive and descriptive detail, their journals would transport readers back to this very moment for generations to come.

I fantasize about my kids coming to me in their twenties and thirties reminiscing about all the incredible scholastic experiences I provided for them.

Without even knowing it, they've already started. I overhear a very detailed narrative behind my back as they mutter about how stupid this project is. Even with my delusions of grandeur, the last thing I thought we'd actually experience at the train trestle was a train; but another blast from the approaching engine spurs me on as I exhort even greater lurching speed from my reluctant students. "Come on, Zi! Riel, you can do it!" I manage to gasp, open-mouthed and panting.

I've been running for over twenty-five seconds and the adrenalin has worn off; I'm dangerously short of breath and starting to hit the runner's wall.

I'm not entirely surprised to discover Riel has cut back to a brisk stroll and Zion is half-heartedly loping as I charge wildly into a thicket of brambles. I claw and clamour my way up the steep slope, pausing to free the video camera in my pocket. More train blasts signal the imminent approach of the hundred-ton behemoth bearing down on our vantage point beside the tracks. This is shaping up to be possibly the greatest field trip ever. Poised at the edge of the bluff the ground begins to shake as the squeal of rust and iron rattle along the metal spine while the train snakes its way past our class of three. Well over a mile long, it takes more than four minutes for the last car to pass. Both kids are snapping pictures of the paintings on parade as the graffiti gallery slowly slides by one boxcar at a time.

The silence grows as the train passes from view. Riel looks over at me and says, "I decided to climb up here on the bank 'cause I thought this might be a once-in-a-lifetime experience."

"That's funny," I said, "that's what I thought too."

We spend the next hour hiking around and across the trestle, examining the concrete and creosote construction, and in the process, face fears of heights and vertigo as we gaze down through the cracks to the creek one-hundred feet below. With the Rocky Mountains visible to the west, we make an eighty acre field our classroom and sit down together under a God-sized prairie sky to write about what we were seeing, smelling, hearing, and feeling.

After writing two lines, Riel claims writer's block.

"Just write about what you're seeing around you," I say. "You could even write about the cows."

"What cows?" she asks.

"The cows right behind you!" I say, shocked that an animal weighing several hundred pounds and separated by nothing more than twenty feet and three slim barbed wires could go undetected. Turning her body less than ninety degrees, she's transformed into an archeologist who had just stumbled upon a previously unknown ancient civilization. She's swept up in describing the "gross, dirty white fur, and stinky, ploppy poo patties". Suddenly the pasture becomes a playground as the kids laugh and point at their bovine classmates, making up imaginary names for the cows that rhyme with bodily functions and work as clever lyrics for irreverent ditties.

As we walk back down the train tracks to our van, basking in the glow of a bloody brilliant field trip, I flippantly describe us as a family of hobos.

"What's a hobo?" Riel asked.

Soon we're embroiled in a fascinating discussion debating the subtle, but significant distinctions between hobos, tramps, bums, vagabonds, and Zion's personal favourite: rubbies.

As we freewheel it back to the road with the canola stubble raking the metal underbelly of the van until it sounds like a torrential downpour coming up instead of down, the kids keep a running monologue going in the back seat. They're too distracted by their clever rhythms and rhymes to realize they've been caught up in the exhilarating experience of learning to tell their own story.

Grinning like a Cheshire cat, I sit behind the wheel, basking in their dirty little limericks and my own discovery, that right now, this is my life and I love it.

Horror Attack is our second movie, and was another great day spent racing around the woods together, this time with a bundle of canine energy that unwittingly played the villain.

HAWAII

The Calm Behind a Medicated Exterior

After spending the first four months of our year on the road traveling coast to coast across Canada, we were ready to hit the international trail. First stop – Honolulu.

We lived in Winnipeg, Manitoba for twelve years, one of the coldest cities on the planet, so it was a calculated decision to chase the sun for a year of summer.

As we arrived at the Calgary International Airport we discovered the terminal was abuzz with excitement and activity. The Grey Cup, which is the Canadian Football League's annual Championship and the second oldest trophy in North American professional sport, had just been played the day before in Calgary. In a nail-biting ending the Montreal Alouettes edged the Saskatchewan Roughriders in the final seconds of the fourth quarter. Down by two points with seconds on the clock, Montreal's kicker had just missed a field goal attempt sending Roughrider fans across the country into victory celebrations. But there was a flag on the play; Saskatchewan had too many men on the field. With a second attempt, Montreal split the uprights and won the game.

We were oblivious to all of this drama and history until we found ourselves going through security with an inordinate number of huge, well dressed, extremely hung-over professional athletes, and a small guy lugging a big silver trophy. For a second I thought my fantasy of being an internationally successful rock star with throngs of fans had somehow been realized, as flash-bulbs started going off all around me. It was only when my seared pupils were able to dilate that I realized I was standing next to the guy holding the cup.

I quickly pulled out the video camera and tried in thirty seconds to explain the "cool factor" to Zion and Riel so they would mug for the camera. They of course, were too culturally savvy to believe their Dad knows anything about what is cool and patently refused to participate. I may or may not have told Riel that the cup was full of free candy, so I could take a picture as she investigated. The security guard chose me out of the fifty people standing around taking pictures and video to loudly scold for taking pictures. Artist profiling; it's not pretty, and it affects all of us ... with piercings and tattoos.

Grey Cup Incident behind us, we turned back to more important matters. The only real objective of the year was to explore and experience cool and amazing things, so I stopped a flight attendant to ask if Zion and Riel could see the cockpit. Before you could say "Maverick, we've got a bogie at 6 o'clock!" they were not only in the cockpit, but Captain Tim had Zion and Riel in the pilot and co-pilot seats yanking on the stick and flashing signals to the ground crew. Go West Jet!

We flew to Vancouver where we had a layover before flying to Honolulu. As we approached the U.S. customs desk, I assumed our piercings and tattoos would draw some extra attention and thought it would be good to review the details of our trip, in the event the agent separated us from our kids. I wanted to make sure we were all on the same page. As Zara searched through her bag for our passports and plane tickets, I looked at Zion, "OK, bud, let's recap: where are we going?"

"Tim Horton's," he said, licking his lips in anticipation of donuts with icing and sprinkles.

"I don't mean in the airport, where are we flying to?"

"Australia," he said, jumping six weeks and two continents ahead in the queue.

"No, we're going to Hawaii," I said while trying to retain a calm, rugged exterior. "And how long are we going to be there?"

"Um, a week," he replied, stabbing wildly at a guess.

Zara and I looked at each other over the kid's heads and

exchanged one of those "we-are-totally-screwed" glances that I've learned parents hide behind a calm, often medicated exterior. As the agent motioned us forward, all I could think was that traveling to the U.S. with Zion was possibly the most terrifying thing I'd done in years. Obama can't shut down Guantanamo Bay and reinstate habeas corpus fast enough.

We breezed through security and started hiking the endless corridors from one terminal to another. As a courtesy cart passed us shuttling an elderly couple to their gate, I jokingly told Zara we should have hitched a ride.

"Wait! Are they driving people to Honolulu?" Zion exclaimed.

"God," I prayed aloud, "this is your son Rik. From one father to another, please help my son grasp a smattering of geography this year."

As I muttered a weary amen, Zion stuck his finger up the nose of a giant bear statue wearing an RCMP costume and told me to take a picture.

The family was famished, so we parked our bags at the Hanami Asian Cuisine and ordered dumplings, sushi, and curried chicken to celebrate our first successful border crossing.

Everything is a first for the kids. Today is the first domestic flight, the first layover, and the first international flight, so when the airline calls for pre-boarding Zion jumps to his feet.

"It's only for pre-boarding," I tell him.

"I want to pre-board!" he exclaims, excitedly confident he can easily outmanoeuvre the elderly and infirm shuffling toward the gate. He pauses before adding, "Wait … what's pre-boarding?"

We finally get on board only to be told we're going to have to sit on the tarmac while they unload all of the luggage because some dumbass was arrested at the gate for trying to fly on a fake passport and they have to remove his bags. The dumplings have worn off, Riel is hungry and we're just sitting there. I slide to the back of the plane and hit up a flight attendant for food. Energetic as a crackerjack he whirls around, and deposits two armfuls of Bits and Bites, cookies, and some juice boxes. I return to our seats where I'm greeted as a conquering hero. Go West Jet!

With our delayed departure, we arrive in Honolulu just before midnight. First flight – first snafu. When our backpacks come careening down the luggage chute, my orthotic sandals are missing. Years ago, I was in a horrific car accident. Chronic pain from a number of broken bones and crushed vertebrae has been the gift that keeps on giving. Orthotics have been a key component in compensating for structural damage, but they are nowhere to be seen.

I find a big happy Hawaiian guy with a clipboard to file my lost items claim. We sit down next to the carousel as he starts taking notes. It's all going great until he gets to the description of the lost item. I tell him I lost my orthotic sandals and I see him write, slippers. I nonchalantly clarify that we're talking about sandals as he nods affirmatively. He asks for the value. I tell him the stupid things cost me $400 Canadian. OK, he nods, and writes $700.00. At this point, I'm picturing a West Jet agent sitting in Calgary reading a report from Honolulu where a guy from Winnipeg claims he lost $700 slippers.

We head to Arrivals where we meet Sean, an old friend of Zara. Something is immediately apparent. Sean is awesome! He tells Zion and Riel he feels nervous meeting such famous YouTube stars as he's been tracking our journey up to this point. We jump into the backseat as Sean whisks us toward Mililani; I'm tired but unbelievably excited to be in Hawaii.

Sean and Zara had met in Hawaii twenty years previously at something called YWAM. To hear them describe the experience, it sounds like summer camp meets spring break for horny kids from religious families. Whatever details their sordid past may contain, their friendship pays off in incredible dividends and we're shown the time of our lives.

In the intervening years, Sean married Alice and they have a little nine-month-old-girl named Caitlin. They live in a quiet complex in Mililani. Somehow they manage to make room for our family of four to invade their home for two weeks.

We pass Aloha Stadium and signs for Pearl Harbor as I try to pronounce Queen Liliuokalani Freeway in my head. I'm surprised Honolulu is so big and it seems surreal that we'd left the snow-covered Canadian prairies a few hours earlier and were now cruising past palm trees in a tropical environment.

On our first day on Oahu, Sean has to work, so Alice and baby Caitlin are our local guides as we head up the north shore. We can't all fit in one vehicle, so we give Zara, Alice, and Caitlin one of our walkie-talkies while Zion, Riel, and I follow. Alice keeps a running monologue going that comes through in static bursts that sound like a snake with a lisp talking with a mouth full of crackers. After each garbled transmission the static disappears and we hear her say, "did you get that?"

We pass rows of pineapples and the Kona coffee fields as we make our way to Turtle Bay, where we go for our first swim in Hawaiian waters. At a little roadside fruit stand a group of Hawaiian Grandmas with sparkling eyes, and laugh lines drawn like road maps across sun-dried faces, introduce us to delicious deep-fried bananas called lumpia and fresh pineapple sprinkled with li hing mui. Riel is immediately a fan.

Twice as we're driving down the coast we pass Terry O'Quinn, the actor best known for playing Locke on the TV series *LOST*. The second time we see him we decide to ask for an autograph and a picture of him with the kids, but Locke is much more than a part of Hurley's subconscious; that man moves like the wind. By the time we circled the block, the only thing left to see is his golden bronze skull disappearing up the road.

We unwittingly arrived in Hawaii at the time of year the island gets its big waves and for the next two days all the kids want to do is head up the north shore where they can get pounded by the surf. Zion's favourite thing is sitting directly in the path of the biggest waves he can find, squealing happily as they pound him repeatedly in the face. He looks like a tumbleweed getting blown 20' – 30' up the beach, scraping his skin along the sand until his body is streaked with thin red lines.

I laugh as I hear him trying to convince Riel to join him. Riel is content to run along the beach trying to stay ahead of the waves.

"Holy crap!" she exclaims at one point as Zion tumbles past her, dragged along by a thousand gallons of ocean.

If we had an itinerary for those first few days, it would have simply been: arrive late morning stay until the sunset. It's a great plan, captured in all its glory in *Zion & Riel – Oahu, Hawaii*. Over the next couple of days, all we do is surf, sand, and sun. On our third day, I decide in my infinite wisdom to teach Riel how to boogie board. The fact that I've never boogied on or off a board in my life and have logged zero hours in the ocean in my life doesn't enter my mind, proving that at some asinine level I really am a guy.

So there we are, maybe 10' – 12' from shore in a sea of dumping waves. I get an incredibly nervous Riel to lie on the board, gripping the front lip and just as I look over my shoulder for the perfect wave … SLAM! A wave smacks me in the face sending us head over heels. Under the water, I feel something slam into the side of my head. Churning under the surface, I can't get my bearings, stand up, or even figure out where I am. I thought we were in shallow water for God's sake! Mostly, I'm terrified for Riel. I can't see her or feel her, and when I come up I can't focus.

Finally I see her closer to the shore than I am, and try to make my way to her, but something is wrong; I keep falling over. Things keep spinning and I keep falling as I try to reach to her. By the time I struggle out of the water, the world grows dark for a bit and I find myself on my hands and knees trying not to throw up. I'm no doctor, but something has definitely gone sideways. I lie on the sand in a hallucinogenic reverie, congratulating myself on the perfect execution of another dementedly whack-ass idea as I look up into the concerned faces of my family.

The next day at a walk in clinic, I discover that when the boogie board slammed into my ear it ruptured my eardrum. The thought that I might lose my musical life makes me emotional, and I involuntarily start whimpering. When the doctor tells me that my eardrum will heal itself if I take care of it and cease my aquatic buffoonery, I burst into tears. The Bible says Jesus wept. I blubbered.

So … yay my ear will heal!

But now I'm in Hawaii and I can't go in the water for six to eight weeks. Sean takes his role as a local guide seriously, so we hit the weekend with gusto. We rent a big van so we can all travel together and take off Saturday morning. On our way through Honolulu, little baby Caitlin has a bit of an episode, known in mom and tot circles as "screaming blue murder", necessitating an emergency stop. Not one to waste a single moment, our intrepid guide stops in front of Duane 'The Dog' Chapman's place. You know Dog, the ex-con, born-again Christian bounty hunter with the TV show.

While Caitlin visits the dairy queen in the backseat, Zion, Riel, and I rattle the door and peer through the blacked-out windows, to no avail. No need to Beware of Dog: apparently he's left the building.

We head up Pali Highway, stopping off for a little hike to a spot known to locals as Jackass Ginger. A handful of black, idle SUVs and some bored-looking body builder types loitering along the highway was our first clue that something was up.

Through a serendipitous exchange as we roll by, Sean discovers *LOST* is filming in the area. We park up the road and hike through a bamboo forest as Zion and Riel exchange *Kung Fu Panda* dialogue. Our attempt to crash through the woods and accidentally stumble into Jack, Kate, and Locke is unsuccessful. The hike is gorgeous and honestly, with all the beauty and ska-dooshing going on, no one really cared.

We continue on to Kailua Beach, the poster child of Hawaii's beach babies. Writers with larger vocabularies than I could dig deep into pockets full of adjectives and still be at a loss to fully describe the fine white sand, jubilant jungle greens, and turquoise-crystal blue water.

After frolicking for a few hours in God's backyard, we head to Waikiki. Along the way, Sean pulls over on the side of the highway and tells us not to ask any questions but just to follow him. We snake our way along a faint trail that runs off into the dense vegetation. In Winnipeg, a trail like that would ultimately lead to a nest of dirty needles, empty bottles and a bunch of guys singing Freebird down by the river. But in Oahu a mere ten-minute stroll off the freeway leads us to a ledge 40' above a pool of water. It's a location from the film *The Run Down*, featuring Dwayne 'The

Rock' Johnson and Seann William Scott. We're standing a stone's throw from the Pali Highway, looking down into the pool we recognized from the scene where the actors plunged down a mountain, followed quickly by a CGI jeep.

With no hesitation, Sean strips to the waist, looks the camera in the eye and says, "This one goes out to the *Run Down,*" and steps over the ledge, disappearing into the water below.

Having blown the hole in my eardrum the day before, I'm relegated to the role of cameraman as Sean makes repeated trips over the edge. I'm not jealous; I'm envious. With the kids chattering excitedly about the "adventure of a lifetime", we head down to Waikiki. We walk along the strip sipping exotic fruit juices, basking in the luxurious humidity and ocean mist, and mugging for the camera in front of the Duke Kahanamoku statue. As the sun slowly sinks into the sea, we grab a front row patch of grass to catch the hula show. Torchlight flickers like fireflies off the palm leaves as Hawaiian hips make grass skirts dance as if they are alive. I get Riel to pinch me at one point just to make sure it's really real. For a nine year old, that chick has nails.

The sun has set and we've packed more into one day than I'd have thought possible, but on the way back to the van, Sean sidled up next to me.

"I know it's late and everyone's tired, but do you think you guys are up for one more thing?" he asks conspiratorially.

With a vision in his creative mind and the wheel in his capable hands, we cruise up to the Kahala Mandarin Oriental Hotel, a swanky place where dolphins, manta rays, and turtles swim in a private lagoon.

That night, I teach Zion and Riel what I feel is an important life lesson. When you are somewhere you're not supposed to be, doing something you have no right to do, and want to avoid detection, sometimes the best disguise is just to stroll purposefully through the grounds as if you own the place. I've never gotten a job or a gig without employing this important technique.

The kids drift into my slipstream like capable little wingmen as we navigate the lobby and lounge. Crossing the little stone bridge, we slip down to the edge where a hand slap on the water is rewarded with the sudden appearance of numerous dolphins just inches away. When it's all over and we're heading home, I let the hypnotic lights of Honolulu carry me away; it seems impossible that we'd had so many exotic experiences in just one day.

From hockey to Hawaii in a matter of hours, this is where the trip went international, and the kids learned how much they love getting beat up by giant waves.

Man-Eating Mandibles and Surly Dispositions

Hanauma Bay was declared a marine conservation area and underwater park back in the late 60s. Legend has it that two warriors fell in love with a princess and hand-wrestled at the bay to decide who got her. When neither guy could get the upper hand, the princess started worrying that they were actually going to hurt themselves. She turned herself into the beautiful mountain that is now called Koko Crater so that these two wrestlers could gaze longingly on her beauty forever. Then her dad shape-shifted into a dragon, curled up at the foot of Koko Crater and became the protective arms surrounding Hanauma Bay.

The curvature of the coast protects the bay from large ocean waves making it an amazing place to snorkel along a reef. I had another fabulous opportunity to bask in the brilliance of trying to teach Riel how to boogie board. With my ruptured eardrum, I got to stand in water up to my chest as Zion, Sean, and Zara snorkeled in the crystal water, chasing fish of every colour of the rainbow. From my vantage point above the surface, it looked like they were swimming in a magical underwater fairytale world with gumdrops and jellybeans. Every time Zion would come up, he'd start jabbering excitedly about what he'd just seen before he'd even broken the surface. It was hilarious watching his lips try to form words around his snorkel. It looked like he was eating excitement with an open mouth.

The next day we headed to Waimea Bay, which means Red Water in Hawaiian. We followed a windy little dirt trail to Pu'u o Mahuka, the largest heiau, or religious site, on Oahu, covering almost two acres. Pu'u o Mahuka means "hill of escape".

Native Hawaiians and kama'aina, people who have lived on Hawaii for a long time, still bring offerings of fruit to the small living altar. We followed a path into the dense under-brush, making me feel a bit like Merry and Pippin running into Fangorn Forest. It looked as if the path was starting to peter out. To my untrained eye it sure seemed as if it could have been made by wild Hawaiian boars with man-eating mandibles and surly dispositions.

My heightened senses and overly active imagination kicked in as I vividly recalled the traumatic events of a harrowing tale in a different forest only months before. It happened when I was up in Inuvik, a community located one hundred miles north of the Arctic Circle. I was performing at the Great Northern Arts Festival with Tribe of One. Wanting to take full advantage of our play day in Canada's arctic wonderland, performance painter Tina Newlove and I headed out with cameras in hand to see just what we could see. We wound our way past the rows of houses brightly painted in primary colours like "Smartie" buildings, perched atop pilings. The pilings are a unique necessity for people building in the far north with year-round permafrost. Power, water, and waste lines run above ground through enclosed tunnels called uti-lidors. These utility corridors crisscross the community, vaguely resembling corrugated row housing for Hobbits. They built stairs at regular intervals for pedestrians to make their way up and over these Shire shanties.

Anyway, we wandered through the community and eventu-ally climbed up a hill where we could take pictures of the endless skyline seen from the top of the world. On our way back down, I saw what looked like a path leading off into the woods. Without a thought for potential calamity I struck off with a purposeful stride, casting some tripe over my shoulder to Tina that "we're going to Rivendell, Master Gamgee, to the house of Elrond," in an extremely lame Aragorn impersonation.

We were well into the woods and far beyond the reach of the most hysterical cries for help, when Tina decided to bring up a documentary she'd seen on wolverines.

"They're like small ferocious bears," she said, succinctly summing up the horrific image of claws and teeth she had just painted in my mind.

Suddenly our midday stroll along the Jimmy Adams Peace Trail took on an aura of evil. I started to envision roaming herds of rabid wolverines with foam-flecked spittle dotting matted fur and upper lips stained with hemoglobin moustaches. I started scouring the woods looking for a stout stick, to what end I have no idea, but each one I picked up had dry rot and immediately disintegrated in my hands. Feeling like every second counted and that we might already be being stalked, I started scrambling around on all fours flinging fallen leaves, picking up sticks and whacking them against trees to test their stoutness, as splinters and slivers flew about my neck and shoulders like Geppetto making hay in his workshop. I loathed the shrill undertone of my forced banter that betrayed my growing anxiety and tried to compensate by talking some pseudo gangsta s#%.

"I pity the bitch-ass mother-f#%ing wolverine that gets up in my business yo. I ain't kiddin ya' ll, I' ll pop a cap in that ass. I don't mess around *Beyotch*, so no wolverine bitches better be messing around with me!"

While my gums were flapping in the breeze, I secretly convinced myself that if positioned just right, I could probably outrun Tina. I justified the selfishness of this train of thought by promising myself that as a wordsmith, I could wax eloquent at her funeral, really put the "her" in "heroic". As we walked, I constructed her selfless eulogy in my mind, how she told me to save myself and only asked that I remind the world of the beauty she brought through her paintings.

We stumbled out of the woods. I had an overwhelming feeling like we'd just "dodged the big one" and started yelling to Tina to keep up as I sprinted for high ground atop the nearest utilador.

That terrifying experience had happened just months ago,

and even though Hawaii was a world away from Inuvik, here I was again, in another forest, being stalked and surrounded.

"Holy déjà-vu man," I exhaled under my breath, trying to be brave for the kids.

"It's amazing how fast a leisurely stroll through a lush tropical forest can turn into such a bloody nightmare," I whispered to Zara as she passed me.

When Sean wasn't looking, I started picking up coconuts and fashioning a palm frond sling, revisiting the more salient details in the story of David and Goliath in my mind. Miraculously we emerged from the jungle without incident. I can only assume the enraged boars were afraid of breaking a fragile truce on sacred land.

We found ourselves high above the bay as Waimea's white sand and giant surf stretched out below us. Sean took a picture of our family and captured one of the most exhilarating moments of our trip. In the winter months, Waimea Bay is a favourite surf destination and home to the Eddie Aikau Big Wave Invitational competition. Eddie is a legendary Hawaiian surfer and the first lifeguard of the North Shore of Oahu. Eddie Would Go T-shirts and bumper stickers abound, immortalizing the courage of this lifeguard who would swim out to rescue surfers when no one else would.

The Eddie Aikau surfing tournament started in 1984, but in the twenty-five years since has only been held eight times due to the condition that waves must be at least 20' high. We just happened to be there for lucky number eight as Waimea delivered an event of legendary proportions as waves of up to 50' rolled in for the 25th Anniversary.

Anticipation on the island leading up to the contest was electric. Everyone everywhere was speculating on whether it would be called today, or tomorrow. The average Hawaiian has an impressive grasp of technical jargon related to weather patterns, barometric pressure, water temperature, and every other variable that contributes to monstrous waves.

Originally, we thought we'd actually go to Waimea the day the event was called, but when we got out of bed, Sean told us that there were already 30,000 people on the beach at sunrise. We chose to sip our coffee and huddle around the TV to watch Kelly Slater, Bruce Irons, and Garrett McNamara tackle the insane waves. Eddie's younger brother Clyde was still in the lineup at sixty years old, but it was a Californian named Greg Long who surfed his way to victory.

Instead of braving the north shore crowds, Sean gave us the Hawaiian movie and TV history tour.

"Over here is where they filmed part of *Jurassic Park III* and over there is where they filmed *50 First Dates*. To my left, your right, is the road from the opening sequence of *Magnum P.I.*"

Around each corner, Sean could rattle off an impressive string of movie deets and trivia. The December we were there, they were filming the final season of *LOST*.

Sean leads us right into the Survivor's beach camp. There is no one around, including security. We wander through the camp past the kitchen and tattered lean-to structures. In a pile of rubble off in the bush we discover a plastic Dharma Initiative white onion can that accidentally falls into my backpack just as a black 4x4 appears. The pounding surf makes it impossible to hear the vehicle before it's on us.

Oh great, we are totally busted. As a performer, I've spent twelve years honing my ability to get out of crowded venues after a concert so as the guy climbs out of the 4x4 I just drift, silently and unobtrusively, into the background. I'm almost back to civilization when I realize Zion and Riel haven't followed my example: I've essentially left my children unattended on private property to be prosecuted to the full extent of the law by a major Hollywood production company. So, I slide back into the picture, where Zara, Alice, Riel, and baby Caitlin have done what girls do best: they've distracted ... The Man.

He's the Director of Photography and tells us that if security had found us they'd bounce our asses off the set in a heartbeat, but admits that he doesn't care and proceeds to regale the ladies with stories of his life. He eventually ends up taking some group photos for us. That night, Sean, Riel, and I film a spoiler for the ending of our latest video *Zion & Riel – LOST!* discovering Bub, the little stuffie Zion had made, hiding in the Dharma Initiative white onion can in the grass.

Über Conservative Christians, Mormons & Mermaids

It's Sunday, December 7th. We woke up this morning at 7:55 a.m. to the sound of the fighter jets flying low over Honolulu commemorating the anniversary of Pearl Harbor. We all head up to Haleiwa and hit the Coffee Gallery where we sip Pipeline Blend dark roast and nibble on papaya and citrus muffins. Surf aficionados mill about, chattering animatedly about waves and the people who are in town to ride them. Rainwater stands in pools and the saltwater mist in the air is almost as thick as the coffee. We watch a glassblower molding a Gecko while schmaltzy Christmas carols play over shop speakers. This world is a world away from anywhere I've ever been before.

Traveling Oahu with Sean and Alice reinforces what we believe to be true, that being a traveler kicks ass over being a tourist. Tourists are relegated to buses, resorts, and buffets, while travelers get to slip off the beaten path to taste and see what life is like from the people actually living there. A couple of nights earlier we followed Sean and Alice through a random maze of suburban streets, winding our way up a hill and parking in front of an empty lot for sale for a cool three million bucks. The house had burned down years ago, leaving nothing but an old concrete foundation and some scattered weeds. Sean grabbed Caitlin and started down a path I hadn't even seen. Hawaiians are pretty militant about public beaches belonging to the public. This means a bunch of rich people can't connect the fifteen-foot walls that surround their ocean-front property to prevent people like us from getting to the sand. We mountain-goated our way down a steep path that led out to a magnificent volcanic shoreline. The lot above us suddenly seemed accurately priced; this really is a million-dollar view. Sean and Alice surprised us with a little picnic of chocolate, mango, green tea, vanilla, and strawberry mochi. Mochi is a Japanese rice cake made of glutinous rice pounded into a paste. Small balls of ice cream are wrapped inside a mochi covering to make mochi ice cream balls.

We could have been in Winnipeg, huddled around our wood-burning fireplace in our drafty, ninety-year-old home that night in December. Instead, we were sitting on a volcanic island in the middle of the Pacific Ocean eating mochi and watching the sun set on another perfect day in paradise.

On Monday, we decided to go to Pearl Harbor, one of the most popular tourist destinations on Oahu with around 4000 visitors a day. We toured the monuments outside the museum, reading stories of courage, bravery, and sacrifice before heading into the theatre to watch the historic footage of the attack. To actually be in Honolulu, watching the film where it all happened, made the fear and horror that much more tangible as the first wave of 183 fighters, bombers, and torpedoes hit at 7:55 a.m. The second wave of 170 planes attacked at 8:54 a.m., the battle altogether lasting for two hours. After the film, we filed out of the theatre and jumped on board the shuttle-boat that takes visitors to the Memorial built over the sunken remains of the USS Arizona. It was sobering and I was glad that real images and stories of real events felt different to Zion after all the video games he plays. I was also thankful to have my own Pearl Harbor experience to assuage the horrific memories of Michael Bay's cinematic cluster-mug.

The Polynesian Triangle encompasses approximately 16 million square miles of the Pacific Ocean, with Hawaii at the northern apex, Aotearoa in the southwest, and Rapa Nui or Easter Island in the southeast.

The Polynesian Cultural Center (PCC) is a nonprofit institution founded by The Church of Jesus Christ of Latter-day Saints to help preserve and showcase South Pacific island cultures. PCC has six different villages that offer cultural presentations from Aotearoa (Maori, New Zealand), Hawaii, Tahiti, Fiji, Samoa, and

Tonga. Since the Center opened on October 12, 1963, over 33 million people have visited and nearly 17,000 students have financed their studies at Brigham Young University (BYU)-Hawaii by working at PCC. It is also where Elvis filmed *Paradise Hawaiian Style* in 1966. There is a great black and white photo of the King hanging just inside the front gates.

The über conservative Christian environment of my youth had a long list of people we were officially against, like Catholics, gays, Liberals, etc. Many of the reasons were colourful and quaint, while some were just bigoted and racially motivated; somewhere in the list were the Mormons. So it was exotic and exciting to discover that Alice was raised as a Mormon. It was like someone saying they were raised as a mermaid.

Not only was Alice a Mormon/Mermaid, but a BYU alumnus to boot. Proving Sean wasn't the only highly connected local with mad hospitality skills, Alice made a call and wham-bam thank-you-ma'am, we had tickets to PCC!

After ingesting heavy doses of religious indoctrination in my youth, I've developed what some pastors and religious leaders have called a Dysfunctional Disposition.

Now I'm not here to argue whether a whack-ass attitude about crazy religiosity is dysfunctional or discerning. But I want to admit I was wondering what this Mormon cultural event was going to be like. We drove up to Laie and met Alice's friend Chailoh in the McDonald's parking lot and honestly, Chailoh was the perkiest person I've ever met. I'm pretty sure she perspires positivity. As we chatted she invited us to a Christmas party she was throwing at her place in Hau'ula that night. The thought of getting down at a Christmas party in an oceanfront home with a bunch of Mormons was frankly just too much to pass up.

We spent the afternoon taking in cultural presentations at the Maori Aotearoa, Samoa, Tahiti and Tonga villages. The highlight of the day was the sexy smartass Samoan making his pecs dance and flirting with the women as he turned a coconut into a three-course meal in under ten minutes. Riel was impressed, in a scandalous sort of way, at how the women from Tahiti could shake their moneymakers.

When the village presentations were over we drove down the coast to this super cute house right on the water for Chailoh's party. I think it was a particularly progressive group of Mormons, as wine was involved, though I have a suspicion it was present to make dysfunctional evangelicals like me more comfortable.

I only say this because a lady came up to me and asked if I'd like some wine.

"Oh, that would be great" I said, genuinely feeling at that moment that the only thing that could make the moment any better would be a glass of red wine.

As she handed me a plastic cup a few minutes later, she whispered, "I'm sorry it's not cold, it was just sitting on the counter."

"No problem, that's perfect," I assured her. After she walked away, I looked down to see she'd added three big ice cubes to my wine. Hilarious!

We headed back to the PCC and thoroughly enjoyed *Breath of Life*, a three million dollar production that combined all the unique expressions into one extravaganza of Polynesian culture. During intermission instead of popcorn and peanuts, the ushers walked up and down the aisles selling bowls of fresh fruit ice cream. It was great.

Sean had warned us that we wanted to get out of the theatre and on the road as quick as we could after the show, because there was only the two lane highway leading back to Mililani, and getting caught behind hundreds of cars would definitely suck. The show ended and the family launched into action. Zion and I threw decorum out the window and crawled over three rows of chairs to get to the aisle. Zara and Riel were behind us, moving fast, bobbing and weaving through the rank and file like wide receivers going long.

We hit the parking lot at different times and from different doors. Hundreds of people with the same expressed intent made it feel like we were in the *Amazing Race*. I was scanning the crowd looking for some sign that Zara and Riel were still behind us when Zion discovered they had actually overtaken us without our noticing. As soon as we saw them, they started to run.

"Come on Dad!" Zion exhorted, "Mom's got her quick feet on," as he sprinted off after them.

As we were two decades younger than 90% of our competitors, we left them behind like a bad smell, and had nothing but clear skies and bright stars before us as we hit the road.

After our day of cultural exploration, I imagined that during the drive home the four of us would talk deeply and passionately about music, art, and Polynesian culture. Within moments, Zion dashed these dreams on the harsh rocks of reality.

"That was a pretty amazing day, hey kids," I said.

Riel agreed it had been, while Zion seemed preoccupied, almost pensive and lost deep in thought.

Thinking to mine some of the wealth of his keen perception I asked, "What are you thinking about, Zi?"

"I was just thinking that it would be awesome if we could change the meaning of penis so I could use it more in casual conversations," he replied.

The family spent the 45-minute drive listening to Zion offer possible new meanings for penis, including how to use them effectively as sentence enhancers. This ultimately led to his question of the day. "Mom, why do people have hair connecting their belly button to their penis?" he asked.

"I don't know, Zi, I guess they're pube extenders," Zara replied.

We spent a day traveling to different locations used for TVs and movies, including the set of LOST, where we were inspired to shoot a 'Lost' scene of our own.

MALAYSIA

Rock Star Swagger With Cock-On-The-Block Pizzazz

The alarm clock says it's 5:00 a.m. When I come out of the bathroom moments later, I find Zara knocking on the kids' door. I look at her quizzically.

"Locked," she mutters with an early morning, I-don't-need-this exasperation.

I know Zion and Riel will never be roused by quiet, polite knocking, and I don't want to wake the neighbours at 5:00 a.m. by pounding and screaming, so I scrounge through my bag for a pen and manage to pick the lock. Upon entry, I turn on the lights and find Riel sleeping in Zion's bed, while her bed lies empty. A quick scan of the room fails to uncover my son. A momentary chill catches in my throat as I imagine some nefarious abduction, my eyes darting to the window for any signs of forced entry. I fall to my knees and shove the mattress on the floor out of the way. I pull up the bed ruffle and peer into the dark abyss under the bed and discover my teen, fast asleep in the fetal position.

Eventually it's time to head out the front door and start loading backpacks into the vehicle. There is a spooky mist hanging in the air and an oppressive silence I assume exists every day in the early morning hours that I so rarely frequent. I feel quite conspiratorial, like we are slipping out of the city in the middle of the night on another whirlwind adventure of international intrigue.

I look down at Riel, who is trudging across the parking lot in front of me with her fuzzy blanket and travel pillow tucked under her arm and her day pack filled with puzzles, books, and snacks.

"I'm so glad I'm doing this trip with you, Riel," I whisper. She beams in response.

Backpacks and gear loaded, we're ready to go. I know Zara finds airports, customs, and all the officials unpleasant, so as she comes across the parking lot I intercept her for a we're-going-to-get-through-it hug. Riel sees us from the car and squeals "family hug!" as she jumps out the door dashing to join us. Never one to be left out of a family hug, Zion scampers out the other side grabbing Sean, and soon we are circled around a storm drain in the parking lot peering up and down into each other's smiling faces.

Pretty damn good life we're living, I think to myself.

We pile into Sean's car and start for the airport. We've left plenty of time for possible traffic snarls and delays but traffic is moving smoothly and when Sean realizes that we can use the carpool lane, we're suddenly flying at breakneck speeds arriving so far in advance that extra-curricular activities are actually required. So we head to Starbucks where I discover my son is one of "those" people, the ones who order coffee as if they're reading a periodic table of contents.

"I'll have a double shot, caramel macchiato, no fat, frappuccino," he says with a smile. Zion only started drinking iced coffees during the summer on our tour across Canada, so how, or when, he picked up these mad skills is beyond me.

Feeling a bit lame with my plain latte I inhale some froth as Zi suddenly exclaims, "Oh my god, my pants are on backwards."

He does a quick "Clark Kent" in the bathroom and grabs his coffee on the way out with rock star swagger and cock-on-the-block pizzazz. We drive to the edge of an airfield and, our last morning on the island, finally catch a sunrise. We will watch the sunset that night in China.

We'd booked our flight to Malaysia in August through CheapOAir back when we were at Ian and Ros' place in North Bay. We still haven't entirely shaken the fear that the deal was too good to be true and have a nagging fear in the back of our minds that something is going to go wrong.

From Honolulu, we will fly to Tokyo, then on to Taipei. We have a fourteen-hour layover in Taipei before our last flight to Penang. Zara had done some research through Lonely Planet and read numerous stories about how hard it was to get out of the airport in Taipei and how you had to hand over your passport. She's now prepared to spend the night in the airport sleeping on a vinyl bench. The idea sucks and I totally admit I'm not on board. As we're pulling up to the terminal we get into this conversation again, when Sean chimes in to say that often airlines arrange accommodations for you if you have an overnight layover. Armed with this small ray of hope I approach the Air China desk with an air of Captain James T. Kirk, boldly going where I have never gone before. I was once again employing the eager, slightly effeminate, flirtatious air as I inquire if they had already taken care of booking this simple thing. They say they haven't but would get someone on it ASAP. I ask every Air China employee I find all day long and by the time we arrive in Taipei they're waiting for us.

We're given a sticker for our lapel, paperwork to sign, directed through a special immigration wicket, escorted outside the airport where a shuttle driver picks us up and drives us to the Novotel Hotel. The swankiest, hippest place we'll stay in all year. The complimentary breakfast the next morning is out of this world. In a culinary celebration of East meets West, there is everything from a fresh fruit bar, waffles, pancakes, bacon and eggs to sushi, grilled salmon, dumplings, desserts, and a cappuccino machine. Our total is $120.00 for the room, supper the night we arrived, and the incredible breakfast buffet.

The coup de grace is when the concierge presents Riel with a Panda stuffie she promptly names Tai. We arrive back at the airport feeling rested, relaxed, and full of good vibrations, vibes we will desperately need in a few short hours when we touch down in Malaysia.

We arrive in Penang, the "Pearl of the Orient", early afternoon December 17. It is +35° C/95°F with 100% humidity. Straight off our exciting experience at the Novotel Hotel the night before, we're feeling great and ready for Malaysia, which is a good thing, because wires have gotten crossed.

We get our bags and make our way to the arrivals lobby where we discover there is no one waiting to meet us. Our distant relatives are still that, distant. Not to worry, we assure the kids, we'll just get a sim card, drop it into our cell phone, call the relatives and find out when they're going to arrive. Zion and I make our way outside the airport to a kiosk where we find an awesome young woman who sells us exactly what we need. She even pops our phone open, inserts the sim card and starts to enter the code to set it all up for us.

This is when we discover that Rogers Wireless even manages to suck on the other side of the world. The phone is locked, which means we can't use the sim card. She pops the card out, returns our money, and twenty minutes later we return to our pile of backpacks where we inform Zara and Riel of our lack of progress. So I head over to a bank of pay phones only to discover there is some incomprehensible reason we can't call the Australian relatives' cell phones from Malaysian pay phones.

Zion is getting increasingly nervous, and asks repeatedly, "What are we going to do?"

Back home the kids have always enjoyed the security that comes from knowing their parents know where they are, where they're going, and how to get there. Suddenly Zion finds himself feeling like a little foreigner in a big foreign country where airport security is dressed in full combat fatigues carrying automatic weapons. Understandably his faith in his father is shaken, especially as he watches me fail at something as simple as using a cell phone. I will happily explain to him in detail for the rest of the year what a crap company Rogers is, but for the moment, it's me, not Rogers, who is coming off as a crappy service provider.

As I stand by the bank of pay phones trying to figure out our next move, a fellow traveler taps me on the shoulder and asks if I'd like to use his cell phone. Soon enough I'm talking to Matthew, our Aussie cousin, asking in a really non-judgmental way if he, or someone else from the family, was planning on making an appearance at the airport any time soon to collect their Canadian rellies.

"Oh, sorry mate," Matthew replied in a really un-sorry "I'm-from-down-under-and-have-no-worries" sort of way. I haven't met Matthew at this point, but immediately start to cobble together a composite sketch of the man. I picture equal parts Baloo and his whole "bare necessities" vibe, with Pumbaa and Timon's "hakuna matata" being sung on a beach by a bronze-skinned Aussie with scores of Great Whites frolicking in the surf just off-shore. As I eventually get to know Matthew I realize my initial assessment wasn't that far off.

Matthew is on the other side of the city. Apparently some-one has written the wrong date and time of our arrival, but he gives us the name of the apartment building where we're staying and directs us to the prepay taxi service in the airport. He even tells us how many ringgits it should cost, and our problems, at least for the moment, are sorted. We hoist our backpacks into the taxi and off we go.

It is illegal in Malaysia for taxi drivers to negotiate flat rate fares, but the rate per minute set by the government is so low the companies would never make a living, so every ride is negotiated by the flat rate. I don't know this as we pull out of the terminal, and am a bit nervous as we approach the line of soldiers with machine guns, when the driver says, "Let me do the talking. If anyone asks you just say you pay this," as he tapped the meter. As we cruise past checkpoint Charlie, I start quietly humming "those bare necessities, those simple bare necessities, don't worry about your trouble or your strife".

I make a mental note to ask Matthew what would be involved in converting to the "No Worries Mate" religion.

Malaysia is one of those countries where I am immediately happy I'm not driving. Traffic is a buffet where the horn is the main dish and signal indicators are at best a superfluous garnish. The dividing lines for lanes seem to be nothing more than a vague suggestion, playful hints if you will, that motorists may or may not want to consider as they are driving. Judging by the death-de-fying feats of insanity, most it seems choose "not".

Cars are grossly outnumbered by scooters that swarm like bees at every intersection. While we idle at red lights, scooters with whole families on board or furniture or fast food being delivered weave through the lanes to the front of the line where they literally swarm the crosswalk. When the light turns green, they take off in a cloud of exhaust and a deafening high-pitched whine that sounds like the Indianapolis 500 on helium. As they get up to road speed, they start to veer to the left of the road and allow the line of cars coming up from behind to start weaving through their ranks. It's kind of like a terrifying video game. Most lights are staggered just far enough apart that we manage to pass most of them before hitting the next red light where the swarming happens all over again.

Zion and Riel are in the backseat playing a game of "Can You Believe That?" pointing and exclaiming at the madness buzzing around us. I was expecting a sticker on someone's bumper to say: *Evil Knievel was a pussy ... I drive a scooter in Malaysia.*

We're going to stay in Batu Ferringhi, which is a good hour from the airport and the drive provides us with our first opportunity to get a feel for the sights and sounds of Malaysia.

Back in the 1800s, a French explorer named Jules Dumont d'Urville came up with the terms Malaysia, Micronesia, and Melanesia, differentiating these cultures from Polynesia.

Malaysia is the state, while Malay refers to the language, culture, and people. Somewhere in the 1860s, Malaysia became a British colony and stayed that way until the Japanese invasion in 1941. A few hours before attacking Pearl Harbor, the Japanese landed in Kota Bahru, so one could argue the battle of the Pacific actually started in Malaysia.

This helps explain the surprising amount of English signs and billboards and the occasional sandwich board advertising a Real English Breakfast.

Our cab driver is a prodigious man who can weave and bob through the hints and suggestions of local traffic with the best of them. Matthew has told me to go to the Eden Fairway apartments in Batu Ferringhi, which is where we're headed. At least we hope that's where we're headed. After driving for about forty-five minutes our cab driver starts making a series of phone calls to his dispatch; there's no preamble or platitudes, just a rapid punching of numbers punctuated by him yelling "EDEN FAIRWAY!" into his phone. He listens for a couple of seconds and then yells again, and again and again. Then he hangs up and drives for a while before picking up the phone and starting to yell again, "EDEN FAIRWAY APARTMENTS!"

Brutally aware of Zion's skepticism with my competency to navigate this foreign culture, I try to lighten the apprehensive mood by pretending to be Phil Keoghan doing a voice over on the *Amazing Race*.

"Teams must now travel through the streets of Penang to Batu Ferringhi where they will find their next clue."

We make it to the right area and the right street, but no address seems to match. I'm sure the driver is blaming me, judging me, with his wide, deep brown eyes and honest face, and just when I think he's going to forcefully eject us from his cab, Zara spies a tiny sign across the street that says Eden Fairway Apartments. Our driver pulls a *Dukes of Hazard* U-turn through oncoming traffic, careening up over the curb where he parks sideways across the sidewalk.

As he's tossing our backpacks out of his trunk onto the sidewalk, the lady managing the apartments serendipitously arrives, along with a van full of our Aussie rellies. With hugs and kisses and introductions all around, we're quickly given directions to the hotels and villas where the rest of the rellies are staying. We wave a quick goodbye as the manager whisks us through security, up the locked elevators, and into our apartment. We've made it! In one piece, with both kids AND all of our luggage. Maybe Matthew and the Pillars of the Assembly are right, maybe there aren't any worries.

The Host of Heaven Laughing Their Asses Off

We included Malaysia on our trip because Zara's cousin Matthew was getting married to Kelly, who had been born in Malaysia. Virtually everyone coming to the wedding was from somewhere else in the world, including Matthew and Kelly themselves. An incredible amount of planning and organizing accommodations and activities had taken place. We were invited to piggyback on those plans, including grabbing an apartment at Eden Fairway. A couple of months out, it sounded like a brilliant idea. It was just a couple of blocks from the beach and the 11th storey balcony offered a million-dollar view to watch the sun set over the ocean.

The problem was everything attached to the balcony was kind of … crappy. It was a combination of things really, the lingering aroma of mothballs, coldwater showers, a kitchen stocked with one frying pan and one pot, both blackened and warped from decades of use. It looked like MacGyver had jimmied a submarine-sized propane tank under the kitchen counter to fuel the gas stove. Thankfully, it didn't explode while we were there, but unfortunately it didn't work either. We were so thankful not to be spending our first night in Malaysia on the street, or curled up in the fetal position in the airport terminal under the harsh, uncompromising glare of our children's "how-could-you-do-this-to-us" gaze, that we happily forked over a princely sum in ringgits for the pleasure of the dodgy accomms.

The next morning Riel and I headed out of our apartment to the day market to try to find something for breakfast. It was still early morning but already the air was hot and wet. Worn and weathered Mitsubishi vans filled with assorted produce and products lined both sides of the side street, funneling the flow of foot traffic into one slow-moving stream straight down the middle. Folding tables were covered with everything from plastic cups and plates to oven mitts, radios, mangoes, and cigarettes. Tarps were laid out on the ground to display an impressive selection of fish, crab, and prawns, but more than anything the tarps were dedicated to pig products. Every pork part was accounted for, the hooves, snout, and ears; even whole decapitated heads were available.

The smell was distinct, the imagery shockingly visceral, making Riel's first twenty-four hours in Malaysia unforgettable. She looked up at me at one point, nose wrinkled in disgust, "Is this why you don't eat pigs?"

I grew up on a pig farm in the Canadian prairies and upon coming of age proudly proclaimed that I would no longer be consuming the cloven-hoofed animal *ever again*. My children have graciously accepted this prejudice without adopting it as their own.

In answer to Riel's question, I nodded sagely, hoping that head bobbing with pursed lips made me look wise and not just simple, as my overactive imagination immediately injected a pseudo "Nam-like" flashback as I was transported back in time to the pig barn.

Flash

I'm back in "The Barn" breathing in the pungent smell of poo and pee while trying to avoid everything icky, gucky, stinky and gross … so, basically everything.

Flash

I see my eight-year-old self receiving fifteen seconds of "basic training" from my dad before I'm sent to the "front lines" to hold a thin sheet of particleboard in front of me as a wild stampede of rabid, frothing swine are driven my way. I am given several assurances that the pigs will see the board and veer happily into their respective crates.

Flash

Little Ricky sallies forth, dreamily imagining man and beast taking a serene stroll down God's garden path Narnia style. (Apparently, someone forgot to tell the pigs … and my brother.)

Flash

Primal shrieks and bellows of profanity pierce the air as my brother hurtles a 250-pound gilt toward me with alarming speed.

Flash

Flailing flesh rattles and crashes as my brother and the gilt, two titanic forces of stubbornness and obstinacy, make their way ever closer.

Flash

Violence erupts as punches are thrown and absorbed – testicles are pawed with blunted hooves and rutting foreheads as sweat flows freely down my brother's furrowed brow, stinging his eyes that are glowing red with fevered intensity.

Flash

Eight-year-old Ricky Leaf, crying unabashedly behind a wafer-thin sheet of particleboard clutches the end of his pee-pee in desperation as his pre-pubescent bladder slips precariously close to complete collapse.

Flash

My brother is towering over me with his arms wrapped around the pig's writhing torso as she rears up on her back legs, swaying in his clutches like a drunken Presbyterian at her first high school dance.

Flash

Trying to comfort me in my abject terror my brother is screaming, "What the hell are YOU crying about? She's not even AFTER you!"

Flash

Little Ricky running pell-mell into the wheat field behind the barn throws himself prostrate into a puddle of salt-water tears, pouring out the first of many penitent prayers asking God to remove the plague of pork from his family!

Flash

God, and a host of heaven are listening in … laughing their asses off.

Anyway, back at the Malaysian market, Riel and I purchased a bag of lychees and pineapple, some ground coffee, and a can of condensed milk and headed back to the apartment like conquering heroes who had passed our first test of cross-cultural exploration.

After breakfast, we headed out to meet up with the rest of the relatives. This was Zion and Riel's first Asian experience so everything was new, bizarre, and exciting. As we were dodging and ducking through kiosks and street vendors trying to hustle a buck, Zion said, "You know, this isn't anything like I thought it would be."

I realized we'd never talked about their expectations of the people and places we plan to visit. So we talked about what they had thought they would find.

"Well, to begin with, I didn't think there would be cars," Zion replied. "Yeah," Riel piped in, "I thought it was just going to be a little village."

As we walked, we talked about how the world has developed and is developing and about what opportunity and privilege look like. As we talked, we walked and walked and kept walking. North American car culture can definitely leave you unprepared for the effort of getting around everywhere else in the world, where hoofing it is still the thing. We ended up outside the Hard Rock Hotel two to three kilometres from our apartment. It was hot and steamy and we were starting to wonder if we were ever going to find the elusive rellies when one of them showed up.

Matthew's brother, Christopher, a doctor from England, was just coming out of the Hard Rock and was heading back to their place. So we struck up a conversation and followed his lead to the Ferringhi Villas where the rest of the crew was staying.

As Chris headed off to collect his kids, Zion, Riel, and I jumped into the outdoor swimming pool. After the three-kilometre walk it was awesomely refreshing and just as we kicked back and started to float away on a waterbed of serenity, around the corner came a herd of squealing rellies. Adults were seriously outnumbered by a gaggle of kids with searing vocal chords and throbbing adrenal glands. Right about the time some introductions would be in order, Zara was invited to go off for the day with the rest of the girls, and with a wink and a wave, she disappeared.

Fifteen kids under the age of thirteen transformed the pool into a cauldron of chaos and mayhem. With all the Brits, Aussies, and a Kiwi in the pool I amused myself by listening to the international sentence enhancers; sunnies were sunglasses, swimsuits were bathers, cozzies or swimmers. There were blokes, corkers, and duffers and one kid was scolded for being a "hideous beast". I did overhear a few incomprehensible conversations about footy (Aussie rules football) and cricket, which I eventually understood, but still don't "get". One guy was gobsmacked and one of the kids apparently gave a gobful to someone else. Gross.

Zion and Riel had a great time. The rellies were loaded up with grandsons; there were boys, boys, and more boys, most around three to nine years old, which made thirteen-year-old Zion kingly in his teenage magnificence. I watched as the little cousins pledged their devotion to their Canadian idol as Zi forcefully threw them around the pool with much laughing and squealing with glee.

Riel found meeting other kids more complicated than Captain Gregarious, and was thrilled to discover Annie. Annie was from England; her mum was a cousin of the groom and was off with Zara and the rest of the girls, so Annie and her brother Eddie were at the pool with their dad, Bob.

Bob is a six and a half foot British surgeon from Oxford and was just what Riel needed. He was great at getting the girls to dive for stones, and race across the pool and see who could swim underwater the farthest and stay underwater the longest. Riel had an awesome afternoon thanks to Bob and Annie.

Once the girls were happily playing, Bob and I stretched out poolside and started chatting. When I told him what our family was doing, he immediately responded by saying, "You should come and stay with us in Oxford!" I was gobstruck, assuming an Oxford surgeon would require a patent of nobility before extending an invitation to an artist from the colonies.

The pool was the perfect place to engage in some leisurely hobnobbing with Zara's rellies. As wedding guests had flown from the four corners of the globe, we were able to spend the next three weeks lounging indolently in the Malaysian tropics, sipping Mai Tais and Pina Coladas, wangling invitations to stay with people from Wollongong to Winchester. Networking had never been so enjoyable.

Eventually the women came back from their day on the town, and our little family of four started the three-kilometre hike back to our apartment. Zara was eager to find out how our day had been with her relatives while she was gone.

"Those were the least annoying, most fun kids half my age I have ever played with!" Zion responded, in a wonderfully descriptive summation.

Riel told Zara all about the games she'd played with Annie and the similar things they were interested in as we dodged and ducked through the swarm of scooters back to our apartment and the fragrant potpourri of musty mothballs.

A Shifty Musician With a Wonky Astigmatism

After an exhausting day, I needed to ramp up my social game as I headed out the door to Matthew's Bucks party. The streets were teeming with activity.

Kabobs sizzled on open grills as cigarette smoke and diesel fumes billowed in aromatic clouds. Neon lights cast shadows and shapes that made graffiti dance to the electronica, pounding like a heartbeat from the pasar malam.

The Malaysian night market (pasar malam) is an incredible phenomenon. Hundreds of vendors arrive at sunset, spreading canvas awnings and sheets of corrugated metal over the sidewalk to create a shantytown that stretches for miles. Tables, racks, and shelves are lined with Dolce & Gabbana, Louis Vuitton, and Rolex knock offs, pirated DVDs, knickknacks, bags, and clothes, as tourists slowly crawl through the excess.

When I got to the outdoor pub, I ended up sitting beside Kevin, a retired sheep farmer from the Australian Outback. Kevin had an expansive laugh, an infectious sense of humour and the look of a man who had spent his life working outdoors in one of the hottest countries in the world. Before the end of the night, he would also say the magic words, "When you're down in Australia, you should come stay with us."

The Bucks party was lots of fun but I've noticed over the years that the limitless capacity I once had for socializing has been slipping and suddenly I'll just be done. That night between one round of shots and the next I was just done.

This condition has forced me to develop a unique set of skills my therapist calls an unhealthy coping mechanism. I've made an art form of fading into the background till I just disappear. It was harder to do in a case like this because eventually someone was going to look for me and realize that I'd buggered off without saying goodbye. But that would be tomorrow's problem, for tonight I just needed to disappear.

I waited until all the bucks were distracted with vodka shots before pulling my best Bilbo Baggins and vanishing. And I'd made it; I had slipped away unnoticed and was striding for home, until I ran into one of Matthew's best friends coming out of the washroom. If I hadn't had my guitar slung over my shoulder we would have grunted some inane bear-like greeting and passed each other without a second thought, but because of my frigging guitar, I had the look of a shifty musician slipping out the back.

"You're not leaving are you?" he said, surprised.

"Oh, no, of course not," I lied, and then kept lying. "I just lost a contact … yeah, yeah, that's it, I lost a contact." With a plausible lie to work with I really sank my teeth into it and started chewing.

"It's my left eye which sucks, 'cause my left eye is already such a bugger, you know, with this wonky astigmatism."

As I listened to the inanity coming out of my mouth, I was aware that I really didn't know what half of it meant. But it was too late to slow down now, so I just kept going.

"So I'm just going to run back to my apartment and get a new contact. I' ll be right back, so don't drink all the rum!" I said, in a really bad Captain Jack Sparrow impersonation.

I got back to our dodgy digs and slid into bed beside Zara, who was barely awake.

"How was it?" she mumbled sleepily.

"It was good. I fake-lost a contact, so that's the story in case anyone asks." But she'd already drifted off before she could answer.

The next morning we packed up our stuff. All the wedding guests scattered around various locations in Batu Ferringhi were consolidating at the Park Royal Hotel for the day before and the day of the wedding. Zara and I were trying covertly to figure out a plan that would allow us to avoid coming back. The manager must have picked up on our vibe and kept asking for reassurances that we were coming back. I couldn't say we weren't because we didn't have anywhere else to go, but I didn't want to say we were because we weren't going to stop looking. It's tricky trying to chart a course with a moral compass that keeps pointing toward self-interest.

The Park Royal was luxurious. An oasis of palm trees, cabanas, and a wrap-around pool were just a stone's throw from the ocean. The pillowy white beach was a playground where brightly coloured parasails rose and fell like bumblebees pollinating the umbrellas planted in the sand like exotic flowers. Jet skis and speedboats swerved around the bobbing heads of those crazy enough to go swimming. It was the kind of place where the only reasonable thing to do is nothing, which is what we did in earnest.

Zion now had his faithful flock of devoted cousins assembled in one place, so it wasn't hard to find him if you were looking. You'd just scan the pool and look for the largest, loudest group of happy, squealing children and he'd be there somewhere in the thick of things. Riel and Annie were usually floating by on an enormous inflatable orca.

For our first night at the hotel we were invited to a party just down the beach where the South Africans, Aussies, and Brits were setting up for a rousing game of cricket on the beach. Watching the men try to teach my son the finer points of cricket made me laugh. Zion had never liked competitive sports and regularly scorned any of my attempts to introduce him to any game of any kind. He loved games with no rules, no winners or losers, just a bunch of screaming and wrestling.

When Zion and Riel were six and two years old, their favourite game was a homegrown brand of tickle tag. Our house was designed with an open floor plan and doorways that connected the living room, dining room, and kitchen. Every light on the main floor would be extinguished and rock music would be cranked to ear-bleeding levels. This rendered the senses of sight and hearing virtually useless. The kids would start on the home-free couch, and would have to make it all the way around the circuit before they could return home. I would lurk in the dark and employ various methods of clothes lining and open-field tackles to take the kids down and tickle them voraciously. When they were captured, they would squeal and shriek for help.

"Save me, Riel, save me!" "ZION, HELP!"

Their little voices would have that mixture of excitement and terror. My favourite part of the game was when they would come to each other's rescue, no matter how terrified they were or in what peril their rescue efforts would put them.

We also used to play Red Rover on the outdoor ice rink across the street from our house. Zion couldn't have been less interested in learning to play hockey, but was totally into a game that involved chasing, tagging, sliding, and possibly some on-ice wrestling. Often it would just be the three of us on the rink, so I would make a big production of getting distracted or confused and narrowly miss my prey several times. One day one of Zion's friends saw us out on the ice and ran home to get his skates. He was a competitive little guy and a good little skater, but he whined like a rented mule any time he was tagged. And if he was IT, he would tag Zion and Riel within strides of them leaving the goal line. So yeah, basically the competitive little bugger killed the fun and subsequently the game. Under the pretext of needing to make supper, we packed up and left. On the way home as we trudged through the snowdrifts Zion shared his philosophy on sports.

"People that want to win just wreck things."

This came back to me as I watched some of the older men try to teach Zion the finer points of cricket. I saw his glassy-eyed indifference and laughed as I watched him purposefully bash the ball into the ocean so he could watch the adults chase after it.

Riel and some girls had discovered their own entertainment. There were large pools filled with hungry little fish that would nibble the dry skin from your feet and ankles. It was incredibly ticklish and they sat squealing and shrieking all night.

It was a gorgeous evening as the sun set on the water and we sat sipping wine with guests from continents around the globe. At the end of the night, Zara and I wound our way through the silhouettes of cabanas and sun chairs emptied of their dark passengers, who would faithfully return in the morning for the divine touch of the sun god. I've always marveled at the piety of the truly penitent sun-worshippers, who bare not their souls in quiet supplication, but come instead with the full measure of their ample girth proudly displayed for all the world to see. With buttock and bosom barely contained, doughy flesh straining the stitching and weaves of banana hammocks and thongs, they are truly one of human nature's seven wonders.

Zara and I were searching for the perfect place to savour the glasses of wine in our possession. I ended up choosing the dark side of a Tiki bar where the stars seemed to burn brightest and the bartenders were cranking *Play That Funky Music* which was a huge step up from the wedding party across the palm trees where a Chinese dance band was butchering Neil Diamond's *Sweet Caroline*.

Zara, however, was drawn to a particularly messy train wreck in the Park Royal lounge that involved *Hotel California* and two female Malaysian performers in short pants singing to backing tracks on a laptop. In front of them, middling groups of tourists were besmirching the good name of dancing with perverse forms of hip thrusting and ass-waggery. Thankfully, the wine, the stars, and the rhythmic roll of the waves were not adversely affected for all the shenanigans and we eventually managed to find our perfect moment in spite of our fellow man.

Today is the wedding day and we are traveling across the city on a tour bus. Kelly's brother is regaling everyone with hilarious stories as we snake along windy roads where lush vegetation hangs like veils from cliff faces as scooters, taxis, and transport trucks narrowly avoid catastrophe. Zion and Riel are on the kids' bus, which they describe later at the wedding as patronizing and infantile. Nothing offends our kids more than being treated like kids.

Matthew enters stage left with his brothers Dominic and Christopher. In their light grey suits they look every inch the part of three millionaire playboys who have just helicoptered in from a giant yacht they sailed down on from the Mediterranean.

I know Christopher is a doctor in England, but no one has actually told me what Matthew and Dominic do. I make a mental note to do some imaginary checking later. They look too suave and debonair to have real jobs, but for the moment, I am too preoccupied just trying to breathe in the stiflingly hot tiny church.

Pictures afterward on the church steps are taken with military precision as different groupings of the family tree are hustled on and off the concrete steps to quickly pose with the newlyweds, who were braving the heat and direct sun with a radiance of their own.

Back at the hotel, we sip champagne beneath the grove of palm trees as a breeze comes in off the ocean and a Malaysian three-piece serenades us. When the Muslim call to prayer is broadcast over the city, it mixes with the acoustic jazz in the garden creating the most erotic sonic hook up I've heard in a long while.

The evening is awesome. Arrangements are made for the kids to party at the Coconut Club in the hotel, where they can play games and raise hell. Everyone staying at the hotel means no one had to drive or navigate the night market to get home. The funniest part of the night is just figuring out how to access the wine. It was cheaper for the family to bring the wine into the country themselves, which means the hotel isn't in the slightest bit motivated to serve it. Their interest is in pushing soda pop.

The servers keep coming around, trying to fill glasses with pop as the guests point at the wine. I eventually take matters into my own hands and manage to pilfer a couple of bottles, returning to the table as a conquering hero.

I assume some backroom conversation takes place, probably by a couple of the bodyguards from the imaginary Mediterranean yacht who persuade the manager that "Mr. Matthew" isn't happy, because eventually the embargo is lifted, the pop is shelved, and the night floats exquisitely away.

The wine also makes all the English, South African, Malay, and Australian accents sound extremely cool. The phrase "Charge your glasses and be upstanding" is a reoccurring mantra, as speakers take to the mic to toast the couple.

Kelly's brother Brandon rips it up in his speech, teaching the crowd to scream "Yum Sing!" which means bottoms up.

With a few "introductory" yum sings, a couple more

"practice" yum sings and a full oration peppered with multiple "energetic" yum sings, no one could have driven anywhere after Brandon's speech. I'm hardly able to press the floor number in the elevator on the way back to our room.

Matthew and Kelly's decision to have the wedding in Malaysia meant that everyone was on holiday. By planning the date in late December, most people had also decided to celebrate Christmas and New Year's Eve there as well.

After the Park Royale, we knew we weren't into moving back into our dodgy accommodations at the Eden Fairway Apartments. Like castaways on *Survivor* we had been investigating possible alliances.

Christopher and Katherine stayed in one of the villas in the gated complex and invited us to move in with them. This seemed like a great idea. Zion and Riel had the loft, Zara and I were in a bedroom off the kitchen, and we were within walking distance of the relatives and the pool. For two days it was great, until the bride and groom wanted to move back in and discovered we'd stolen their room!

So we packed up and prepared to move again. But Zara's relatives weren't ones to leave us to our own devices. Inquiries were made; perhaps money exchanged hands or Matthew's Mediterranean bodyguards from the imaginary yacht made some visits. All I know is another apartment was discovered.

One of Kelly's aunts had rented an apartment for the month, but had already left and it was just sitting vacant. It was back at Eden Fairway, which was cause for some skepticism, but we discovered that not all apartments at Eden Fairway were created equal. This apartment was wonderful. A big, bright three bedroom with a working kitchen and hot water in the shower AND it was free.

After the wedding, there was Christmas. Most of the parents, including us, had tried to pack a few presents into their luggage, but we all still hit the night market looking for presents for our kids.

Everything at the pasar malam is a knock-off, but if you don't care about brand names in the first place, who cares?

Unfortunately, in the end pretty much everything was junk. The $1.00 pirated DVDs would play two-thirds of the way and then glitch out. I don't even know how that's possible.

Zion and Riel found Christmas in Malaysia very un-Christmasy. No tree, no decorations, they just rolled out of bed in their bleached swimmers and staggered into the front room of a strange apartment where some gifts were wrapped in plastic bags and old newspapers. Having all these DVDs crap out two-thirds of the way through a movie was the coup de grâce. They'd open up *Star Wars* or *Pirates of the Caribbean* and start to watch, as disc after disc would suddenly die.

We weren't talking about a lot of money, but it sucked to have bought these things and have none of them work. We decided to try to return them to get a refund and go to another stall. But of course there are no receipts, there's no customer service desk or return policy, so as I walked up to the crowded stall I had little anticipation for a happy resolution. I figured the guys would just deny they'd ever seen me before.

The first guy asked if he could help me, so I told him what happened. He slipped away behind the table where he had a covert conversation with the boss. As the boss looked over the tables piled high with his shoddy DVDs crowded with tourists pawing through the stacks I realized how this could all work in my favor.

With a big goofy smile I yelled, "Yeah, they didn't work! None of them worked. They were ALL CORRUPTED!"

As I was yelling I waved the bag above my head in a vigorous manner, making the plastic billow and flap like a flag in the wind. Before I could utter another word that could affect potential sales, my bag of useless DVDs was exchanged for a full refund and I was given a playful push back into the stream of humanity.

The Demonic Roar of Genetically Modified Vocal Chords

As we entered our last week in Malaysia, we got word that Kelly's aunt, who rented the apartment, was actually coming back sooner than later. So we started scrambling for new accommodations for our last three days in the country. We eventually settled on the Ferringhi Hotel located across the street from our apartment. The hotel was only a block off the main strip, and the lobby was classy and clean with an upscale vibe, but we soon realized we were off the beaten path and felt as if we might be beaten on the path at any moment.

The staff was all smiles and full of assurances as we checked in, but the longer we stayed at the EQ Hotel Ferringhi the more expendable it felt we had become.

When we went out on the first morning, I told the front desk I didn't want them to clean our room. No problem, no problem. When we came back, of course, someone had been in our room. Initially I was most concerned with the fact that my bottle of gin was gone. With a lime in one hand, a cold can of tonic in the other and a major case of liquid expectation, I was crushed.

I charged down to the front desk to lodge my complaint, which was right about the time everyone in the hotel suddenly stopped speaking or understanding English. I flapped my gums and arms as I besmirched the service and staff for cruelly stabbing me in the back. In the end, the manager produced some twenty-year-old dude who said he threw the bottle out, likely into his open mouth. From that point on, we were definitely on our own.

For weeks after checking out, we discovered an impressive list of items that went missing during our three days at the EQ Ferringhi Hotel: hats, belts, and all the Christmas presents and gifts we'd bought to send home. So yeah, factor that into your budget if you ever plan to stay there.

For days, I've been waking up in this tropical paradise, taking my morning coffee outside on the deck and looking up at the amazing mountain scenery rising behind us. The subdivisions in this part of the city look brand new; brick walls with private electric gates and manicured lawns surround each home. I love walking and exploring new areas, and for the past two days I've seen what looks like a winding road climbing up the side of the mountain. From the balcony, it appears the road running right by our apartment leads up to the base of the mountain where it connects. I decide that this morning is the morning I'm going to investigate.

While Zara and the kids are watching movies on the laptop and building Lego, I get my hiking shoes on and head out the door. It couldn't be a more perfect day; it's warm without being too hot, the sun is up and there's nothing but blue skies as far as the eye can see. As I walk through the neighbourhood, I pass a few gardeners and see a couple of moms outside with small kids. On the right side of the road there is a tall, chain-link fence about twelve to fifteen feet high with three strands of barbed wire running along the top. Without any real development on the other side, it seems like it could be a private golf course or something.

About six blocks from our apartment, I come to the end of the subdivision and start trying to figure out where the street connects to the road running up the mountain. I turn right and follow a little scrub of a trail around the far side of the last house, but the trail immediately fizzles out into a disgusting creek. It looks as if people dump their garbage and all manner of debris there.

Determining that this definitely isn't what I was looking for, I turn around and head back to the street to follow the subdivision in the other direction. As I'm walking back, I see a medium-size dog standing at the end of the sidewalk watching me. There is something about the stance and the look that makes the hair on my neck start to stand up. As I pass behind a bush, I quickly reach down and pick up two stones. They are the only things I can see that might possibly be useful in a self-defense situation. As I come around the edge of the fence, the dog is waiting for me, still just staring. I walk by, trying not to appear aggressive, but also not wanting to exude a "pussy head-hanger" vibe.

As soon as I walk past, the dog immediately starts to follow me. Well, isn't this just great, I think to myself, glancing periodically over my shoulder to make sure Woofie stays a good eight to ten feet back.

Within the next twenty steps, Woofie's friends, Ass and Hole show up. Strength in numbers and all that seems to encourage them and they start getting closer and closer in an emotionally detached sort of way. My mind and my heart are racing, trying to figure out what the hell the protocol is in these situations.

I stop and turn to face them, not saying a word, just an acknowledgement that I know they are there and on the record (at least officially), I'm not scared.

When I stop, they stop. No one says anything. I turn around and as soon as I start walking, so do they, getting closer and closer. This happens a couple of times until I'm convinced this really isn't working.

The third time I stop, I turn around and say something to the effect that they are D-bags who don't respect people's boundaries and should go engage in carnal relations with themselves. When I yell they start barking like mad; their lips pulled back into snarls as they crouch down in a posture that seems to indicate we have reached "go time".

What do behavioural scientists say about the animal kingdom, it's either fight or flight? I'm not fast enough for flight, so I start moving toward them hard and fast yelling random school-yard filth that comes to mind. I ask them, incredulously, if they want a piece of me, and if so, to come and get it. But they should also know that after school, they're totally dead because I'm going to kill them.

It dawns on me how ludicrous it is to be yelling at a pack of feral dogs. I'm in Malaysia … as if they understand English!

But when I move toward them, they turn around and run off. I don't wait a second before I turn in the other direction and start making for home with all haste.

At this point I have a lot of adrenalin in my system that I need to work off, so I set a brisk pace. I walk for a couple of blocks, muttering to myself as I try to get my heart and mind back from the grip of terror. That's when I look around and realize that I can't see anyone anywhere. Where are all the people that live in this brand new subdivision? It's weird that it's so deserted.

About two blocks down the road, I'm finally dialing down. The moment is over; I can see the top of my building over the trees and can't wait to tell Zara this story. This is when I hear the clicking of claws on pavement. I whirl around and see five dogs spread out in a V, charging at me down the deserted street. On one side is a fifteen-foot-high chain-link fence with barbed wire running along the top. On the other side are endless blocks of houses with six-and-a-half-foot brick fences and electric retractable gates. I only have a split second to decide what to do. I figure I' ll make for the fence in front of the nearest house. As I run across the road, I see that the gates are all attached to brick pillars that look maybe seven feet tall, with flat concrete caps on top that might be a foot in diameter. It looks like my best bet. If I can scramble on top of a post before the dogs reach me, I hope I' ll be able to pull my feet up high enough that they won't be able to bite me.

At that point, I can scream for help until someone comes to my aid. But just as I get to the fence, I think maybe I should just vault over the actual gate which is about four feet high and run up to the door and ask for help. The five dogs are almost on top of me as I plant both hands on the gate. Just as I am about to hurdle the gate and launch myself into the yard, the two biggest, most vicious guard dogs I have ever seen launch themselves at the inside of the gate. They must have had genetically modified vocal chords to produce such a demonic roar. It is deafening, and terrifying, as the force of their bodies practically twists the metal gate.

"Jesus!" I scream. "No fucking way this is happening !"

At first, I just didn't want to get bitten by some idiot dog and have to get a shot in Malaysia. Then when there were three of them I was thinking I was at risk of getting badly scarred. But now, I'm seriously thinking my big, bright, beautiful sunny day with blue skies and chirping birds might actually be the day I'm mauled to death just two blocks from my apartment.

I freeze. I don't climb. I don't hide because there isn't anywhere to go. I spin around to face the feral pack and at least go down swinging. I'm just in time to see them hit the brakes, turn around, and start running like hell in the other direction. I can only assume that the feral dogs think I'm at my own home. That death-dealing Cerberus and Barguest are on my side and I'm about to throw wide the gates to hell and release the hounds.

Honestly, I'm so terrified by now that as the pack of dogs runs up the street one way, I run as fast as my wobbly legs can take me the other way. Less than two blocks down the road, I round the corner and am right back into the busy bustle of the market area. The isolation and barren wilderness of Malay suburbia is nothing but a memory.

The downside of having an imagination like mine is moments like these. My mind still replays the event over and over again, reliving the snarling teeth, the sound of the claws on the pavement, and of course, all the "what ifs".

What if I'd taken the kids with me? What if I'd tripped? What if I'd vaulted over the gate?

For the rest of the trip those twenty minutes of hell were the gift that just kept giving.

AUSTRALIA

Horror Porn For Overactive Imaginations

We have arrived in Sydney! Making our way through the sea of humanity to collect our backpacks I realize Australia is one of those places I never thought I'd actually get to see.

It's early morning in January and Zara's uncle Peter is waiting for us when we finally clear customs, which is no mean feat. Zara had been to Australia just over a year ago and had a suitcase full of stories about clearing customs. While Aussies have no worries, the immigration officers positively obsess over them. The major worry seems to be organic materials that will adversely affect the ecosystem, so we jettisoned all our food before the luggage carousel. Except, of course, for the jar of Marmite that the other three Leafs have to travel with. With a conspiratorial wink and a nod, the border guard writes vegemite, in place of marmite, and we're through.

Driving through Sydney we're all eyes and ears soaking it in. The billboards and ads display a uniquely Aussie sense of humour. From Air Asia's "Cheap Enough to say, Phuket I' ll Go", to the Department of Health warning about sexually transmitted infections, "YOU'LL FEEL LIKE YOU'RE PEEING RAZOR BLADES".

At one point, it feels like a futuristic cityscape, as every skyscraper has huge corporate billboards on the top. And the tolls! The privatization of the roads in Sydney has let someone put up tolls like lemonade stands, making the trek across the city an expensive venture. But, we're here!

Peter and Christine live on the outskirts of Sydney in

Turramurra. After the Ferringhi Hotel debacle, it's an incredible relief to feel safe and secure. We lug our backpacks upstairs where Zion and Riel have their own room and Zara and I have a great big, beautiful queen bed, in a room with air conditioning.

Christine is a therapist, and has a home office situated under the stairs in a configuration the Dursleys' would happily have bestowed on Harry Potter. The back deck is a rambling affair, with multiple levels that wrap around the back of the house and give a bird's eye view of the jungle-esque backyard. A gaggle of kookaburras wake the neighbourhood early in the morning with their insane cackling.

After dumping our backpacks in our rooms, the rellies give us the grand tour of the house. Dishes are over here, cutlery over there, food is in the pantry, help yourself, that sort of stuff. "There is a cute little lizard that lives under the mini fridge," Christine mentions, "you might see him from time to time."

For days, that cute little lizard keeps scaring me silly. I'm helpless to prevent womanly screams of panic from erupting as I burst into tears and clamber for the highest chair. As a northern hemisphere Canadian, co-habitation with lizards has never been part of my experience. At one point, as Zara is trying to talk me down off the dining room table like a police negotiator, she asks, "If you had to choose between a lizard or a mouse, which would you want?" Surprising myself, I choose a lizard.

It's apparent that Aussies have a different perspective on reptiles, insects, and predators, so I'm not sure if Christine has given me a gag gift or a lifeline when she hands me a Snake Survival information wheel. I lay in bed spinning the selector to dozens of different species that slither around the country, each apparently more capable than the last of ending our lives in horrific fashion. Time will tell.

Looking for some late night reading material, I put the snake wheel down and grab an Australian tourism book from the shelf. Big mistake! Aussie tourism literature is like horror porn for overactive imaginations like mine.

The first line I read says that eight out of the ten deadliest creatures in the world live in Australia. That's how the frigging book starts. Because of the sheer volume of potential calamity, Aussies quite understandably prioritize their interest based on how efficiently and effectively said beastie will kill you.

Take Huntsman spiders, for example. They are HUGE, furry, fast, and virtually impossible to keep out of the house. Which is what makes Cousin Vanessa's offhanded comment so chilling, "Oh yeah, and you might see a Huntsman spider in the upstairs bathroom if you go in at night."

When I ask about the Huntsman, the family's collaborative description is hardly comforting.

"Well, they are big, like really big, brown and hairy," offers TC, Vanessa's husband, spreading his hands in the shape of a plate.

"And they're quite fast, so it can be startling to see such a big spider move so quickly," Vanessa adds helpfully.

My overactive imagination immediately slams this information like thirteen lines of coke and a dozen Red Bulls and begins constructing night terrors that will wake me in a cold sweat for the next six weeks.

"But they can't DO anything to you; they're harmless," they conclude optimistically. This is when I realize why Aussies have no worries. There is so much they could, and probably should, worry about that if they lived like the rest of us, they would not have time to do anything else. Arachnology feels like a life and death decision. The book says Huntsman spiders often hide behind picture frames and come out at night. Lying there in bed I look up, and no kidding, hanging on the wall right above me is a gigantic sinister picture frame.

"What kind of a country makes you fear art, for God's sake?" I mutter aloud. According to the horror porn book, I'm a sitting duck and didn't even know it. As I lay there all I can think is, "Aussies have worse things to worry about than Huntsman!" I am not comforted by the thought.

The book has pages and pages dedicated solely to the lethal dangers of visiting the country. Don't camp beside saltwater, because the saltwater crocs may drag your dumbass out of your tent in the middle of the night and stuff you under a log until you decompose. OK, no worries, we just won't camp by the ocean. Oh, hold on there, Canadian camper, the next paragraph tells you why you shouldn't pitch your tent beside fresh water lakes, lagoons, or rivers. The freshwater crocs, or "freshies" as they're known, might attack you.

The book makes a half-assed attempt at assuaging the fear it has generated by saying most adults should be safe because freshies are smaller than saltwater crocs and not as aggressive. But just when you're about to file freshies as a nuisance like flies or mosquitoes, you read "Small children should not be left unattended in their presence". So yeah, that's super comforting. Mom and Dad are safe, but the kids are on their own.

Tonight I'd snuck out into the front yard after everyone had gone to bed. I just wanted to finish my glass of wine under the stars in the southern hemisphere. I managed to walk thirty feet from the front door before terror struck. Every stick was a snake; every cluster of leaves a herd of marauding Huntsman. I lasted less than five minutes before the wind rustling through the foliage sent me running for the house.

For our first exploration, we borrowed Christine's car and GPS and headed off to the Koala Wildlife Preserve. It was the perfect introduction to Australia. We wandered through the grounds feeding and petting kangaroos, wallabies, wombats, echidnas, and emus, as koalas slept in trees above our heads. On our way into the park, we passed a sign that said "A Koala is resting in a tree nearby." We all started peering up into the dense foliage playing "spot the bear" when Zion called out, "See him, Riel, can you see him! He's nuzzled in that tree. He's the little grey fuzz."

We had just left the little grey slumbering fuzz behind when we came face to face with our first kangaroo. Zion kept creeping closer and closer with his camera until it hopped off into the bush.

He turned excitedly and exclaimed, "He bounces like a master."

When Riel got to pet her first kangaroo she looked up at me and whispered, "Holy crap, he's unbelievably fuzzy."

The park sold a bag of feed for a couple of bucks, which actually turned out to be a little sandwich baggie of cheerios.

Just as Zion handed a Cheerio to a receptive kanga, it got distracted with its ass, first scratching, then probing, finally craning its head around to really start digging for gold. Zion saw me coming with the camera to capture his two-handed petting job and without missing a beat he turned it into a spa treatment and started speaking in a soothing tone, "You're so tense, you're so tense, you guide me, you guide me."

As Riel came over to see what we were giggling about, she happily jumped in with her own two hands, "Oh, he likes tummy rubs!" she exclaimed.

Zion was petting a Joey hanging out of its mother's pouch and talking in the little baby voice adults save for newborns. "Who's the little pizza pocket, who's the little pizza pocket? That's right, you are the pizza pocket!"

Riel waxed eloquent on how the wallabies look like the swamp rats in *Lego Star Wars* and called me over to check out an emu. "See the holes in his head … those are its ears," she said spookily. It was great Aussie interaction for *Zion & Riel – Australia.*

We rode the train downtown on Saturday to catch the Sydney Festival. Walking through downtown Sydney on a blazing hot Saturday is an experience Zion and Riel discovered is not their cup of tea. Amid their colourful crabbing and complaining, we stumbled onto a great street magician who was busking.

We went up after his performance to tell him we thought he was amazing and he gave us a little additional private one-off, involving Riel. He got Riel to write her name on a card and then she was supposed to snap her fingers and the card would jump to the top of the deck. The only problem was, Riel had never really mastered snapping her little fingers at that point and was put on the spot trying desperately to engage the magic. The magician kindly lent a snap of his own, and magic was produced as the card with her name on it appeared from his mouth.

We were all left suitably impressed by the trick, but it was the hands on part, being right on top of the action that made it compelling for Zion, and Riel.

As the sun started to go down, hundreds of gigantic flying

foxes filled the sky transforming Sydney into Gotham City. We all started nonchalantly searching for the bat signal in the sky.

We were hungry and found a burger joint where everything was fresh and homemade. The food came and so did the calm that descends on a group when famished mouths are too busy eating to talk. Zion looked across at Zara and said, "Wow Mom, you're really attacking your food with your face." As we all laughed, he turned to me, "You should write that down."

The next day we decided it was time to head to Manly Beach. We navigated a couple of trains downtown where we caught the ferry and steamed through the harbour, past the Opera House, as sailboats and catamarans cut back and forth across our wake.

As we hit the beach and started looking for a patch to call our own, I heard the lifeguard making an announcement over the big megaphone.

"There are a lot of blue bottles washing up on the shore," he said, in what I assumed was an anti-littering message, reminding people to throw their water bottles into the recycling bin and not the ocean. I was trying to figure out if surfers took bottles of water with them so they wouldn't get dehydrated and then just chucked them into the water when they were done. That seemed pretty irresponsible, I thought to myself as the lifeguard continued.

"If you step on one, it will sting for a couple of hours."

I was just about to comment that the last bit didn't make any sense, when I noticed a small blueish-looking jellyfish on the sand in front of me. Suddenly the light bulbs came on and I looked up to see the sand littered with blue bottles.

This little development meant Riel wasn't going anywhere near the water. It was hard to know what to say. I mean, I was the guy that tried to teach her how to boogie board in Hawaii and that memory still hadn't faded.

To be honest, it wasn't super comforting to see hundreds of Aussies swimming around in the water. The riptides and currents meant that the lifeguards had put the flags for the swimming area close together. This packed hundreds of bobbing heads, flying fiberglass boards and stinging blue bottles together in the choppy surf. But if it's not going to kill you in less than five minutes … no worries mate.

Australia started with petting kangaroos and koalas and quickly moved onto exploring beaches and giant surf down under.

Barrel-Assing Into the Pit of Hell

When I was in my early twenties, I was in a car accident that almost killed me. I was air lifted to the hospital where I woke up days later on life support.

After numerous reconstructive surgeries, the insertion of metal plates and pins, and a year of physiotherapy, I regained much of my life. But I've lived with chronic pain pretty much every day ever since. Some years have been better than others and there are many things I have simply been unable to do since. I need to stay physically active, but have to choose low or no impact activities, like skating, cross-country skiing, and biking. If I stay active and exercise regularly, I can have a decent quality of life. Biking in particular has been a passion. Back home I rode every day. Not having a bike has been one of the things I actually missed on this trip.

When I saw Peter had a couple of bikes in the backyard, I was eager to get back in the saddle and go for a ride. Soon I was coasting down a hill that went for miles and miles. It eventually petered out into a trail and the trail led down a gorge, and as I kept descending, it dawned on me it was very quiet, too quiet. I realized I was all alone and hadn't passed anyone else since I'd gotten on this trail. I stopped and looked around. Once again, I was off in the weeds, literally.

There were waist high weeds on both sides of the trail, the perfect height for hiding anything from genetically modified kangaroos to deranged dingoes to any possible amalgamation of Huntsman spiders, viral snakes, salt-water crocs, and freshies. I started to feel that coasting downhill was some sort of religious metaphor, that I was barrel-assing my way straight into the pit of hell, slackjawed and vacant-eyed like the poster-child for the very type of slumbering souls our straw-haired hell-fire-and-brimstone preacher used to scream about.

I could hear the incredulous exclamations of the Aussie relatives at supper. "You rode where? OMG! Didn't you see the signs that warned cyclists not to ride through the gorge from 12:00 – 3:00 p.m. because of the herds of rabid blue-tongue lizards and migrating salt-water crocs?"

I decided Mrs. Leaf 's son had more common sense than that, and immediately turned around and rode like a man possessed back the long, uphill path to Turramurra. But it felt great to be back on a bike.

The next day, Zara's cousin Louisa and her husband Greg invited us to their place for a BBQ. They'd made it back from Malaysia as well, and were enjoying the last couple of weeks of summer holidays before school started. As we hung out on the back deck, drinking beer and throwing shrimps on the barbie, I told Greg about my ride. A fellow bike enthusiast, his eyes lit up and he offered to bring his bike over the next day so we could go for a ride together. Greg could make being kicked in the plums sound like a great idea, so in no time at all we'd made a date.

Our bike ride was like the story of the city mouse and the country mouse. The day before I'd been content to get on an old borrowed bike, wearing my billowing hiking shorts and substantial shoes. But I felt conspicuously inadequate as Greg walked out the door in his bright red, form-fitting cycling shirt that showed off his exquisitely sculpted pectorals and ripped biceps. The black bike shorts left little to the imagination, and more than adequately showcased Greg's firm landscaper's glutes.

I strapped on a bulbous bike helmet I found at the bottom of a potato box in the pantry. I caught a glimpse of my shadow as tufts of hair stuck out through every gap making my head look like a pregnant possum having a bad fur day. There are times it's satisfying to look artistically disheveled but this wasn't one of them.

Greg clicked into the clips on his pedals and suggested that I go first. Now, I'm not a competitive person in the sporting, show-off kind of way, but I am painfully aware of the impossibly high, unspoken standards others set for me. But I took the lead and tried to ride in a way that would keep Greg interested in me as a person as well as an athletic sojourner. As the first five miles were all downhill, I just kept my hands off the brake and freewheeled it as fast as my bike would go. I think for the first five miles everything went great. We caught all green lights and didn't even have to slow down. We got to the part of the road that turned into a trail and just kept going. Down into the gorge we flew, as I grew a little concerned about the smoking brake pads that might indicate the type of heat that would warp a rim, but as I was effectively out of control, I really didn't have a choice and just kept going. Eventually we reached the bottom, crossed a little bridge, and started back up the other side ... up the other side of a gorge. I really poured on the gas and pedaled in a serious way. I didn't want to look back to see if Greg was still with me in case that seemed condescending in some way, as if I doubted his ability to keep up with me after the blistering pace I'd set. But I did and he was right behind me, just sort of coasting along uphill.

I decided I'd really pour on the jets. I dug down deep, way down deep, where the really secret stuff I'm made of is supposed to live. I admit it's an area that has gone largely unexplored in my life ... an area frankly I've tried my best to avoid. My vision started to swim a bit and the pounding in my head grew uncomfortable as I started to draw ragged breaths that did not quite provide enough oxygen, but I kept going. Around the next turn I stole a quick glance behind me, to see how far I'd left Greg behind. But there he was, even closer and looking even more casually bored and bronzed than before. He gave me a playful encouraging smile, the kind people commonly reserve for toddlers and inebriated seniors, but as I looked forward I could feel his kind, Kiwi eyes watching me, judging me, mocking me!

Greg didn't give me any choice, I was forced to throw open the floodgates to my overactive imagination. I needed to relive every horrible childhood memory I'd ever endured in a desperate attempt to propel myself up the gorge on raw rage, shame, and bitterness.

I dwelled on the grade fiver that twisted my nipples every morning on the bus. The debilitating shame as the rest of the grade seven boys pulled my pants down and laughed at my pubeless balls. I relived the day my friend punched me in the stomach as I was asking out my first girlfriend and I farted. I took back all the forgiveness, undid all the therapy. I tore the bandage off all my emotional scars and let the torrents flow like hot rivers of rage through my veins. On the outside, I was just an out-of-shape, middle age guy with a possum-shaped head sucking wind ... but on the inside I was the Demon Lord of Turramurra.

Ten years previous, I had been diagnosed with a heart murmur, which came back to me as my heart started beating hard enough to crack a couple of ribs, but did Greg care about that? Of course not, and I suddenly realized why ... Greg was trying to kill me.

This also explained why he was wearing the sexy tight shorts and shirt. He was into some sick, twisted Erotic-Cycling Asphyxiation fetish. I pictured the evening news, the cameras rolling as Greg, bronze skin glistening in the setting sun, like a Kiwi God, described my last gasping moments.

At the top of the hill, I faked a chain malfunction and crawled under my bike like a mechanic just so I could lie down. We rode around a university campus for a while before heading back to the gorge and the five-mile uphill ride. We were within sight of the house when Greg really poured the salt into the gaping wound, blasting past me like the memory of a man I've never been. His legs moved like pistons propelling him with the speed of a cheetah, the grace of a gazelle, and the raw, primal passion of a lion.

I wanted to yell something witty and biting, but only managed to scream, "Louisa is a lucky woman!"

As Greg disappeared over the horizon, it reminded me of the first time I watched the Olympics as a kid. I barely understood the games, but I loved cheering my little head off for the Canadian athletes. But they never seemed to win. As Turramurra drew closer, I felt my adult self, disappointing my child self in that same way.

My inner child was tantruming, "No, no, don't let him get away, pedal, pedal. Why aren't you peddling! Oh dammit! We lost to the Kiwi. What the frig!" Greg was chilling like a villain on the back deck by the time I finally arrived. Thwarting Greg's master plan by returning alive, I gasped, "I win," as I collapsed.

The Only Thing a Loving Father Could Do

There was no way we could have planned every detail of our trip before we left home. A few dates, like the wedding in Malaysia, were set, but everything else was arbitrary. We'd just decided to spend two weeks in Hawaii. We spent three in Malaysia, mostly because that's how long everyone else was there.

We decided to spend six weeks in Australia. Countries like Australia require a departure date before they let you in so we also knew when we'd be heading to New Zealand. Traveling this way meant we were always trying to lay the tracks in front of the train as we traveled. We'd worked on Hawaii while we were in Canada and organized a few Malaysian things when we were in Hawaii. But internet was so hard to come by in Malaysia that we hadn't organized anything in Australia before we arrived.

After Zara and I spent a few full days on our respective laptops eating up a massive amount of Peter and Christine's monthly internet usage, we had a working plan in place.

We rented a car and headed down to Wollongong where Zara's cousin Dominic and his wife Emma live.

The first day in town, Emma took us all down to the beach where massive waves were breaking. Zion was instantly back in Hawaii mode, throwing himself recklessly into the churning water and tumbling ass over teakettle up onto the beach. I was still officially supposed to keep salt water away from my ruptured eardrum, which was starting to feel like the most inconvenient consequence of staggering stupidity in recent years.

It had also produced a healthy paranoia regarding the power of waves to kick ass and take names, namely mine. So watching Emma at the beach with her kids was terrifying. I knew she'd grown up in Australia and lived her whole life on the coast. For all I knew she was part mermaid. But she kept heading out into the massive dumping waves, holding her daughter Laura in one arm and hanging onto her son James' hand in the other, as set after set of huge waves crashed all about and over them. At one point, a rogue wave smacked them all in the face sending Emma's sunnies flying. James completely disappeared in a writhing swirl of sea foam as did mother and daughter. I was on my feet racing toward the water when Laura's head popped up spluttering and blinking in confusion. Before I could even reach her to comfort and console her, her face broke into a huge smile and as Emma picked her up she squealed, "Again, Mommy!" At that point, I decided it would be a good time to go for a long walk and meditate on the true meaning of "no worries".

We'd made a plan to spend the next two weeks hitting every beach we could between Wollongong and Melbourne, nothing but surf, sand, and sun.

Bateman's Bay YHA was our first hostel experience as a family. We followed the Princes Highway down from Wollongong and arrived in late afternoon. As we pulled off the highway into the grounds it felt as if we'd time-traveled back to 1972. A variety of old mobile homes and holiday trailers were lined up, most with some sort of extension built on with wood paneling and a few with tarps.

We pulled up to the main building and all four of us climbed the stairs to the second storey office. This was another one of those inexplicable experiences for the kids that just seemed to come out of nowhere. They had gotten used to checking into hotels and motels, scouting out the facilities for pools or tennis courts while I was checking in, but the hostel was something other. After getting a key, the manager plopped a couple of square plastic milk crates onto the counter, filled with dishes, bowls, cups, and cutlery. I could tell Zion and Riel were confounded when I handed them kitchenware and sent them out the door.

"Do these come with the room?" Riel asked.

Before I could answer Zion said, "Do we have to fit all this in the car for the rest of the trip?"

I think initially they thought hostels were one part garage sale and two parts accomms. Then the manager gave us a tour. We entered the common room, filled with Germans watching the Australian Open, as we passed through the kitchen and on out the back door where the washrooms, showers, and pingpong table were.

We drove around back and discovered a row of old mobile trailers vaguely resembling a refugee camp, or an old time construction site from a period film. We parked beside our unit and opened the sliding glass door where we discovered two metal military bunk beds, some dirty brown curtains with faded orange flowers and an olive green vinyl chair. There was a tiny toilet and sink, so at least there wouldn't need to be any midnight runs through the grounds to the loo. There was a bit of shade on a third of the trailer, but the other two-thirds of corrugated tin was laid bare under the Aussie sun. Welcome to the world, kids!

Riel loved hostel life. She made any excuse to take the keys and run down to the main building where she hung out with an international collection of twenty-something backpackers jabbering away in a variety of languages.

Zion, on the other hand, had some serious doubts about the whole thing. When we hauled our groceries into the kitchen, proceeded to put them in the communal fridge on the shelf marked by our unit number and turned to leave, he was incredulous.

"What are you doing? Are we just leaving them there!" he sputtered. "They'll be fine," Zara said. "Look, everyone else has their food in here too." "But what if our food is better than theirs," he argued.

Zion has always been our laid-back kid, the one who gets along with everyone and anyone. It was funny to discover that underneath his accepting demeanour lay an under-current of deep suspicion of his fellow man.

The next morning I knew it was going to be a great day when we asked for directions to a nice spot on the water and someone told us just to take Beach Road, where every beach is the most beautiful one you have ever seen.

We grabbed some food and headed down to Sunshine Bay. The day was perfect. I was out in the water with the kids as they bodysurfed and frolicked in the waves. I was still trying to be very careful of my ear, hoping it was already healed but not wanting to complicate things by swimming too soon. Time restraints, pressures, stress, and busyness were all things from another life. We were just floating free in the waves.

Over the steady thunder of the surf, I thought I heard a voice calling somewhere off in the distance. Bobbing there in the water, at least sixty feet from shore I turned to see Zara standing at the water's edge yelling to us and pointing behind us. I spun around as my heart skipped a beat: twenty-five feet away I saw not one, but five dorsal fins cutting through the water.

"Absolutely no f#%ing way is this happening!" I screamed and inadvertently gargled a salt-water wave with my ill-timed profanity.

It was too fast, too gruesome. There was absolutely no way I could get to Zion and Riel in time, and with less than one of us per shark, the odds were not stacked in our favor. I wanted to be brave, I wanted to be a hero and save my kids, so I did the only thing a loving father could do. I started splashing epileptically, fingering the fins and screaming profanely. "Over here! I'm over here. Come and get me, you shark pussies! You want some of this? I dare you to eat me!"

That is when I saw the first body come out of the water. It was the most beautiful, playful dolphin I'd ever seen, with the kindest Santa eyes and a sweet knowing Mona Lisa smile. We paddled with glee as the little pod swam back and forth parallel to the beach for fifteen minutes before disappearing.

We're in Manna Park, an eco-preserve located nine kilometres north of Merimbula off Sapphire Coast Drive. English Karen, voice of our GPS, didn't actually have Manna Park in her extensive library, so we ended up on a little dirt road at the back end of nowhere. Nothing like driving into the bush in Australia to make you feel like you are watching the opening sequence of a horror picture.

Australian tourism has filled my mind with a vast array of horror potential. Zombie kangaroos, a crazed pack of feral wombats, a forgotten race of ancient warriors that throw venomous snake boomerangs. When we finally find the main entrance, it still seems like we're following a bush trail worn down by woodland creatures. One of the kids admits from the backseat that they are starting to feel like Harry Potter and Ron Weasley heading into the Forbidden Forest. We all pray there isn't a blue-tongued lizard named Aragog waiting for us at the end of the road as we pull up to a ranch-style structure.

From the moment we get out of the car, Manna Park is a fabulous experience. Salah is the manager of the facility and doesn't waste time with introductions or handshakes, calling us straight over to see a wombat nibbling on the lawn. At dusk, a mob of kangaroos comes out of the forest to graze on the grounds surrounding the buildings. A flock of bell miners in the trees around the clearing keeps up a constant pinging sound, that sounds more electronic than organic. My first thought was that Australia must have a Homeland Security of their own; just with more obtrusive gear at their disposal than the Americans.

The facility operates in a number of capacities. Throughout the year, university students study the ecosystem. There are also a number of facilities the organization rents out to groups, including families. We arrived on Sunday, January 24, when most Australians were getting ready for school to start up. Salah tells us that from the beginning of December until two days before we arrived, the facilities had been packed.

We found it while we were searching online for accommodations. At $75.00 a night it was the cheapest lodging we'd found and jumped at it. But Manna Park is one of those miraculous treasures you accidentally discover.

We're one of only two families sharing the entire eco resort. When Salah gives us a tour of the place, he invites us to pick any room we want. We choose a big dorm room with seven bunk beds. Down and around the corner are immaculate washrooms and showers and a huge common room with a sprawling kitchen. Outside the door is a veranda that wraps around the pool. Morning and night we sit outside watching kangaroos, wombats, and a vast array of exotic birds, reptiles, and insects cohabitate.

Manna Park is a great learning experience for all of us. In some situations, you need someone to teach you how to see what's right in front of you. But sometimes you still need someone to explain what you're seeing, and we find Manna Park to be the latter. Salah is a great teacher, pointing out the bell miners, the St. Andrews Cross Spider, bandicoots, and Cicadabird. He points out the bees that line channels around doors and windows with honeycomb and feed off a certain kind of spider, feeding the larva to their babies.

Horror Picture People

One night Salah saw me preparing to take a walk. I had built up the courage to walk the road we drove in and out on day by day. Seeing me with my Burmese Army trekking stick, he encouraged me to take the path that led off the road opposite the woodworking shop.

"Just veer to your right when you get to the bottom of the hill and you can follow trails all through the forest, it's very beautiful," he said encouragingly.

I believe I was humming a happy little ditty as I veered off the beaten path and into the untamed forest, home to over 700 different species of lizards. But within moments of skipping merrily down the path, I heard a massive crash off in the bush to my left. It was *Jurassic Park* crashing, with the tops of trees swaying as some giant creature galloped off. "Holy soil-yourself-in-the-trees," I exhaled, deeply horrified and descriptively aware of how close I'd come to doing just that.

I started walking slowly, which I suppose was a cautionary reflex to avoid startling any beasties that might lash out wildly with armored tails covered in poisonous spikes. But then it dawned on me, I had made myself the slowest moving target in the jungle, which I did not need *National Geographic* or *Planet Earth* to tell me is a place on the food chain I don't want to be.

I was sure I could feel the heat rise from smoldering eyes as herds of predators watched from behind the foliage. I imagined them deciding to let the young inexperienced hunters and the old geriatric wizened ones have a go. I suddenly remembered a nature show where a mother killer whale caught a sea lion and swam with it gently in her teeth out into the open water where she whacked it with her tail sending it fifty feet in the air. Her surly teens spent the next half an hour pummeling this sea lion, learning how to approach and connect with the tail swing. I started feeling very sea lionish.

I walked about 200 metres down this creepy path, at one point pulling out the Flip, thinking that I could offer some measure of closure to my next of kin by, at least, letting them know what devoured me. Maybe it was the presence of a camera rolling but it dawned on me I'd become a "horror picture person".

Horror picture people are a rare breed. Alone in a strange house, the power suddenly goes out and they hear a noise in the basement ... something like a chainsaw working its way through a femoral artery. Horror picture people will creep to the top of the stairs and call out: "Hello, is anybody there?"

The top step can be littered with torn, bloody fingernails from previous occupants who have tried to escape their gruesome fate and horror picture people just clomp down the stairs. Through pools of coagulated blood, slipping and sliding through sacrificial entrails, past spectral shapes hovering above pentagrams and decapitated ghosts carrying their own severed heads, they go. They have to; they just have that "gollygee-wilikers" curiosity.

I suddenly realized that if I proceeded in the lunacy of sauntering through a forest that proudly boasts 700 different species of lizards, many of them presumably ill-tempered and peckish ... I would die, and subsequently be judged for all eternity as a horror picture person. That is a fate my soul could not bear, and so I did the only sensible thing. I turned and ran like a little princess back to the road.

I hightailed it back to the safety of the camp and met up with Salah on my return. No sooner had I relayed a subdued version of my events than he chuckled. "Well, you know the area behind your room, have you seen the little holes in the ground?"

Indeed, I had seen these holes as I'd walked around with nothing but my naiveté and open-toe sandals for company.

"Those are Funnel-web homes" he said, "the second deadliest spider in Australia!"

I must have turned green because he quickly added, "But I

have no problems with them. They stay outside; they never go in the cabins."

Well, isn't that special, inside the cabin all I have to worry about is the gigantic, brown, hairy Huntsman. As I gingerly tiptoed back to my room careful to stay on the boardwalk, Salah called after me good naturedly, "No worries, mate, enjoy the rest of the day!"

It's Australia Day, and we are definitely smack dab in the heart of the Aussie heartland. The little wombat is happily munching grass on the front lawn, and as we watch, six kangaroos pogo around the grounds as a Crimson Rosella lands on the tree in front of us, dazzling us with its bright blue cheeks, shoulders and tail, and a deep rich crimson body.

The Mandeni Family Fun Park is located on the far side of the eco preserve and we decide to head there for some holiday fun. We rent mountain bikes and get suited up for a cross-country circuit that winds around the sanctuary.

They don't really have a bike the right size for Riel, so we end up getting her on a bike that is a bit too big and just give her some time in the parking lot to get used to handling it. When she finally feels comfortable we take off down the trail.

I'm in the lead with Riel right behind me. She's already dealing with a lot of nerves because of the size of the bike, so when we come around our first turn and something large and reptilian crashes off into the bush in front of us, I definitely want to keep moving and not alarm her or anyone else. But Riel managed to catch enough of a glimpse that she calls up to me, "Dad, what was that?" in her, I'm-totally-on-the-verge-of-freaking-out, voice.

"Oh something fuzzy and cute," I reply through clenched teeth.

The trail markers are virtually impossible to find and in less than ten minutes we're completely turned around. A couple of hours later, after dodging snakes and lizards and God-knows whatever it was that crashed off into the forest, we finally make it back to the centre. As I drop the bikes off, I ask the lady at the counter what the big beastie might have been.

"Oh, it's probably better you don't know," she replies in that sweet no worries way. Aussies!

After the bike ride, we decide to take a drive and explore some of the New South Wales coast on our way down to Eden. Salah told us we could get the best fish and chips down by the wharf. We are barely on the road before Zion starts to complain that he doesn't feel good. Promising the bracing effects of some fresh air and a stiff walk, I pull into the parking lot at an outdoor market. As providence would have it, there is a parking spot right at the front gate, just off the main road. We all pile out of the car, ready to join the teeming throngs of people streaming into the fair grounds.

Two seconds into the bracing fresh air Zion power pukes, right in front of a solid dozen or so folks entering the fair. I take a quick step back to avoid the backsplash as Zion takes a step forward to avoid his own puddle of filth. Then he spewed again, closer to me than last time.

"Oh, Zion, I'm so sorry," I call comfortingly as I start to move laterally, hoping his forward momentum will carry him past me.

Perhaps tuning into some instinctive primal connection to his loving father, his head swivels with my movement and he projectiles a third time, in what has started to seem like a deliberate stalking manoeuvre.

"Stop chasing me!" I blurt in a schoolgirl register.

"Aggghh," he grunts, wiping spittle from his chin as he continues to plod toward me.

I'm sure at this point that he's saving up for the coup de grace. "Piss off!" I squeal frantically as I abandon my firstborn in his time of need. He raises his blood shot eyes accusingly, judging me for not pulling over earlier.

At this point, Riel comes around the car, unaware that the porridge-like substance spread across the parking lot isn't part of the craft show. Then the smell hits her and she reels backward as if she's been punched in the face.

Zion groans, "Oh gross, it tastes like spaghetti and eggs."

"Don't explain it," I beg, "that will only make it worse." For me at least, I think ungenerously.

"Together they taste like lasagna," he mutters.

Dealing with my own gagging reflexes and the weight of disapproval from passing pedestrians, we duck into the change room at a public swimming pool where he tries to clean up. If Zion was unimpressed with the drive and the idea of stopping at a country fair before he got sick, he is downright incredulous that we still plan to stroll leisurely through the grounds.

We walk past the baked goods and homemade knitting to Zi's steady stream of guttural derision, until he finally decides that I'm just not getting it and he explodes.

"Imagine you puked on yourself, and then Riel and I made you walk really slowly through Toys R Us; that's what this is like. I smell like barf!"

I concede his valid point and we make our way back to the car.

It had been a long, event-filled day and we were all exhausted and ready for bed. I'd crawled into Riel's bunk bed to read her a bedtime story. I was in the process of describing different constellations in the southern hemisphere pointing at the ceiling as we imagined the stars when we saw … IT.

Different cultures have different names to describe evil that takes physical form and walks the earth: demons, the Devil, Diablos, Satan. Staring into the eight eyes of pure, unadulterated evil, we called it, The Huntsman.

Evil incarnate was hovering right above the bed. Riel managed to exhale in a quavering voice, "Daaaaad." before being paralyzed from the neck down.

The air was sucked out of our lungs as the temperature in the room dropped. Zara and Zion stopped what they were doing and looked up. Eight human eyes stared into the eight eyes of the Huntsman. It hung above the bed, all eight legs splayed like tentacles covered in coarse brown fur with razor sharp fangs; it was the single most disgusting spider I've ever seen.

Scientists will tell you Huntsman grow to the size of an adult hand. This one was easily the size of an hors d'oeuvres platter and weighed seven, maybe eight pounds. It obviously had supernatural powers and a surly disposition.

I had never wanted to be a burly, testosterone-fueled man's-man in my life until that moment. This was one of those animal kingdom situations where the person with the penis is supposed to man up, and protect the women and children. But who was going to protect me?

I looked around the room for inspiration. There was no way we were going to turn out the light and go to bed. Just the thought of this nocturnal nightmare crawling around the room in the dark: what if it slipped and fell into my bed? What if my mouth was open and after falling into my bed, the beast crawled up into my mouth? What if it crawled into my mouth and decided to lay 200-300 eggs?

I don't know what I hoped to find, maybe a flame-thrower, or a shotgun. There wasn't anything big enough and besides, if we killed a spider in cold blood on an eco-preserve we'd probably be cursed. I did the bravest most courageous thing a loving, caring father and husband could do: I walked out the door and across the pitch-black parking lot, ignoring the thumping, crashing sounds moving in the foliage, and knocked on the door of the resident biologist. Salah had introduced me to Tony earlier in the week. Through the window, I could see the flickering of a TV screen as I quietly called out, "Tony? Hello. Tony? I need help, please Tony, if you can hear me, please answer."

With Tony not answering, I tried to go over his head. "Oh Jesus. Oh God. O Lord in heaven, hallowed be thy name ... please wake Tony the frig up."

From my lips to God's ears, like an angel of light Tony appeared. After explaining our dire circumstance, he disappeared inside, I assumed to don riot gear, face shield and flak jacket, and probably to grab some neutralizing nerve gas and a high security, industrial-strength cage.

He returned seconds later with a plastic lid from a CD spool and a piece of paper, which is when I knew: Tony was a badass ninja. In the bedroom, he hopped up on the bunk bed, lowered the plastic see-through lid down over the Huntsman, slid the paper along the ceiling and plucked the Huntsman from its perch. We gathered around as he showed us the fur, feet and fangs. As he left the room, he told us that Huntsmans were attracted to the light. As soon as he left, we plunged the room into darkness and lay in our beds quietly humming the tune for Kumbaya. This made for gripping drama in *Zion & Riel – Viva Australia*.

Viva Australia pays homage to some of the Aussie wildlife that kept scaring and startling us, as we journey from Melbourne to the Outback and end our trip on a sailboat.

A 12-Foot Tall Naked Hairy Man

Founded in 1949 as a peace movement, Servas International is a non-profit organization run by volunteers in over 100 countries working to build understanding, tolerance, and world peace. The organization accomplishes this by coordinating a network of hosts who are interested in opening their doors to travelers. The idea is to create an opportunity for people to share their stories with one another, and in the process recognize our similarities. No money is exchanged. Travelers stay for a maximum of two nights, and the hosts provide breakfast and supper. As travel is the common denominator, most hosts travel extensively themselves, which provides lots to talk about.

I found out about Servas a couple of weeks before we left Canada, leaving us just enough time to have an interview and to get the paperwork done. As registered Servas travelers, we were able to request a book that listed all the Servas hosts in Australia. The hosts are organized by region, along with a list of information that includes languages spoken, countries visited, education, interests, and whether they have room for a single person, a couple, or a family. I'd sent out some email inquiries and got an invitation back from a couple in Moe. Our first Servas experience was absolutely brilliant.

We thought the drive from Manna Park to Moe would take us about two-and-a-half to three hours. It was actually closer to six. I'd tried to call ahead to our Servas hosts to let them know that we were on our way. I wasn't aware we were jumping state lines with different area codes so when I tried to leave a message it said the number was no longer in service.

Salah told us we had to stop along the way and explore an ancient forest he claimed was unlike anything else on the planet. Following his directions, we headed off down some gravel trail in our rental vehicle but after about ten miles decided we were risking life and limb and possibly a guest appearance in a remake of *Deliverance*, and decided to turn back.

I was in the middle of negotiating a twenty-three-point turn on the narrow dirt trail when the phone rang. Zara pushed answer and thrust the phone at me as if it were burning her hands. It was Anthony, wondering where in the Sam Hill we were. Literally, at that moment I had no idea, but generally I was able to give him an approximate area. "So we should be there in about an hour, I suppose," I told him.

"An hour!" he exclaimed. "You're over four hours away."

I apologized as he muttered something in the background about trying to salvage the dinner meal. We drove like mad banshees and got to their place just before 7:00 p.m.

Anthony and Bernadette were awesome hosts.

They live in a farmhouse on rolling hills, with cattle lowing in the paddocks outside the window and two whippet dogs, Georgie and Bonnie. As this was our first Servas experience, we had no idea what to expect. I guess I was thinking people would show us to the corner of a basement with some old moldy mattresses and a couple of sleeping bags. I wasn't expecting separate bedrooms, our own bathroom, and a dinner of roast beef and vegetables right out of the garden with a wonderful bottle of Australian red wine.

The next day they sent us to Toorongo Falls in Noojee State Park about a twenty-minute drive away. Halfway there we turned off the highway onto possibly the worst gravel road I have ever driven. In Canada we would call it washboard; in Australia they call it corrugated, but you get the point. We arrived with compressed vertebra, loose fillings and some serious movement of internal organs. But, we had an entire rain forest to ourselves. We hiked for hours without seeing a soul through a spectacular jungle forest of Manna and Mountain Grey Gum, Blackwood, and Austral Mulberry trees.

Hiking in forests always triggers dialogue from fantasy stories. Zion and I were bantering about his bag of chips being lembas bread.

"All right, Mr. Frodo, get your ass moving; we've got to get to the top of Cirith Ungol," I said.

Riel was in one of her moods, and wasn't interested in any banter, joking, or horseplay. As she passed me I said, "Here comes Samwise," hoping for a smirk or grin … nothing.

As the kids disappeared up the trail, Zara passed me, laughing at my failed attempt with Riel. "If that's Frodo and Sam, I guess that means you're Gollum," I called after her.

As Zara passed me she covertly gave me the finger behind her back so the kids wouldn't see. But of course I was still filming, and the whole exchange became a featured part of our next video *Zion & Riel - Down Under.*

Much to the admiration of a growing number of viewers who started writing to say they wanted more footage of Zara giving me crap. There just aren't any discerning audiences these days.

We bid Anthony and Bernadette goodbye and headed to Melbourne where the Australian Open was in full swing. We ended up in a funky little economy hotel in the St. Kilda district. St. Kilda is situated on a picturesque point of the Bay, with lots of cafes, pubs, and shops just a short walk to the water. For decades, Melbournites apparently shunned the area because of its unsavoury elements, but it certainly seems to be enjoying a resurgence. Basically, we look for four things when booking accommodations: cheap, clean, quiet, and safe. We found all the above at the Easystay Motel.

Our room was upstairs on the third floor around the back of the building. Zion stayed in the room building Lego and watching the Australian Open on the little TV while Riel, Zara, and I headed out into the shops and cafes to find something for supper. We returned with pasties and pizza and all walked down to the harbour where the sky was full of the U-shaped sails of kite surfers racing back and forth parallel to the beach.

I wanted to film Zion and Riel running barefoot along the sea wall with the ocean and setting sun behind them. My plan was to hold the camera down at knee level and run alongside them like a camera on a moving dolly. I got my talent ready and yelled action! They started running and I started running. But they're young, lithe and energetic, and I am not. So there they are leaping like jackrabbits, sprinting along as I gamely try to keep up, lumbering along bent over at the waist trying to hold the camera steady. My kidneys seem to be compressing my lungs and the stitch in my side starts to feel more like a rupturing suture.

"Cut!" I wheeze. "OK, let's do that again, just not quite so fast."

We get back to first position, I get the camera rolling, and with "action!" off they go again like Usain Bolt's little Canadian cousins.

"Come on, guys," I gasp, lurching like Frankenstein's Igor, "stop … going … so fast." Miraculously we got some great footage. Hopped up on his success at reducing his old man to the shell of his former athletic glory, Zion turned his sights on Zara and challenged her to a race across the beach. Before the words were fully out of his mouth, she yelled, "Go!" and took off. Her subterfuge secured her a tie, but the moment was not lost on either of us. The kid is growing up!

The waterfront was such a beautiful setting we were back again in the morning, sipping coffee and nibbling on breakfast pasties, as a scraggly contingent of surfers crawled out of their VW camper vans in the parking lot. It was a cultural collision of our life past and present. Behind us were the long hair, dreadlocks, tie died and flower prints of our early twenties when Zara and I met. In the harbour in front of us was a sailing club of kids Zion and Riel's age who spent most of the time beating the crap out of each other with paddles and ramming their boats like bumper cars.

We checked out of the Easystay and headed downtown to the National Gallery of Victoria. We had tried unsuccessfully on a couple of other continents to get to a Ron Mueck exhibition. Mueck is an Australian hyperrealist artist who creates sculptures mostly of the human body, with the most amazing detail. He also plays around with scale, which is alternately cool and creepy.

I first experienced Mueck's work at the National Art Gallery in Ottawa, Canada when I was on tour with Tina Newlove, the principal artist in Tribe of One. I thought I was in for a hell day going to the National Gallery with a visual artist. I assumed she would spend hours in front of obscure paintings, deeply impressed with some quality a mere mortal like me could never appreciate. The reality was, the size of the sculptures and their incredible detail totally affected her and she blasted through the exhibit as if the place was on fire. I'd wanted Zara and the kids to be able to see his work, so when we saw an ad for a Ron Mueck exhibition we had to go.

As I gazed up at a twelve-foot-tall naked hairy man, Riel sidled up to me and whispered, "The guy who made this even put pimples on his back."

Zion added, "And you can see his flat bum cheeks."

A twenty-foot newborn baby creeped Riel out with his huge umbilical cord. The size and scale of the sculptures made it an absolutely amazing experience. For reasons I cannot begin to fathom, people were allowed to take all the pictures and video they wanted, so I ran back to the car and got the Flip, and Mueck's sculptures were the guests of honour in our next video.

From the art gallery we headed out of Melbourne to Ocean Grove to meet Graeme and Margie, our next Servas hosts. Graeme and Margie live a couple of blocks from the ocean and so moments after arriving we took a stroll down to the beach. The path took us past the Begola Wetlands (Place of Many Frogs) as Graeme regaled us with stories of local folklore. My favourite story was about a guy named William Buckley, a British convict who had been transported to Australia. Old Bill escaped from custody in 1803 and lived with the Wathaurong people near Ocean Grove for over thirty years, becoming so much a member of the tribe that when he was discovered in 1835 he could not speak a word of English. His story spawned a common expression, Buckley's Chance, that basically means something almost impossible with little hope of success.

So far, Servas had been an awesome type of accommodation. It was great to meet people drawn together by a love for travel and culture. We had a great afternoon on the beach, walked over to a super little pizzeria where we met up with Margie.

The next day was absolutely gorgeous, and we spent all of it in the sun as Graeme taught us how to body surf. (No dumbass instructors from the prairies blowing their eardrums out this day.) With some wet suits, boards, and informed instruction, we got it. After one particularly spectacular ride as Zion and Graeme raced side by side for the shore, Zion jumped to his feet and exclaimed, "Graeme is the master and I am his willing disciple!" We filled up our waterproof video camera with great footage. That night we enjoyed a spectacular meal together. Zion curled up in the basement to watch his hero, Roger Federer, soundly beat Andrew Murray in theAustralian Open final.

Monday morning dawned bright and beautiful as we headed off down the Great Ocean Road. The road was built after World War I by returned servicemen and was constructed as a permanent memorial to those who died while fighting in the Great War. Recognized as one of the world's most scenic drives, the Great Ocean Road stretches over 200 kilometres along Victoria's coastline. It takes a hell of a long time to drive 'cause you just can't help stopping every fifteen minutes to take pictures as the road winds along cliff tops and plunges down to the edge of beaches, offering panoramic views of the Bass Strait at every turn.

Down Under is action packed footage as we learn to body surf, cruise the Great Ocean Road, hike through a tropical jungle and finally catch a Ron Mueck art installation after chasing his work around the globe.

A Metallic Gunshot As Stars Explode In My Eyes

After spending two weeks exploring the southern coast it was time to head back to Sydney. Greg and Louisa had pizza and beer waiting for us when we arrived at Turramurra and we had a mini reunion, sharing stories from our adventures.

By this point, we were getting better at knowing what worked best for us. Everyone had suggestions; we just to see Byron Bay and the Great Barrier Reef and Uluru was a must. The thing is, Australia is frigging huge and we are not exactly rolling in dough. So we decided to add The Outback to our Australian adventures. Kevin was the retired sheep farmer I sat with at the Bucks party back in Malaysia. I can't remember how many rounds of drinks Kevin and I had consumed when he slapped me on the back and shouted, "Mate, you've gotta come stay at our place when you're in Aus."

I convinced Zara we should take Kevin up on his offer, regardless of his blood alcohol level when he made it.

From Sydney we drove a couple of hours north to Nelson Bay. Zara had booked us two nights at the Samurai Beach Bungalows in Port Stephens. When we arrived, we discovered that the Samurai hostel was actually a series of individual bungalows, each one buried deep in the lush, tropical jungle. There was a funky outdoor kitchen located in the centre of the camp along with a luxurious salt-water pool. As we were checking in, we asked the manager what she'd recommend we do while we were in the area. She handed us some custom-made "Samurai" sandboards and gave us directions to Stockton Beach, located at Anna Bay.

There we discovered a thirty-five kilometre long beach with breathtaking sand dunes and endless waves. We walked off into the desert under a charcoal sky with billowing white clouds tumbling overhead. As we walked, the wind picked up, making me feel like Lawrence of Arabia in a giant sandblaster. We waxed up our boards and proceeded to learn how to navigate the forty- to fifty-foot sand dunes. Riel had an instant knack for it. After slipping and sliding a couple of hours away we found a decent grocery store and picked up everything we needed for homemade hamburgers. Each cabin at the Samurai had two separate rooms with a shared bathroom in between. Part of the reason we love staying in hostels was cheaper rates, but the other, and equally important reason, was the opportunity to meet other travelers. Just before supper, our neighbours arrived.

Rob and Nikki were from Cornwall, and had two girls, Toots and Eliza, who were the same ages as Zion and Riel. Eliza was nine and suffered from spinal muscular atrophy. SMA is a genetic disease that breaks down the anterior horn cell in the base of the spine, which is responsible for sending messages from the brain telling the muscles to grow. As Eliza's body grows, her muscles don't, meaning she gets weaker as her body gets bigger. The first time I saw Eliza she just about ran me over, as she flew around the foliage in her motorized wheelchair laughing wildly as she was being chased by the resident German Shepherd.

The terrain around the hostel grounds was totally wild; paths were lined with bark mulch, but Eliza tore around like a mad woman with an infectious smile.

Rob and Nikki exuded a laid-back surfer vibe, which we discovered was actually quite genuine. They were from a small village along the southern coast of England where they owned a couple of retail shops. As the sun set, we sat out on our veranda with our bottles of wine and packets of rolling tobacco and shared an incredible night in a tropical paradise.

The kids raced back to the cabin at one point to tell us that the owner was letting people hold his giant boa constrictor. I grabbed the Flip and got footage of the giant snake draped over a grinning Eliza as Riel kissed it on its lips. Who knew that a couple of nine-year-old girls would go bonkers for a boa?

Rob and Nikki couldn't get a second night at the hostel because there was a naturalist convention rolling in for the weekend and all the rooms were booked. When I jokingly told Zion and Riel that the campground was going to be filled with naked old people they were horrified and wanted to stay indoors until dark. Rob and Nikki did find accommodations at another place in town, so we made plans to meet up later for a barbie in a park.

We were loading our daypacks in the car when Rob came scampering around the corner looking a bit wide-eyed.

"You can't walk anywhere in this bloody country without running into something a bit mad," he said. "I just about stepped on a six-foot lizard in the garden."

I knew exactly how he felt.

We explored Tomaree Head during the day. It was hot and the kids complained mercilessly as we climbed. At one point while I was filming the magnificent view, Zion stood behind me providing a running commentary on my commentary.

"Wow, look at that view," I said, panning slowly across a million dollar panoramic view.

"It looks like garbage," Zion interjected beside me.

"Folks watching at home, today we are in paradise, but Zion says this spectacular odyssey looks like garbage," I continue.

"It's rubbish," he mutters.

"Why don't you grow a pair," I taunt. "I've already grown a pair," he volleys.

"Why don't you grow a bigger pair that can walk up a hill without bitching," I reply.

"If my pair were any bigger, they'd be dragging on the ground," he retorts. I know what you're thinking, and you are right ... I deserve Zion.

Late in the afternoon, we met up with Rob, Nikki, Toots, and Eliza at a public park. Parks in Australia have free outdoor BBQs that make it super easy to have a picnic. Rob already had prawns and baby squid sizzling when we arrived.

Zara and Nikki were whipping up something amazing as we opened a couple of bottles of wine. I got into an impromptu game of catch with Zion as we chucked a tennis ball back and forth. Zion long bombed the ball high up and over my head. I faded back like a wide receiver, putting my quick feet on, sprinting with all possible speed to chase down this incredible throw. All of a sudden, it sounded like a metallic gunshot went off as stars exploded in my eyes and the world went black. The next thing I knew I was staring straight up at the sky and it felt like my face on fire.

The metallic gunshot was the tennis ball hitting the corrugated tin roof over the top of the barbie a split second before I ran face first into the metal pole supporting the roof.

Oh great, I thought. Rob and Nikki had just invited us to come visit them in Cornwall and now they're going to remember me as the guy that ran his face into a pole. Pole-face, that's probably what they'll call me. Years from now they' ll meet someone from Canada and Rob will say, "Oh, yeah, we met some Canadians awhile back. Nik, what was that Canadian guy's name again that we met in Australia?"

"Oh, right," she'll say thoughtfully, trying to pull my name from thin air, "you know, I can't remember. Do you mean Pole-face?"

Then they'll laugh and tell the story. As this is running through my head, Zion's face looks down at me, less concerned with my welfare than he is with trying not to laugh. He says, "Sorry you ran your face into a pole, Dad."

Both families disintegrate into gales of laughter as Zion receives a rousing round of high fives and backslaps. They all walk back to the food leaving me to lie in the peace and quiet of my own shame.

The next day we veered inland. Enroute to Kevin's sheep farm in Coonamble, we decided to spend a couple of nights in Dubbo, best known for the Taronga Western Plains Zoo that sprawls over three square kilometres and offers a safari-style adventure to experience walking around with over 700 animals.

We arrived at the Blue Gum Motel where we met an outrageously apathetic manager who just didn't give a kangaroo's fart about anything. This guy seriously took "half-ass" to full-on. As I was checking in, I saw a sign behind the counter about an additional discount if we purchased tickets for the Zoo right at the front desk. I asked him how much of a discount it is. "Aahhhh," he exhaled, like he needed to steel his nerve and dig deep to drum up the energy necessary to tackle such a huge question, "It's ten per cent off."

"Is that off the family rate?" I asked.

He looked at me as if I was an insurmountable obstacle the good Lord would need to give him grace to overcome. Whether it was apathy or arithmetic, his final price was actually higher than purchasing full rate tickets at the Zoo. He so obviously couldn't give two hoots that I decided not to mention it.

The Dubbo Zoo was OK. The highlight wasn't the elephants, giraffes, rhinos, or monkeys: it was a wombat off in a little pen so far away from the action I'm not really sure what was up. It said not to pet the wombat, but he seemed so lonely and kept standing up on his hind legs to reach his little snout and paws over the edge of the pen, it was impossible not to. The lonely little wombat was the hit of the day.

The next day we headed up Highway #55 for Coonamble and Kevin and Louise's place. We were cruising along when the phone rang; it was Kevin.

"Hey mate, how're ya doing? So yeah, we're not going to make it back there in time, we're still down here in Sydney."

As I listened to Kevin, I mentally scrambled to figure out what exactly we were going to do with ourselves in the middle of nowhere. But Kevin's not the kind of guy to leave you high when he leaves you dry. He passes you off to someone else.

"Tell you what, mate, why don't you stay with our daughter Liz. Let me give you her number," as he proceeds to fire it off.

Now this was awkward. I only know one Buck's party and seven-Malaysian-beers-worth of Kevin, which was barely enough to build travel plans on. But to show up at his daughter's house, whom we'd never met, that felt weird. But ... and this was really the most important thing, we were in the Outback in Australia and hardly in a position to worry about feeling guilty.

So I dialed Liz.

"Oh hiya, mate!" she greeted. "Yeeah, I talked to my Dad; you guys can totally stay here, no worries."

Thank God for this whole "no worries" thing. Liz gave me directions to their place that involved landmarks more than street names or signs.

"On your way through Coonamble, do you think you can stop at the grocery store and pick up a box of food? I' ll just tell them to have it ready and you can pick it up," she said. We passed some landmarks to the little store. I walked through the door and before I could say a single word, the lady looked up and said, "You must be the Canadian."

That's when I knew we were in a small town in the Outback. With groceries in the front seat and a map in hand, we headed for the ranch.

Liz and Ben had three kids: Hamish, Cameron, and Helen. Hamish and Helen were the same ages as Zion and Riel, and within minutes Wii, Lego, and a swimming pool provided all the common ground necessary. After enjoying a cold beer, Ben invited us to take a tour of the property. The kids jumped into the box of the truck as Zara and I jumped into the cab and off we went.

The area had just experienced the wettest spring Ben could remember, making everything green and gorgeous. We were greeted by a mob of kangaroos racing pell-mell alongside our vehicle, until the curvature of their scimitar-like tails disappeared in a cloud of red dust and our exuberant cheers.

As we sat around the table chatting that night, we discovered just how small the world really is. Liz started to tell a story about traveling to Canada twenty years earlier with her friend Louisa. At the same moment, Zara and Liz realized they had met before, as the Louisa in the story was "Cousin Louisa", the one we'd been partying with in Sydney.

Twenty years earlier, the two Australians had stayed with Zara and her family during their tour around Canada.

The next few days were a blur of activity. Riel learned to ride the quad and Helen's dirt bike and was soon racing around like a crazy woman, while Zion went yabby hunting with Hamish and Cameron. A yabby is an Australian freshwater crustacean in the Parastacidae family. They looked like disgusting, blue baby lobsters to me.

As you may have realized by now, I have a tendency to scream in a shrill womanly fashion when I'm scared by wildlife. It's not a big thing, and I've realized it doesn't have any real bearing on the quality of my character, so much as it's just awesome fodder for mocking and derision. When Cameron pulled a net full of yabbies out of the creek and dumped it on the ground right behind Zion, who was crouched over doing something busy, I tried to casually get his attention, thinking I would save him the embarrassment of shrieking in a high womanly manner. But Zion has a Dad filter that seems to reduce all frequencies associated with the timbre of my voice, thus enabling him to "cut out" the white noise of parental instruction and correction. I started to sound like an insistent toddler.

"Zi, Zi. Hey, Zion, Zion, ZION!" He finally turned to acknowledge me as a half dozen yabbies were closing in on his feet, their pinchers primed and clicking inaudibly in frenzied anticipation of seizing his unprotected toes.

"Oh cool," he said, unfazed and unflappable, picking them up ever so gently between his thumb and forefinger before tossing them playfully back into the water.

That night we really headed out into the wild for a barbie beside a big beautiful pond. Ben was describing how clean the water was, but when he said you could drink it, Zion thought that was going just a bit too far.

"Yeah right," Zi scoffed. "I'd like to see you do it."

With no worries or even a moment's hesitation, Ben leaned down with his cup, scooped up a half glass of pond water and downed it. I think I threw up in my mouth a little, but everyone was busy watching Ben.

Having grown up on a farm in Canada I really appreciated the culinary application of a common discer, which is a piece of equipment used by farmers to plough fields. The round, concave disc had been welded to a metal tripod which was set over the fire. It worked perfectly as a cooking surface for sausages and yabbies. I pulled out my guitar and an ice-cold beer and played some songs, as the kids swam in the pond and the sunset filled the immense Australian sky with an amazing kaleidoscope of colours.

When we got back to the house, we discovered hundreds of bright, lime green frogs about the size of a computer mouse. The kids were having a great time, catching them and holding them and oohing and aahing at their little eyes. I took the Flip out to get some footage and when I leaned over to see a little guy, one of his brethren jumped onto the top of my head. I've mentioned the high womanly shrieking, right?

I danced in one spot, spasming and swatting as the kids dissolved into gales of laughter. Unfortunately, the Flip was still rolling and this also became a featured part of *Zion & Riel – Viva Australia*.

Our time in the Outback was over and our time in Australia was quickly coming to a close. But we were heading back to Sydney for one last great adventure.

Viva Australia pays homage to some of the Aussie wildlife that kept scaring and startling us, as we journey from Melbourne to the Outback and end our trip on a sailboat.

Swarthy Swashbucklers and Nautical Hazing Rituals

Today I was a millionaire. Well, at least I lived the way I'd live if I were a millionaire.

It all began with a magnificent invitation to join Zara's uncle, Peter, aboard his sailboat for a couple of days. That was how we found ourselves heading out of Pittman Bay under the beautiful, bright Sydney sun attempting to tackle the challenging world of sailing aboard "Sail La Vie", Peter's thirty-seven-foot Sea Odyssey.

Initially, the experience reminded me of my early days as a theatre stagehand trying to remember which was stage right and stage left, front, and back of house. We were not even out of the harbour before we were scrambling about the deck like a herd of landlubbers, stumbling over winches and cleats, and getting tangled up in ropes and rigging.

Peter tried valiantly to teach us some simple nautical terminology like port, starboard, coming about, and tacking. But honestly, my affirmative head-bobbing and grunts of understanding were really just reflexive "learned behaviour" I'd acquired growing up on a farm surrounded by burly, bearded men who wore tool belts and carried wrenches in their pockets. As usual, I had very little idea of what was going on around me.

Amid the chaos, I amused myself by muttering piratey phrases to Zion in a swarthy brogue every time we passed each other. "Why is the rum gone?" I'd say or "Do we have an accord?"

This was all the *Pirates of the Caribbean* dialogue I had time to channel between stubbing my toes and repeatedly drilling my head into the mast.

We headed out to Broken Bay where the Pittman and Cowan Rivers meet the Pacific Ocean.

"Hey, Zi and Riel," I yelled over the sound of flapping sails and swelling waves slapping noisily against the hull, "you might want to wave … Just over there on the other side of the world is Canada."

We headed down the Cowan River as a northerly came steaming toward us with her dark eyes and stormy skies intimating harsh intentions. Oblivious to the impending deluge, I stood slack-mouthed and gaping like a swashbuckling idiot savant until Peter nudged me to take the wheel. No sooner had he disappeared into the cabin than the heavens opened up and nature started screaming like a banshee. Wind and water stung my skin and blinded my eyes as I pointed the prow of the boat toward nothing, deciding that under my command I would prefer "Sail La Vie" to run into nothing rather than something.

Just when I was starting to suspect that Peter was engaging in some bizarre nautical hazing ritual, he was back on deck in his rain gear and more than happy to take the wheel from my incapable hands as he guided us expertly into Refuge Bay.

We arrived at low tide and moored as near to the little beach as we could, to make going ashore as convenient as possible. Just behind the beach, a picturesque waterfall poured over a ridge from fifty feet up.

After securing the lines, the adult portion of the crew reclined on the deck to sip chilled wine and dine on mango salad, ripe olives, brie, and crackers. The perfect moment was only diminished by my inability to speak with an exotic accent.

As the winds died down we found ourselves looking out over the deep, dark water, as still as glass reflecting the billowing clouds overhead.

Back in 1943, Refuge Bay was known to a select few as Camp Z, a top secret training spot for the Australian army. At a time when the Allies were looking for ways to strike at Japanese strongholds in the Pacific, a twenty-something Brit named Ivan Lyon, and a sixty-something Australian named Bill Reynolds hatched a plan to attack Singapore harbour.

Reynolds owned a beat-up Japanese wooden coastal vessel he had used to smuggle refugees out of Sumatra. Their plan was to use the old ship to sail into Singapore harbour under the cover of darkness carrying commandos who would attach mines to the Japanese shipping vessels.

In September '43, the ship headed off carrying a crew of four Brits and eleven Australians. When they reached Singapore, the commandos assembled a bunch of collapsible canvas, folbot kayaks, before slipping over the edge and paddling off into the darkness. Working through the night they attached bombs to a number of vessels and sank or damaged at least six ships before slinking out of the harbour at first light.

I admit none of this was on my mind when Zion and Riel said they wanted to go ashore and explore. I had not quite finished my wine and I wasn't prepared to go when they wanted to, but told them to take the dingy and I would join them shortly by swimming to shore.

Soon my salad was gone, my wine was sipped and I was at the back of the boat in my swimmers staring at the water. Refuge Bay suddenly seemed cold and forbidding and anything but a refuge.

Movie reels started to spin in my mind, the kind starring sexy, rich kids languishing on yachts much like the one I was on, suddenly attacked by mammoth, genetically modified sharks. Those movies always started with some dumbass dangling his feet in the ocean, kicking back and forth, begging great incisors to chomp them off. As soon as the thought crossed my mind, I stopped kicking and quickly pulled my feet out of the water.

I looked at the beach. It seemed to have floated a lot further away than I had initially imagined. Whatever the case, the kids were already pulling the Zodiac up on the shore and starting to scamper around.

Predatory pictures from the Australia horror porn book were flashing through my mind. It wasn't just Great Whites; there were Bluebottles, salt-water crocs and the Blue Ring Octopus, one of the most toxic sea creatures in the world. As I stared fearfully at the water I was pretty sure I saw a Box Jellyfish flip me off.

I thought of diving off the side of the boat and gaining some forward motion toward the shore, but the thought immediately seemed ill advised. I might as well ring a doorbell.

I thought it might be best if I just slipped into the lethal waters quietly and didn't make a big deal about my presence. I was sure that said predators could smell fear, so I tried to exude a no-aquatic-bitches-better-f#%with-me persona as I crept toward the water.

Which was right about the time my foot slipped and I fell unceremoniously, ass-first into the bay, committing the classic horror movie blunder by broadcasting my presence.

"Oh that's just perfect," I muttered to myself, thinking that I should probably get the hell out of the water, right frigging now. But that seemed like such a pussy thing to do; what would I say to Zara? What would I say to the kids?

"Sorry guys, I just didn't want to be the victim in the imaginary horror flick playing on the screen behind my eyes."

I decided to swim purposefully toward the beach with damnable disregard for the Australian netherworld. As I swam, mind, body, and soul fell into a penitent rhythm.

"Oh God. Oh s#%. Oh God. Oh s#%," I prayed fervently with each stroke. Reality teetered precariously on the edge of my overactive imagination. I was sure at one point I saw a squadron of jellyfish fanning out in a flanking manoeuvre.

Consumed with the anxiety of my own creation, I screamed with surprise and relief as my flailing arms and legs suddenly made contact with the sand. Zion and Riel waded into the water and started pulling on my swimmers, eager to show me what they'd discovered.

Filled with inexpressible joy that I'd survived another one of my imaginary experiences, I kissed my children with wine-scented breath and looked around at the world with new appreciation.

A waterfall cascaded over the sandstone cliffs rising fifty feet above our heads, thundering into a bubbling pool that churned up to our knees. Zion and Riel scampered over the slippery rocks glistening in the mist as the three of us forced our way through the watery veil to huddle like smugglers in the little cave behind the water.

As day gave way to night, sailboats, cabin cruisers, and one home-made-looking houseboat slid into Refuge Bay. Zion and Riel were on the bow spitting pieces of apple over the side to schools of fish, giggling that their spit was delicious special sauce. We ate late, long after the stars had filled the sky and their reflection danced on the surface the sea. I pulled out my guitar and started to play. Knowing how sound carries across the water, "Sail La Vie" felt like a stage as I played a private show to a scattered crowd of twinkling lights.

I was looking forward to falling asleep lying on my back looking up at the stars, but it was raining and we had to keep the hatches closed. It was also Australia, so it was hotter than Hades in the cabin.

The next morning was the only morning I have ever woken up on the ocean. I felt as close to heaven as I've ever been, sitting on the deck sipping a coffee and nibbling on fresh fruit. Until Riel came over to whisper conspiratorially that she couldn't get the toilet to flush. I went to give it a whirl and couldn't get it to work either. Soon Peter was on his phone talking with the guy in charge of maintenance trying to get it to work. Zara and I were oblivious to everything, consumed as we were with lounging on the deck, when Peter walked by with a bucket. "I'm just going to empty the toilet with a bucket and dump it overboard," he said.

As he disappeared down below Zara muttered under her breath without even looking up, "Well, good thing that's a one man job."

NEW ZEALAND

Defense of Persecuted Penguin Retinas

From Australia, we were heading to Aotearoa, the land of the long white cloud. Christine gave us a ride to the airport where our flight departed at 7:00 p.m. from Sydney. We'd decided to fly into Christchurch and explore the South Island first, and then gradually work our way north, eventually departing from Auckland.

We'd given ourselves about six weeks to explore New Zealand and planned to split that time fairly evenly between the South and North Islands.

It's only a two-and-a-half-hour flight to Christchurch but with the time change we touched down just after midnight. It probably took us as long to get out of the airport as it did to fly there. New Zealand is possibly even more anal about keeping organic material out of the country than Australia. Every inch of every bag of every person was searched. As we stood waiting for the customs agent to stamp our passports, we were suddenly joined by an incredibly large female agent, who asked Zara to follow her. Zion, Riel, and I kept moving, getting a cart, collecting our bags, and lining up for yet another inspection. The closer we got to the front of the line, the more I started wondering where Zara had gotten to and what exactly we were supposed to do if she failed to reappear. About six feet from the next agent she slipped back into line and tried to covertly whisper that she'd been detained because her name had apparently set off some security watch. Not wanting to attract any undue attention or additional scrutiny as our bags were being searched, she tried to give me the condensed version and waited until we were out of the airport to reveal the whole story.

It's one of the mysteries of life how the same kids that never hear you shrieking their names, or instructions to pick up their clothes, eat their crusts or brush their teeth, can zero in on the subtlest nuance of the slightest whisper when you do not want them to hear.

As Zara covertly whispered, "My name set off a security watch," I just kept looking forward, totally cool as a cucumber.

That was when Zion's incredibly brilliant voice cracked like an inquisitive whip, "WHAT SET OFF A SECURITY WATCH?"

"Shhh, we'll talk about it later," I muttered like a ventriloquist, my lips moving imperceptibly.

"WHAT IS A SECURITY WATCH?" Riel seemed to scream at the top of her lungs. When her parents didn't show any inclination to answer she turned to her all-knowing brother, "ZI! WHAT IS A SECURITY WATCH?"

"IT'S LIKE A POLICE ALARM THAT ALERTS THE AUTHORITIES TO BAD GUYS!" Zion seemed to bellow.

"AND MOM SET OFF A SECURITY WATCH!" Riel projected at ear-bleeding levels. "WHY? WHY DID MOM SET OFF A SECURITY WATCH?"

Before Zion could respond with any more security watches, I managed to get them to shut up, promising tubs full of chocolate ice cream and pop. Miraculously we got through phase two without any more security watches or problems.

Then we needed to stand in line at the one bank machine to get some Kiwi cash, and then stand in another line for the shuttle van to take us into the city and drop us at our hotel. I'm not exaggerating when I say that it took us as long to get out of the airport and to our hotel as it did to fly from Australia.

Around 3:30 a.m., we arrived at our hotel. The owner had left our room unlocked and we all piled in and gratefully crashed in our beds.

The next morning it was a bit cool and rainy. Since leaving Canada, we'd had nothing but hot and sunny. We spent the day kicking around our little hotel room, watching the winter Olympics back home in Vancouver. It was funny to watch the Kiwi coverage; with only a handful of athletes in a handful of events, they certainly didn't take themselves or the games too seriously. The commentators routinely made jokes about spills and crashes, often inserting a sexual "in-your-end-O" to their banter. As a family of snowboarders, we were excited to watch Shaun White win the half-pipe with his latest aerial invention called the Tomahawk. Around noon, a shuttle bus from El Cheapo came by and we headed off to pick up our rental car. We'd done lots of research online comparing possible modes of transportation while we were in New Zealand. El Cheapo rents older cars, but they let you pick up in Christchurch and drop off in Auckland, and the price includes the ferry crossing from the South to North Island. The company even makes the ferry reservation for you, so it seemed like the best bet.

On the way to the rental agency, Zara told me to look at the gas prices as we passed a station: $1.89 per litre. I thought it must be a typo, but, of course, it wasn't.

After getting our car, we headed downtown to explore Christchurch. It was a big day for Riel as our little tomboy bought her first pair of dangling earrings, before we wandered around taking in the sights and sounds including a Maori haka in the city square.

Friday we headed down the coast to Oamaru and the Chillawhile Backpackers Hostel. We'd arranged for a whole room for our family for $80.00 a night. We had lots of room, on the second floor just around the corner from the kitchen.

Chillawhile was a really feminine hostel; the vibe was clean, artsy, and felt great. We headed out after supper to the blue penguin colony on the coast to watch the smallest penguins in the world come in to shore for the night. We managed to see one.

He/she was mostly obscured by foliage and made even less accessible by the sheer number of tourists crammed onto a tiny little viewing platform. There were about fifty or sixty tourists, a mish-mash of middle-aged officious types. There was a sign that asked people not to use flashes on their cameras so as not to disturb the penguins. But let's face it, cell phones have been around for twenty years and people still forget to turn them off in movie theatres, so, of course, someone was going to forget to turn the flash off.

Heaven pity the fool that took a picture with a flash. It was kind of like a library or a mortuary, everyone standing around quietly whispering until a flash went off. Then a militant strain of loud, vocal tourists would rush to defend the persecuted penguins' retinas. "Who did that!" would echo from all directions simultaneously.

"No flashes! No flashes! Read the goddamn signs! GEEZUS SOME PEOPLE ARE IDIOTS!"

I started to worry more for the penguins' endangered eardrums than their retinas. The turmoil would eventually taper off and an oppressive hush would fall over the crowd. But, of course, this was a popular beach for sighting penguins so people were constantly arriving and this scenario repeated itself every three-and-a-half-to-four minutes the entire time we were there.

It's part of humanity's hypocritical charm; we become self-righteous knobs defending the world from belligerent dicks.

The next day we headed out to Elephant Rocks. The kids immediately recognized this amazing rock formation as the location of Aslan's Camp in *Narnia* the movie. Although to be fair, Zion did go on at length about a section of *Halo* of which they also reminded him.

I learned an important lesson the day we explored Elephant Rocks. If I ever want to know what my son is thinking, feeling, or dreaming, or if I just need to distract him for a while, all I have to do is ask him a couple of simple lead questions about *Halo* and he's off. As we climbed and wandered around, Zion regaled me with tales of sniping Brutes and Elites and Grunts. On one particular rock, we looked across the little valley and saw a movie set. We started dreaming and scheming about what movie it probably was and how we could sneak onto location.

The proximity to Aslan's Camp from the first movie led us to speculate that it must be for a new *Narnia* film. And that led to further speculation on which book they would be filming next. Zara and I started cobbling together storylines from the different books, doing that classic discussion-debate, which book came before which and who the main characters were and which of the Pevensie kids were still allowed in Narnia.

There was a guy sitting in a lawn chair on the top of the hill looking across the valley toward the rocks. But as we watched him watch us, we realized he never moved ... ever. Someone had propped a mannequin up in a lawn chair in an effort to defend the movie set. But we were not so easily dissuaded, so we hiked up the road to check the perimeter. We could tell there was an actual security guard sitting in an Atco trailer on site, so we wandered up and down the road talking loudly to our kids in the most distinctive Canadian pronunciation we could muster, and sure enough, after two to three minutes, an old guy came out for a smoke.

One friendly greeting led to another and in less than ten minutes, we'd talked ourselves into an unofficial tour of the movie set. It wasn't a Narnia movie but a Jesus movie and, according to the resident security guard, a Jesus movie bogged down in pre-production but reported to be the biggest-budget movie ever to be filmed in New Zealand. He repeated the phrase so many times I assume that it is the movie mantra since LOTR. While the guy gave us the tour I kept pulling the Flip out of my pocket and filming every time his back was turned. It was one of those moments where I could just ride the comedic energy.

I would somehow instinctively know every time he was about to turn around and I would hide the camera.

When he was all done, I asked if we could take a picture and he freaked out and said he'd lose his job for sure if he let that happen. Which is the one piece of dialogue that would have made the video priceless, but walking back to the car Zara put her pre-emptive foot down and forbade me from using any of the footage in *Zion & Riel – New Zealand Adventures*.

One of the bonuses of producing our "Where in the World are Zion & Riel" videos was having such great material to introduce ourselves to people we were contacting along the way. We could just direct them to our YouTube channel and they'd be able to get a feel for who we were and what we were up to.

After watching some of our videos, the owner of the Chillawhile hostel had offered to exchange a night of free accommodation if I made a promotional video for her. I worked on it throughout the day on Monday, and had fun putting on the finishing touches with Ashley, Daisy, and Karen, woofers who were working for their room and board.

In the end, we decided Daisy's English accent was the best and collaborated on a script, and got her to do a few takes before sealing the deal and uploading the video.

I'd just gone to bed and was lying there reading when someone knocked on the door. Daisy stuck her head in and asked what the name of my song was that I'd used at the end of the video. When she left, Zion's voice floated down from the top bunk, "Wow, Dad, you must have been embarrassed, lying there with your big beer belly hanging out."

In New Zealand Adventures we explore Elephant Rocks, instantly recognizable for anyone who saw the first Narnia movie, laugh at Zion's epic face plant racing down a sand mountain at Seal Point, luging in Queenstown and hiking along Lake Wakatipu.

It Might Not Be Art But It Sure is Creative

I'm not sure when Zara and I gave up on our lofty aspirations for homeschooling, but somewhere along the way reality was just too gritty to ignore. But that doesn't mean I still don't have to submit a mid-term report to the authorities. I have just taken BS to a whole new level. It might not be art, but it sure is creative.

To: The Homeschooling Authorities of Canada, Re: Zion & Riel Leaf, Mid-Term Report

Travel, geography, different cultures and history have been our primary focus and are all subjects we have incorporated naturally, as we have been traveling. My wife and I both work in the cultural industry and have made a point of including workshops, theatre productions and arts presentations into our itinerant curriculum. These have included the Polynesian Cultural Centre and Pearl Harbor in Hawaii and local and international theatre productions and art galleries in other cities.

Zion and Riel have both been writing extensive journals about their experiences.

I am of course, referring to the doodles of stick men battle scenes on napkins and placemats that litter our vehicle.

They are learning to write descriptively and vividly of their many experiences.

Mostly when describing how the stick men are dying and why their heinous deaths were warranted.

We have also insisted they both read daily and have been

buying many books along the way to focus on their reading and comprehension skills.

This at least is true. We continue to insist and they continue to resist and every book we've bought remains as untouched and unspoiled as Merry and Pippin in a sea of Saruman's orcs.

We have also been working through Grade-appropriate Math textbooks we bought before we left Canada.

This is also true, as we've needed to light a few fires along the way and the ink they use for textbooks is a great kindling substitute.

Both of the kids are bright and inquisitive. Traveling has opened their hearts and minds to the world of possibilities that exist for them and has caused numerous in-depth conversations.

Zion is still lobbying for penis to have a more inclusive defini-tion so he can work it naturally into more conversations.

They are experiencing the world in ways they could never have imagined before this year.

Zion contends that being forced to leave his X-Box behind con-stitutes cruels and unusual punishment.

We are thrilled with their development so far this year and believe they will return to Canada filled with indispensable knowledge and life experiences that will empower them to face the challenges of returning to school.

What I mean is, they will have to work their asses off to catch up as we have failed to teach them anything.

After emailing the report to our liaison back in Winnipeg, I returned to our hostel room and read the official memo out loud. Our pillows glistened with tears of mirth and merriment as we collectively laughed ourselves silly by the absurdity of it all.

As Riel drifted off to sleep she chuckled, "Dad, you're funny."

The Asylum Backpackers hostel is located in Seacliff, just up the coast from Dunedin. It used to be the site of an asylum built in 1879. Where Chillawhile felt very feminine, the Asylum felt totally male. There were lots of vintage cars in various states of restoration sitting around, boogie boards, wet suits, and tennis courts, all free to use. The manager seemed to think either we'd want a really quiet place or maybe he thought the kids would be really loud and disturb everyone else. He walked us across the yard from the main building to one of the only original buildings left standing on the site. It was built back in 1800 and something. In one corner were the remains of a blacksmith forge with scorched brick and the lingering aroma of soot and ash.

The floor was rough blocks of stone and there were shutters instead of windows and gaping holes in the roof and walls. I wouldn't have found it remotely surprising if there were a family of possums living in the east wing. One big room had six single beds all lined up, military style. The manager thought we'd like the vibe.

It was old and crazy and I knew I was going to write this story. I thought it would be great if we stayed in the oldest building on the Island, a creepy old insane asylum telling ghost stories to the kids and scaring them silly.

I was the only one that thought that sounded fun. As soon as the manager disappeared, Zion and Riel put their emphatic little feet down and ordered me to take care of it.

We grabbed some boards and directions to the beach in Karitane and took off. I have lost track of how many times we just took off with no plan, no books or maps, nothing premeditated, just a willingness to see where the road took us. This was one of those days and it was magical.

The kids and I swam for a while, but after the waves in Australia, New Zealand didn't really compare. While we were paddling around, Zara hiked up the hill beside us. Just over the ridge, she discovered the Huriwa Historic Reserve and a path that circled the point. We spent the next few hours hiking and filming and exploring together.

Then we jumped in the car and headed for Dunedin. Zion and Riel thought every town must have a Lego clearance warehouse and forced us to prove otherwise.

After wandering around Dunedin, Zara suggested that we hit up Seal Point on our way back to the Asylum. We followed a little road down toward the ocean and came to some tiny, nondescript parking lot. We got out and started walking down a totally forgettable path, came over the hill and found ourselves wandering through a farmer's pasture.

Only the aimlessness of the day and the complete absence of an agenda provided the impetus to keep going. The path eventually came to a little gate hidden in some scrub brush, where we passed some out-of-breath tourists. They were our first clue that we were headed in the right direction. We went through the gate, down into the brush and popped out at the top of a steep cliff, covered in deep, silky fine sand that flowed like a duvet as far as the eye could see. Riel took off first, running pell-mell down the hill, her little legs sinking deep into the sand with every step. Zion went next, and in an effort to out-do his little sister, over-extended himself in a way common to thirteen-year-old boys. Just as he was passing some hikers coming up the cliff, he bit it, literally. Face-first, ass-over-end, spine bending the wrong way as his downward momentum carried his feet high up and over his head.

When he emerged from the cloud of dust, he was spitting sand out of his molars and digging it out of every crook and cranny while Zara and I laughed ourselves silly. We stuck around for another uneventful attempt at seeing penguins come ashore, although this location had an actual blind we could hide in, and the rest of the tourists weren't self-righteous knobs.

We headed back to the Asylum where we started making supper. As was often the case, we were the only family, and that made the kids a novelty. I struck up a conversation with a girl from Portugal and another from Spain who were making their way around New Zealand in the opposite direction from us. We swapped stories of good hostels to stay at and the best things we'd done and seen. In an off-handed comment, I told them that we'd sold our house in Canada and were spending a year traveling the world as a family.

After supper when everything was cleaned up and the kids were busy building with Lego in our room, I took the New Zealand hostel map out to the common room to circle the ones that they recommended.

As I sat down at the big table, they immediately launched into the topic most on their mind. "Do many people in Canada do what you are doing?" one of them asked.

Not really, I responded.

"Because in Portugal people would think you crazy," she said, obviously feeling that way.

This led to one of those interesting conversations that strangers can have. We never shared our names, where we were from, or any chitchat about the weather. We started talking about values, and risk-taking, family and marriage.

Just before we left Winnipeg, I went to an industry event and ran into an old friend. I was excited and told him that the sale of our house had just gone through and we had an actual departure date. I guess he'd had enough to drink so he could say what he really thought, and exclaimed, "What brings a person to the point where they'll destabilize their life like that?"

I finally heard what people tell themselves. I finally understood where the craziness comes from. I've met a lot of people over the years through touring, and we've stayed with a lot of people while we've been traveling. I've never understood why people choose to sacrifice their health, their peace of mind, their marriages, and relationships with their kids until that moment. My friend's security, actually his identity, was his house and his job. Which is a totally foreign concept to me.

The year we were traveling was the year the world was freaking out over the global recession. The people who were playing it smart and safe by putting their security in their jobs and houses were actually the worst off. They were not suddenly just out of work and losing their homes, they were losing their foundation and sense of stability in a volatile world.

We liked our house, but we didn't LOVE our house. And if Zara and Zion and Riel weren't in the house, I wouldn't have given a shit about the house, I wouldn't care about it at all. We'll buy another one someday. We took a bunch of money from the sale of our house so we could travel for a year together. We'll make more money.

After my conversation with Ms. Portugal and Ms. Spain I got back to our room and relayed the talk to Zara. We lay in the dark as the kids slept, whispering about how thankful we were that we were doing what we were doing.

Last Night I Paid $50.00 For Sex

Traveling around the world for twelve months on a shoestring budget can wreak havoc on a sex life. Day and night, 24/7, we're in our kids' space and they are in ours. We're in the car during the day and sharing four bunk "family" rooms at hostels in the evening. We've had great experiences meeting people from all over the world at hostels, but all this togetherness can really put a kink in sexiness.

This is also further complicated by the ages of our kids. They are no longer naïve, innocent lambs; they are sleuthy and crafty and at an age where you can never be 100% sure they are actually sleeping.

And let's face it, no one wants to even *think* about their parents getting busy, let alone be stuck pretending to sleep while they rustle the sheets about in a secretive manner.

Riel has never met a parental hug she didn't want to convert to a family hug, which adds to my paranoia. Just the thought of her misinterpreting the signals as a burgeoning family hug, and leaping into the bed is enough to keep me sequestered off on my side of the bed fearing my wife's body might lead me into temptation.

So last night I got in touch with my inner Justin Timberlake and decided it was time to bring Sexy Back. I coughed up an extra $50.00 to rent a hotel room that had a bedroom. In fact, I was so set on rectifying our situation, I booked the room for two nights.

I gave the kids a stern admonishment, "All right, Mom and Dad are really tired from driving all day, so when we close that door it better not open again until morning unless there's a fire or a scary-ass mo-fo breaking in the window, understood?"

I thought of joking to Zara that it would be *unbelievable* if the moon, with all her complicated and various effects on oceans and women's bodies, conspired to make this the night the red tide came in. I didn't, because that would be ludicrous.

But as we passed in the hallway instead of exchanging knowing glances, winks, and nudges I saw the pad of destiny clutched in her hand.

"Damn the spiritual forces bitter and benign that set their will against me!" I said, shaking my impotent fist in vain at the ceiling. That's life traveling with kids.

Queenstown calls itself the Adrenalin Capital of the World, so everywhere you turn there are posters and kiosks celebrating the many exciting ways Kiwis have created to separate you from your money. We chose the Shotover Jet Boat that screams at breakneck speeds down Shotover Canyon. Back in Canada, only a couple of weeks into our trip we'd stayed with Doug and Sharon in Fort St. John. The day we left, they gave us all sorts of going away gifts, books, and different things for the kids, along with an envelope filled with cash.

"We believe one of the ways to invest in our own dreams is to invest in the dreams of others," they had said on their doorstep. They included a note that said we should use the money for something we'd really like to do but couldn't really afford. On the other side of the world almost half a year later, we had our moment. We boarded the bus that shuttles people out to the canyon. There we got decked out in long black raincoats and bright red lifejackets and jumped into the front row of the boat. Since the company started in 1970, 2.5 million people have taken the ride of their lives. The jet boats can skim along in a few inches of water and the drivers have perfected the art of racing at breakneck speeds a breath away from the canyon rock face.

It was simply spectacular, and an experience unlike anything we've ever done before as a family.

Shotover jets do a 360-degree spin on the open water wherever possible, so we were flung back and forth, up and down being sprayed and soaked along the way. At the far end of the river the driver kills the motor and turns around and asks everyone how they're doing. He throws a few fun facts out before sliding back in his seat and calling out, "Well, that was a good warm up, how about the real thing?"

Riel took him at his word and looked up at me with huge eyes, "If *that* was a warm up, how crazy is this going to be?"

Back on the banks of the river, I turned the Flip on each member of the family to get their reactions in the moment. When it was my turn, I started to thank Doug and Sharon for their gift that allowed us to have such an incredible experience, and got all choked up. Someone had created an incredible memory for my kids. What changes a person's world more than that? *Zion & Riel – Queenstown* celebrates this experience.

We took the bus back into town, grabbed some lunch and had a picnic in a park. From where we were sitting, we could look straight up the mountain where the gondola swept people to the top and the Skyline Luge run. You don't go to Queenstown to sit in your hotel room, so up to the top we went.

Before the trip, Riel was anything but an adrenalin junkie. Looking at her in a big red Luge helmet, riding her first chairlift to the top of a mountain so she could race to the bottom in her own little sled, made me so proud. Before I could say anything she looked up at me with excited eyes. "I never thought I'd do any-thing like this in my entire life!"

The road between Queenstown and Glenorchy runs along-side Lake Wakatipu. The whole country is filled with beautiful drives, but that drive was spectacular.

Lake Wakatipu is shrouded in myth and mystery as the water level rises and falls by about five inches every five minutes. A Maori legend says the lake used to be the resting spot of a giant. When this giant stole the wife of a local Maori, the Maori set fire to the giant, burning him and leaving a big reversed N-shaped hole in the ground where the giant had rested. The hole was filled with the waters of the surrounding mountains forming Lake Wakatipu. The legend says, today the giant's heart still beats within Lake Wakatipu, causing the fluctuations of the water level.

Of course, scientists weigh in with some banal drivel passing off the phenomenon as a seiche, or a periodic oscillation of water level set in motion by some atmospheric disturbance passing over a Great Lake. Phtzzzpt, whatever!

Honestly, I can't imagine being in a relationship with someone whose genetic makeup is wired to deconstruct all of life's great mysteries with jargon and periodic tables. I'm inspired by the poet, who climbs the vines to the second storey window, where he creeps on cat's paws into the lady's room and whispers (in an Antonio Banderas accent), "Senorita, long have I desired to speak French and Latin between your legs as I drive you to Spain with my tongue."

I picture the scientist removing his pocket protector, in a suggestive manner, as he begins to lecture. "Your sexual arousal has initiated enhanced genital blood flow, leading to the formation of a neurogenic transudate. This lubricates the walls of your vagina, buffering its acidity and increasing oxygen tension, which as you may know enhances spermatozoal function." Oooh baby, slip out of that smock and slide your test tube into my beaker. Anyway … it's possible I digress.

When we got to Glenorchy, we went to an information centre to get ideas for a hike. We talked to the girl behind the counter, got her advice, took some maps, walked out the door and started driving, and I have no idea where we ended up. Even Google Maps was like, WTF? We followed a gravel road for thirty miles at least. We crossed slow-moving water, went through some gullies, across sheep and cattle guards, and just kept going and going. We saw a couple of land cruisers from a LOTR tour company with personalized license plates sporting names like Faramir, Frodo, and Bilbo. But it didn't really instill any confidence in us, coming around a corner and finding a bunch of fantasy geeks nerding out in the middle of the road in Gondorian helmets, pleated shorts and crocs.

After slowly weaving our way through one such encounter, Zion broke the silence. "Oh, my God, that was so embarrassing!"

We drove through a river crossing where the water was almost up to the doors of our rental car, came around a corner and discovered half a dozen cars parked beside a porta-potty. The sign said we were at Chinaman's Bluff, on the Dart River.

We started hiking up an incredible trail that hugged the side of a rocky cliff as it wound its way through a dark shadowy forest. The trail eventually opened up into a field with waist high grass that reminded us of the Fellowship running into Lothlorien after Gandalf fell in Moria.

Just as I was launching into an enthusiastic Gimli impersonation, counseling my young hobbits to stay sharp because some said a witch lived in these woods, we stumbled into a retired couple setting up a tent. They were going to spend the night in the woods studying a rare type of bat that crawls along the ground. They were incredibly excited about this bat. If they could document irrefutable proof of these bats in the area, it would guarantee protected status for the region and ensure additional funding for more research.

The thought of spending a night sleeping in woods filled with crawling bats made my skin creep. It's like they say, one man's research project is another man's night terrors.

On the way back to civilization, after navigating all the water crossings and natural hazards, we lost a hubcap. We pulled over and all got out to go find it so we wouldn't get charged when we returned the car. We were all wandering around, combing the grass along the road, when I saw a giant 4x4 tour bus roaring up the road behind us, filling the valley with gravel dust that hung like a giant 747 chem trail. The thought of getting caught behind that for the next fifteen miles spurred us into action. The kids found the hubcap and held it aloft like a prize as I yelled at them to run.

We all started sprinting back to the car with Riel peppering us with questions as she tried to figure out what in the world was going on. We threw the recovered hubcap into the back seat and punched the gas. In a flurry of spinning tires, spraying gravel and whoops of excitement we blasted off, leaving the bus driver and God knows how many tourists cursing us for the next fifteen miles, instead of the other way around.

We stayed at Kinloch Lodge that night where most of the guests were seniors. We were heading up to Aoraki/Mt. Cook in the morning and I needed to book a room, only Kinloch was buried too deep in the mountains for our cell phone to work.

There was Wi-Fi in the lounge so I decided to use Skype to make my calls. Carrying on a conversation through my laptop meant all the seniors in the common room could listen in. Card games continued in silence, so they could keep up with my progress and compare notes on my negotiation skills. After my second call, any pretense of privacy was abandoned as one old lady looked over at me and said, "That seemed a little steep, didn't it?"

Soon tables four to seven were chiming in with names and places I should call. Between the gin rummy gang at table four, Google, and Skype, I finally managed to book us a room for the following night. I'm not sure who felt the most satisfied with their performance as I closed my laptop and bid the room adieu amid a smattering of applause.

The next morning we sallied forth from Kinloch to Glenorchy, back along Lake Wakatipu to Queenstown then up and over to Twizel.

We got checked in and made ourselves some supper. While I was cleaning up our dishes after dinner, a tall, grey haired gentleman came in and started preparing his meal. He didn't seem the least bit inclined to chitchat, but having grown up in a small town, I am often unable to prevent the mindless non-sequiturs that fly out of my mouth.

When I asked how his day had been, he spun around and as his face split into a huge grin, he exploded, "It was awesome!"

His name was Richard; he was a semi-retired interior designer from England who loved motorbikes. It was one of his lifelong dreams to motorbike around New Zealand, and here he was, living his dream. He told me where he'd been so far on his trip and where he was going.

When I shared our story, he invited us to come stay him when we got to England. I got back to the room and started telling Zara about the conversation as the kids eavesdropped and built Lego. When I got to the part of Richard inviting us to stay with him, Zara said she thought that was a great idea. This was too much for Zion, who has, like every other kid in the world, been taught not to talk to strangers. To Zion it seems the rules are out the window, and not only are we talking to strangers, we keep planning to go stay in their homes.

The next morning we packed our lunches, jumped into El Crapo and cranked some *Billy Talent* as we drove the hour from Twizel to Aoraki/Mt. Cook.

At 3754 metres, Mt. Cook is New Zealand's tallest peak. In 1998, the government officially changed the name to include the Maori title, Aoraki, combining "ao" which means world/daytime/ cloud, and "raki" meaning day/sky/ weather. Early Polynesian inhabitants of Aotearoa called the South Island, Te Waka aAor-aki, or, Cloud Piercer.

Mt. Cook was another reference to Captain James Cook, the guy who has been coming up everywhere, from Hawaii to Australia and now in New Zealand.

I'm starting to think some serious investigation needs to go into this Cook fellow who seems to be credited with an inordinate amount of discovery.

The hike to Aoraki was a serious tramp and I was incredibly proud of the kids, especially Riel. This little nine-year-old trudged all the way to the base of the mountain. By the time we arrived she was officially knackered and flopped down for a well-deserved lunch break. While Zara and I were happy as clams to be chasing the sun for a year and avoiding winter altogether, the kids were missing the snow. As we sat at the base of the mountain eating our lunch, the kids noticed a large block of ice in the middle of the glacial stream. We decided to build an inukshuk. An inukshuk is a human figure built out of rocks. It originated with the Inuit people of northern Canada, and was used historically to guide travelers, designate food or shelter, or to mark sacred spots. It felt right to commemorate the hike that led us to the first ice and snow we'd seen on the other side of the world. We took our time, found just the right rocks, and arranged them high up on a boulder at the water's edge with Aoraki rising directly behind it. After we finished, we returned to our lunch rock and kept eating.

As we sat there, we began to notice a curious thing. Tourists and other hikers, and there were many arriving by the minute, were filtering down to the riverbed and taking pictures of our inukshuk. So many people started taking pictures that we started taking videos of them taking pictures. We started giggling as we imagined hundreds of European tourists returning home to show their vacation slides to friends and family, describing the ancient Maori artifact they saw at the base of Aoraki.

Searching for a way to motivate the kids for the long hike back, I asked Zion some leading questions about *Halo*. As we walked Zion talked, and talked and talked, regaling me for over an hour with all the many things he loves about *Halo*. He finally took a breath and said, "It's so good being able to talk to you about this. I've spent this whole trip talking to myself!"

This video honours the financial investment from friends who gave us an envelope of cash for something we would like to do, but couldn't afford to do as we raced down the Shotover Canyon in a jet boat.

Giggles, Guffaws and Fruity Tears of Mirth

Our northern migration took us back through Christchurch where the obstacle course of a lifetime awaited us. There are six levels of adventure at Adrenalin Forest, with one being the beginner level and the rest moving up from there. Riel just met the height requirement for being allowed to do the whole course. We all donned our climbing harnesses and received a five-minute safety course from the Dutch guy running the place and we were off.

I was at the back of the pack, trying to film everyone. The kids were eager to tackle the course but I was a bit surprised that Riel took the lead. By the end of the first stage, I was coming to obstacles that made me think Riel probably couldn't do it. But of course she'd already done it, and was at that moment tackling even more challenging tasks.

Early on in the fourth stage, Riel came to something that went beyond her severely maxed out comfort zone, and decided to call it a day. The guide climbed up to her platform and lowered her down and she ran off to play with the resident dog, Snoof.

That left Zara, Zion, and me. We finished off that stage and eagerly tackled stage five, at which point everything took a decided turn. We were suddenly forty to fifty feet in the air clambering along forty-foot cables that moved, tightening and loosening as the trees swayed in the wind. I wanted to quit but there was no graceful way to do that, so I dug deep in the old testosterone well and tried to find some of that latent male stupidity to override my common sense.

At one point, I was shimmying along a death-defying, ass-puckering cable. I made it to the platform and shrank down with my back against the tree thanking the gods, pagan and sacred alike, that I'd made it. Then I looked back down the cable and saw my son step off the platform and start to make his way across, which was worse than doing it myself. He was not even midway along and he was hitting the wall.

Trying to exude a sense of calm neither of us felt, Zara and I took turns calmly calling out encouragement. "You're doing great," Zara called, "you're almost there."

It was all I could do to swallow my panic and not scream, "OMG he totally is not. He's barely half way!"

In my mind, I had the conversation that was long overdue, "Zion, oh dear, sweet, precious Zion, if I never get another chance to tell you, I just want you to know that I love you and I've always been proud to be your Dad!"

With my mouth, I played my part and started yelling encouragingly, "You're a monkey, Zion, a monkey, with balls of steel!"

When he finally made it to the platform, the two of us crowded together, making good and damn sure that our carabiners were attached to the safety cables. Zion looked up at me and said, "It's not about having fun anymore, it's just about trying not to die."

I decided not to share with Zi that all I could think was that we were risking our lives after an asinine five-minute safety instruction. Of course the pain wasn't over, because now it was time to watch my beautiful wife step off onto the same cable. The three of us managed to hang on to the end of stage five and then called it a day.

I wept unabashedly as the last flying fox deposited me in an emotional heap on an assortment of used gym mats. But Adrenalin Forest was everything we could have hoped for. Our litigious society has banned almost every adrenalin-inducing thing I remember doing as a kid. To find a place where adults and kids can actually scare the bejeezus out of themselves in the name of good, wholesome, family fun was awesome and produced *Zion & Riel – Adrenalin Forest*.

From Christchurch we were heading to Abel Tasman where we've rented a cabin for a week. It was 6:30 p.m. when we pulled into Nelson and there was no point in arriving at our cottage without food for supper, so we did the unthinkable and stopped in at the golden arches so the kids could grab a burger. There are times Zion's inability to whisper drives me to distraction. But there are times I absolutely love listening to him make pointed observations with his bright, energetic voice that carries like a ship under full sail.

He was comparing the burgers pictured in the giant illuminated signs above the cashiers and how awesome they look and how in reality, the burger in his hand looked like "some stinky fat guy sat on it and squished all the life out of it so the only thing left is death". I couldn't have said it better, brighter or louder myself.

Zara had hiked down a few doors from the golden arches to order some Thai noodles. On our way out of the parking lot, she ran up and jumped in as we peeled out into traffic. She'd no sooner sat down and shut the door before the Thai noodle aroma went up Zion's nose sideways, and he blurted, "All right, who just farted!"

Zara had her chopsticks poised an inch from her lips, but before she took the mouthful she muttered, "No one. It's my noodles."

Zion and Riel disintegrated into gales of laughter until Zion lobbed one of his famously insincere apologies into the front seat. "Sorry for saying your noodles smelled like farts, Mom," he said, as he and Riel laughed their heads off.

We'd rented a little two-bedroom cottage for a week on Kina Peninsula Road in Abel Tasman. We were literally forty feet from the ocean and just minutes down the road from Motueka. The next morning Zara was up early and went for a walk along the beach. On her way she encountered a bird that kept swooping down around her; she stood still and raised her arms at right angles like a scarecrow and the bird landed right on her arm, looked at her for a few seconds and then flew off.

After a month of hopping from hostel to hotel every night or two, we were stoked to be in one place for a whole week. With two bedrooms, a living room and an actual kitchen, we felt like we'd won the lottery.

I'm what some people call accident-prone. My shins, knees, toes, and elbows have paid a heavy price in this life. But even after all that I've been through there are incidents when even I am shocked, like last night.

The other three were off doing their own things as I slipped into the bathroom with my book and ran a nice hot bath. I just wanted to soak in the hot water with the window open so I could hear the ocean waves off in the distance as I read. It wasn't a complicated plan; it didn't sound dangerous. And it wasn't … until I tried to slide further down in the water. Somehow, the sloping back of the tub perfectly contoured the curvature of my lower back and created an airtight suction. At first I wasn't exactly sure what had happened, I just felt this tightness in my lower back and couldn't slide back up into a sitting position. Then suddenly pins and needles shot through my body as the muscles in my lower back went into spasm. But I was glued to the bottom of the tub. My feet and ankles thrashed in the sudsy water. My book went flying as my arms began to paw in the air, flailing wildly as I tried to claw for the towel rack to pull myself up. I couldn't breathe properly or call for help, though even in my distress I felt a heavy weight of embarrassment and incredulity. How the hell can soaking in a tub turn into a thrashing sea of shame?

I mostly grunted and squirmed, inhaling sharply, making weird whistling noises through my clenched teeth. I finally managed to break the vacuum seal and was eventually able to resume my life of leisure. I had no intention of telling my family what happened; I get teased enough for accidental injuries that happen in public. I'd actually forgotten all about the whole thing until two days later when we got to the beach and I took my shirt off ready to swim.

"Oh my God, babe!" Zara exclaimed behind me. "What happened to your back?" Zion and Riel immediately dropped everything and ran over to see.

"Oh Dad," they said in shocked stereo. "What is that?"

A solid dark purpley-yellow bruise stretched from my mid back to the elastic waistband of my swimmers. As I tried to describe the excruciating event, their supportive looks of concern soon transformed into giggles and guffaws as fruity tears of mirth rolled down their cheeks.

"Only you babe … only you," Zara sighed. "Nothing surprises me anymore." The following day we headed to the Ngarua Caves, located 2000 feet above sea level at the top of Takaka Hill, between Tasman and Golden Bay. The caves themselves are an amazing marble formation with stalactites hanging like gothic chandeliers. As the four of us walked through the gothic chamber, the kids snapped pictures and I daydreamed of recording an acoustic guitar in the resonant chamber. Zion looked over at me and said, "It's not a mine, it's a tomb," in a spot-on Boromir impression.

After some subterranean exploration, we crawled back to the surface and followed some directions to where the River Resurgence emerges from the base of the mountain. A beautiful little path led to the Crystal Pool. The water was so clear you could see every mossy vibrissa in vivid detail. Zion and Riel both had their swimmers on and decided that a pool this clear, this quiet and turquoise needed to be jumped in. This was a lesson we learned in our first few weeks traveling at Elk Falls on Vancouver Island.

They found a rock ledge five feet above the water, and tried to find the courage to jump as Zara and I took turns coaxing and counting down to give them the little emotional nudge they needed.

The whole situation really took me back to my own childhood. I remembered pudgy little six-year old Ricky Leaf standing on the dock at Pine Lake, immobilized by an incapacitating fear of waterskiing. My family would take turns trying to motivate me too. I remember my older brother yelling exuberantly, "Get the lead out, you little pussy, 'cause I don't get a turn until dad drags your chubby butt around the lake!" My big sister would laugh and poke my baby-fat thighs quivering like Jello. Mom was usually drinking martinis in the boat, waving her olive-laden toothpick like a baton, sharing at length what a disappointment I was to the entire family, as my Dad growled that he could give me something to cry about.

Good times. Good times.

As a glacial-fed stream, the River Resurgence was practically subarctic, which made the kids surfacing loud and colourful. Zion could barely dog paddle, his arms and hands seizing into little stumpy claws as the breath was sucked out of his lungs. Even after watching Zion's reaction, Riel still flung herself off, wanting to have a war story of her own to swap in the backseat. The experience made for wonderful viewing in *Zion & Riel – Damn You New Zealand!*

In Riel's case in particular, I realized it was one of a thousand moments this year that show how much she's changed. All the new experiences and situations have drawn her out of her comfort zone and empowered her to do things she would never have imagined doing before we left Winnipeg. After sunning ourselves like lazy seals, we made our way back to Kaiteriteri.

Kaiteriteri is a gorgeous little seaside resort town in the Nelson region of Abel Tasman right at the top of the South Island. The formation of the beach includes a really fun channel that acts as a river when the tide is going out. You can ride the current all the way out to the ocean where the waves are rolling in. The kids and I did the ride repeatedly. We were having a ball jumping into the channel and being swept out to sea, where we would be pummeled by the in-bound waves. About the third time, I suggested that instead of dropping in where all the locals were, we should go even further inland and really get a great ride. It was so obvious I couldn't imagine why no one else was doing it. I waded purposefully out into the channel, rolled over on my back with just my feet, head, and hands out of the water and was immediately drawn into the fast moving current.

"This is the life, eh kids?" I started to say when, WHAM, my tailbone collided with something really hard.

"Sweet mother," I exhaled, trying to flip over to see what I'd run into and driving my knee straight into a submerged rock in the process. The strength of the current left little manoeuvrability as I pin-balled my way down the channel, slamming knees and elbows, spine and vertebrae into an incredible array of giant submerged rocks. I know I was narrating the experience in my outside voice because people on the beach kept turning their heads and pointing in my direction as I was swept by.

"Ow! Oh, God! Son of a … umph! Oh, that's going to leave a mark!"

At one point I managed to wedge myself between two rocks and wrapped my legs in a scissor hold around one of them for a brief respite. Just when I thought I'd figured out how to get off the watery ride from hell, the current pried my fingers free and I started to slide, slowly scraping my clenched inner thighs along the barnacled surface.

I remember screaming "Oh it burns!" before briefly blacking out. Eventually the sea finished kicking my prairie ass and I stumbled up the beach, a shell of my former self, nursing bulbous swelling joints. I had a bright pink road-rash that looked like dozens of tiny fingernails had burrowed into my inner thighs.

"You're bleeding," Zara understated. "Seriously babe, nothing surprises me anymore," she said, not for the first, or the last time on the trip, as she went back to reading in the sun.

Adrenalin Forest was an amazing day, as we pushed ourselves way beyond our comfort zones and into the realm of full-on adrenalin.

Damn You New Zealand was our recurring joke, as we'd pretend to burst into tears because of the incredible beauty that seemed to wait around every damn corner!

An Agonizing Belly Crawl of Pain and Shame

At the end of a glorious week, we headed to Picton to catch the Inter-islander ferry to Wellington. As the kids sat inside watching Glee on one of the laptops, Zara and I sat on the deck finishing a bottle of wine as we tried to figure out where we were going to live when we got back to Canada. We'd exchanged a few emails with Paul and Corey, the friends we'd stayed with in Canmore. They were thinking about moving to Vancouver Island to be part of an emerging community and we were starting to think it might be worth investigating ourselves.

In Wellington, we'd arranged to stay with another Servas couple. After our GPS finally got herself together, we managed to find our way to John and Marie's place. It was a beautiful home with massive windows in our second-story bedroom with a million dollar view overlooking Porirua Harbour.

We began our adventures with Te Papa Tongarewa, New Zealand's national museum. Their website explains that in Maori, Te Papa Tongarewa literally means our container of treasured things and people that spring from Mother Earth in New Zealand. From the museum we headed for Weta Cave. We are all fans of *Lord of the Rings* and have watched all the behind-the-scenes and extras of the making of the movies. Then with the Narnia movies, *King Kong, District 9, Black Sheep,* and *Halo, Weta Workshop* is synonymous with New Zealand.

According to the little promotional film, fans of the movies kept showing up, but there was nothing to see. They would line up along the chain link fence and stare at the outside of the warehouse. It just seemed pathetic.

So Weta developed The Cave, a small corner space filled with paraphernalia from the various movies. There were life-size statues of Gollum and Lurtz, the leader of the Uruk-hai from *The Fellowship of the Ring*, guns from District 9, swords and costumes from a variety of movies.

After Wellington, we headed to Hawera to stay with Don and Judy, another Servas contact. Don was a no-s#% guy, and I mean that in a no-s#% way. I can't remember what he'd done for a living, but it had damaged his hearing, so he was also forceful in how he spoke. I'm pretty sure he has no idea what Riel's voice sounds like, because the louder a no-s#% man talks to Riel, the softer and quieter she responds.

Don gave us directions to Wilkies Pools, a series of 20,000-year-old pools created from lava fields in Egmont National Park. The road leading up to the pools was like driving through a maze. The jungle rose up in solid walls fifteen feet high on both sides of the narrow, windy road that kept zigzagging around bend after bend after bend. It was hypnotic and kind of mysterious. It felt like we were kids inside a fort.

It was an overcast, foggy day, which made the hike through the forest wonderfully ethereal. I hid with the camera in a little gully waiting for the other three to catch up, hoping for some spontaneous footage. At the foot of a steep incline and a number of steps cut into the hill, Zion took it upon himself to lift Riel onto the first step. Riel was in one of her independent moods, and didn't want any help from anyone, especially her big brother. As Zion wrapped his arms around her waist and lifted her off the ground, Riel squirmed and writhed, making her body stiff as a board, her little fists pummeling his chest playfully as she screamed, "No! No! No! I'll do it myself!"

Zion eventually let her go and trudged off up the trail with Riel hoofing it behind him on her own steam. "Just another beautiful hike in the woods with Zion and Riel," I whispered into the camera in my best David Attenborough impersonation.

On our way back to Hawera we stopped at the Tawhiti Museum, the creation of Nigel Ogle. The website touts that it is the best private museum in the country, and certainly it was impressive as a private undertaking. Ogle uses lifesize exhibits and scale models to present New Zealand heritage in a series of super realistic and engaging displays.

When we were there a new exhibition called "Traders & Whalers" had just opened. It took two years of planning and over two years of building to create a really cool environment depicting the Taranaki coast in the 1820 – 40s period. Illuminated only by the twinkling of lanterns and candles, we drifted in a boat guided by a submerged track through a life-size diorama full of birds and dripping water from mossy banks as burly sailors bartered with local Maori for pork, potatoes, and flax in return for European goods especially that most sought after item, the flintlock musket.

Having recently watching *Iron Man*, Zion decided Nigel was the Tony Stark of dioramas.

According to Maori legend, Taranaki is a mountain with some serious relational baggage. Taranaki used to live with Tongariro, Ruapehu, and Ngauruhoe, but then went and fell in love with Pihanga. She was a pretty little hill on the shores of Lake Taupo and the wife of Tongariro. Tongariro exploded in a fiery rage, spitting fire, lava, and burning ash making the earth shake as he fought with Taranaki. Brokenhearted and banished, Taranaki headed toward the coast, his tears creating the Wanganui River as he moved westward to his current resting place.

I'm sure the scientific community has some banal story of their own.

We were heading to New Plymouth, located at the base of Mount Taranaki, where we'd arranged with our next Servas hosts, John and Jean, to arrive in early afternoon. I talked with Jean on the phone and she told me they had two kids, Amy, who was sixteen and Jeremy, who was thirteen. Zion was excited to find out they had a kid his age and started fantasizing about possible shared loves, like *Halo*, X-box, and Lego. The first thing that took his breath away was the fact that thirteen-year-old Jeremy was 6'1. The second was an invitation to join Jeremy and some friends who were going to play paintball. Not even in his wildest dreams had Zion imagined something so glorious.

We met them at the outdoor game centre, passing a sign that said "No Mercy". I heard Zion chuckling in anticipation. The guy running the place was either ex-military, or a crazy farmer. His safety instruction amounted to him pacing back and forth, daring any ten to thirteen-year-old kids to speak out of turn or even look at him. He punctuated his safety points with multiple blasts from his semi-automatic into a loose metal sheet, to produce optimum sound effect.

"If you get hit in the eye!" BAM, BAM, BAM. "You will go blind!" BAM, BAM.

"If you take your mask off and get hit in the face!" BAM, BAM, "the skin will split wide like a ripe melon and without proper medical attention," BAM, BAM, BAM, "you will likely DIE!"

Instead of having any cautionary effect, all the talk did was whip the thirteen-year-old boys into a killing frenzy as the audible clicks of safeties being disengaged echoed around the room. Before Zion's mother could offer any words of caution, her son fled the building into the jungle to experience his own *Lord of the Flies*. Zion had the afternoon of his life. His team had left him to guard the base from enemy capture, which was boring, but also allowed him to conserve ammo. Forty-five minutes into the match as his team made their way through the brush, the Crazy Commander, feeling that the game was taking too long, blew a horn and through a megaphone announced that the rules had changed, there were no longer any teams; it was every man for himself.

As Zion tells it, he wasted no time, turning on a dime and opening up at point-blank range on his previous teammates. As the only shooter with any bullets left, he decimated the field. Jeremy and his friends dove for cover, trying unsuccessfully to hide behind thin trees as Zion systematically blew them away.

They headed for the water, jumping into the creek hoping to splash their way to cover. Only they all bogged down in thick, viscous mud, slowing their progress to an agonizing belly crawl of pain and shame. From the top of the riverbank, Zion dealt deadly deathblows as he mowed down the field with heavy suppressing fire.

Without cover, without bullets, scrambling on their hands and knees in the mud and muck in a total rout, Jeremy and his friends tried berating the crazed Canadian, screaming and swearing in vain, demanding a cessation of hostilities. As he got to this part of the story, I interrupted him and said, "You were laughing, weren't you?"

"Oh, Dad. I was laughing so hard I could barely breathe or see through the tears … but I managed," he added unnecessarily. Those are the stories of youth.

The next day we headed out for Mount Taranaki and a hike through the Goblin Forest. There was something magical about this day: the hike, the sun, the trees, the conversations and laughter we were having as a family. We had packed a spectacular picnic in our backpacks and found a dry riverbed to camp in for lunch. We were lounging, in absolutely no hurry to go, get, or be anywhere, feeling like we were the only people for a hundred miles.

All of a sudden, out of nowhere, a pear-shaped guy came reeling over the riverbank, skidding and sliding down the trail like a pack of Warg riders were chasing him. Even with rivers of sweat pouring down his blotchy red face, he exuded the Kiwi generosity of spirit as he passed. "Oh, hello, wonderful weather today isn't it," as he puffed and panted his way back up the riverbank on the other side and disappeared. We sat in silence for a couple of seconds and then all burst out laughing. Zion and Riel love to reenact things that have just been said or done, and took turns, reenacting the scene keeping us all in stitches.

From New Plymouth we took the Forgotten World Highway to Taupo. The highway is rugged and remote and winds its way over four mountain saddles, through an eerie one-way tunnel and along a sinuous river gorge. The only significant settlement on the way is Whangamomona. In 1998, the government apparently shifted local district boundaries. Half of the Whangamomona District went from the Taranaki District to the Manawatu District. This did not sit well with the locals, who soon after declared Whangamomona an independent Republic! The twentieth year celebration happened a few weeks before we were there. But we heard that Republic Day celebrations swell the Whangamomona

Village from forty people to around 5,000. Country activities such as Sheep Races, Gumboot Throwing, Gutbuster Races, Whip Cracking, Possum Skinning, Hold Ups, and Shoot Outs all take place in the main street. Over the years, a goat and a poodle have been elected as presidents. Passports can be purchased at the Hotel to ensure safe passage through the Republic.

As we hit the outskirts of Taupo, the sky was suddenly filled with bright coloured parachutes as dozens of skydivers landed beside the highway. We pulled into a rest area and lay in the sun for an hour watching plane after plane dump their human cargo out.

It felt like a great picture of an adventurous life. You can pay for some instruction, even surround yourself with your best friends, but eventually you have to throw yourself out the door and just go for it.

We hadn't booked a hotel in advance, so when we drove into Taupo we split up into two teams and wandered up and down the strip. Riel and I scored a hotel with a loft, heated pool, and a hot tub. As I worked online, I listened to the kids killing themselves laughing in the hot tub making beards out of chemical foam and dry skin flakes. Zara capitalized on the kitchenette and we feasted on a homemade meal.

On our way to Rotorua we stopped at the Craters of the Moon, a geothermal area with pools of boiling mud and fissures that release clouds of sulfurous gas. The burning clouds of thick humid steam rising from boiling pools of mud made it feel very apocalyptic. All of my film footage features the kids with their jackets pulled up over their mouths and noses, screaming indecipherably about the smell of death and sin and the Devil.

Once, it sounded like Zion was yelling at me. It was hard to tell as his faced was buried under his hoodie. I eventually realized he was singing his own version of Rage Against the Machine's *Killing in the Name Of* "eff you I won't smell what you tell me." I gave him full marks on the homeschooling interpretive music class review.

We got to Rotorua and landed a hotel that must have been built in the 1970s.

It had two bedrooms, a living room and full kitchen, outdoor pool, a mini golf course, and a tennis court. The kids immediately created an entertainment circuit starting with a round of golf, then a dip in the pool before playing some tennis out back.

The kids were excited. They'd heard about Zorbing, and Rotorua was renowned for it, so we took a drive out to the site.

ZORB® Rotorua is reportedly a must-do New Zealand activity. In fact, ZORB® Rotorua was the Winner of the Visitors Choice Award for the things to do in New Zealand. At least according to their own website, which also claims it's number #1 on many people's list of things to do before they die.

If Zorbing in Rotorua is number one on people's list of things to do before they die, they need to get out more. Understand, we were sold on the idea of Zorbing before we ever saw it. We came prepared to drop our money and have the experience of a lifetime.

We went out on the little deck outside the office, looking up at the hill. We thought it would be bigger. It looked like a beginner run at a ski hill, with a gentle, straight slope. The ball looked to be about eight feet in diameter and rolled down the slope in a bit of a trough. Two people could go at a time and would actually crawl inside the ball and roll down the hill.

We watched as a young couple came out of the change room in their swimmers and were driven up to the top of the bunny hill. We watched as they climbed inside the giant ball and a worker put a garden hose inside and filled it with a few gallons of water.

Then we watched as they ever so slowly, at times almost imperceptibly, rolled down the hill. It was as if the ball was made of lead and the hill was magnetic.

The most amazing thing was how unbelievably slow and boring it was. It couldn't have taken a minute for the ball to make its agonizing way to the bottom where two other attendants stood, looking as bored as we were. One guy had a football that he tried to throw into the hole in the side of the ball just before it came to a stop. The couple crawled out as dry as they had been when they got in; there wasn't even enough speed to toss the water around inside the ball.

Zion took the disappointment personally and started to expound loudly and at length.

"I would feel like such an idiot if I did that," he shared, unconcerned that we were walking through the main office.

"And it's $50.00 each!" he punctuated incredulously. "That would be like $200.00 for our family to pathetically flop down a hill." So, needless to say, no Zorbing for us.

A Psychosomatic Figment of the Collective Imagination

We continued to the Thames area and our last, and certainly most colourful, New Zealand Servas hosts. Howard and Pauline run a boarding house for pets. They organized a little picnic for our first night and took us to the Miranda Hot Springs thermal pool. Zion and Riel ran around playing on a giant inflatable bladder filled with air that acted like a trampoline's ugly cousin, while we floated and soaked in the hot springs.

After a leisurely soak, we sat out under the stars at the bottom of the world eating and feasting. Howard and Pauline are one of those couples that tell different versions of the same story at the same time. Occasionally they repeat each other's punch lines and salient details or they veer off in different directions focusing on totally different things. Their best story was about a group of friends that all liked to go canoeing and camping together as couples. They have a tradition around the campfire each evening in which the guys throw their hats in a bucket and then pass the bucket around and the women each fish a hat out; whoever's hat you get is the canoe you spend the next day in. Apparently, one year, they were out in the bush when they heard cries for help. A young city couple, unprepared for nature and the elements, had capsized their canoe and become hopelessly lost in the dark. Howard and Pauline's group welcomed them around the fire, gave them some food, warmed them up and offered to give them a ride back the next day. Then it got to the time of night when all the guys threw their hats in the bucket and the women fished them out. When the bucket came to this young girl, she apparently sat there for a moment or two before saying, "Oh, what the heck, why not," and dug out a hat. The thing was, she thought that the game meant she had to sleep with whoever's hat she pulled out. It took Howard and Pauline a couple of minutes to even get the punch line out between the whooping and hollering, laughing and crying and then a couple more minutes of repeating the punch line amid tears of laughter. It was impossible not to get caught up in the hilarity of their storytelling.

The next day we headed up the Coromandel Peninsula to Cathedral Cove. After a long hike in, we made our way down to the beach. There was a giant flat rock a couple of hundred metres offshore that people could swim out to and jump off. Zion and I talked about swimming out together, but in the end I took off on my own. I battled against the waves and the current, and was very glad he hadn't come, as I started to flounder.

I'd been in the water at least six or seven minutes, and exercise for that length of time is bound to wear a guy out. I dragged myself across the jagged rocks, silently thanking God I'd survived the grueling journey and started looking for the perfect spot to jump from. Perfect at that point, meant somewhere I wouldn't hit submerged rocks and become a paraplegic.

Zara was on the shore ready to film my dramatic leap as Zion narrated. "That's my dad out there, jump! Jump!" he yelled, thinking I could actually hear him. I jumped, didn't hit any rocks, surfaced and started off back for shore with what felt like long, powerful strokes. Must have been the limitations of the camera or the cloud cover, because on video it looks more like ragged dog-paddling.

No sooner had I jumped than a super fit, young Kiwi guy stepped up to the spot I'd just vacated. Wanting to clarify for viewers back home, Zara pointed out that the guy standing on the rock wasn't me.

"That guy's bald. Dad is way cooler than that guy," Zion said, right as the guy laid out a perfect back one-and-a-half-gainer with a twist garnering a massive cheer of appreciation from the bystanders lining the beach. I doggy-paddled in to shore, gasping for breath, unaware that my family's disappearance was an attempt to distance themselves from my lame performance.

Just a few minutes down the road from Cathedral Cove is Hot Water Beach. An underground river of hot water flows from the interior of the earth and surfaces under the sand. For two hours on either side of low tide, visitors flock to the beach to find hot water bubbling through the golden sand. We needed to wait around until 6:30 p.m. for low tide. As we waited travelers from all over the world descended, eager to dig holes for their own personal hot tubs. At first no one wanted to cooperate, bringing their "me first" attitudes. A number of eager beavers started digging randomly.

I saw a guy who looked like he knew exactly where to stand, who was also in no hurry to stake out his own ground. I struck up a conversation and discovered he was a local B&B owner who had brought some Japanese tourists to the beach. He eventually convinced everyone to work together and soon we were building the Hot Tub of Babel. Every nationality and language on the planet seemed to have sent a representative. Huge elderly women and incredibly hairy men could be seen digging in the sand with plastic pails and converted food containers, next to dreadlocked surfers and little kids.

Everyone everywhere was digging as if their lives depended on it. It looked like a church picnic threw up on a state fair. But soon there were wading pools literally filled with boiling hot water. I started filming the skeptics who figured the whole thing was a scam created by the guy renting shovels for $5.00 an hour in the parking lot. I'd watch them stride into the pool to prove it was nothing but a psychosomatic figment of the collective imagination, take two or three steps, and then start to do a little Looney Tunes dance into the Pacific to cool their scalded feet. Except for one old guy who walked in and just stood there with a bored look on his face. I assume he either suffered from a total lack of circulation in his extremities or had titanium ankles.

Zara is a natural firstborn child, and spent a good hour building retaining walls with the pierced/tattooed dreadlock contingent, wielding a Tupperware bowl with amazing dexterity. Zion's firstborn contribution was a steady stream of mockery and derision, but he eventually got chilled just standing around flapping his gums and ended up jumping into the pool Zara had built.

From Howard and Pauline's we headed just north of Auckland to Brown Bay where we'd rented a chalet. For the first time since leaving the country, we were meeting up with some friends from Canada. Meaghan and Kevin had been living and working in Korea for several years and were in the process of moving back to North America. They decided that while they were on the far side of the world they'd tour around Australia and New Zealand.

I met Meaghan and her family in Sarnia, Ontario, back in 1999 when Tribe of One was doing a benefit tour across Canada. It started an amazing relationship that has lasted for over a decade. I've been back to Sarnia numerous times for concerts since. As I was setting up tour dates in 2005, Meaghan and Kevin's mothers contacted me to see if there was any way I could play at their kids' wedding. I told them it could work out, and that's when the mothers got creative.

We all shared a love for Baz Luhrmann's *Moulin Rouge!*, so their plan was to sneak me unawares into the church where I would wait backstage until the pastor said, "Does anyone have any reason this couple should not be married?"

At that moment, they wanted me to belt the line "my gift is my song", like Ewan McGregor's character in the movie. At that point I walked out, sat down at the grand piano, and sang the rest of Elton John's *My Song* to the happy couple. That was the last time I saw Meaghan and Kevin as they headed to Korea shortly afterward.

They'd been following our journey online and emailed a month or two earlier about connecting. We managed to work out our schedules so we could spend three days together in Auckland. As a family, we were pretty exhausted at that point, and so thankful for the chalet. Staying with people is great, but you don't really feel as if you have the luxury of just hanging around the house.

We'd stayed with five Servas hosts since arriving in Wellington and it was great to just kick back. Sleep in. Leave clothes and Lego scattered on the floor. Sit on the deck and read a book or write a song. The chalet was built on a hill overlooking the ocean. There were three decks, one for every floor, basically providing a private oceanside view for every man, woman, and child.

Finding high-speed Wi-Fi was difficult and expensive in New Zealand. When we discovered the chalet came with free Internet and it had an Ethernet cable, we went to work. Meaghan and Kevin each had a laptop as well as a spare and Zara and I both have our own. Kevin created a wireless network and soon all five laptops were going, as we downloaded and swapped movies, TV series, and music.

We headed to Piha, New Zealand's most famous surf beach. Situated on the west coast of the North Island, Piha is about forty kilometres from Auckland. Lion's Rock sits commandingly on the black iron-sand as the surf roars in from the Tasman Sea. The road to Piha was definitely one of the windiest, steepest and narrowest we drove and Zion started to play the old "I'm going to puke" game.

As a way of commemorating the Kiwi roads, we stopped and let Zion film a sequence where he piles out of the car to throw up. He left the back door of the car open as Riel crouched down inside with a water bottle. While I called comfortingly from off camera, Zion hid his head behind the door and made loud retching noises while Riel squirted the water bottle on the ground. Zion was so pleased with his gritty performance he encouraged me to use the footage in our next video, *Zion & Riel - New Zealand's North Island*.

Our time in New Zealand is up. Meaghan and Kevin take Zion and Riel out for the day to explore the area. Zara is once again trying to make all our stuff fit into four backpacks as I head down to the village to buy some travel Lego. The flight from Auckland to Rome is going to involve a lot of hours cooped up in cramped, uncomfortable quarters. Purchasing Lego for long flights is always a win-win. Having children gleefully preoccupied with building and playing with medieval villages allows parents to drink and watch movies.

Our time in New Zealand and Australia has really been all about nature and the outdoors. We spent most of the last three months hiking and lounging around in some of the most beautiful places in the world. But as we look forward to the next phase of the journey, we are all incredibly excited to be heading to Europe.

New Zealand's North Island video follows our journey from Cathedral Cove and Hot Water Beach to the Goblin Forest and the stinky clouds of sulphur at Craters of the Moon.

ITALY/FRANCE

A Pint-Sized Grim Reaper & a Weird Ass Creepfest

A herd of Italian cattle just blew by our window. We're riding the high-speed train out of Rome heading north to Milan where Zara's youngest sister, Amanda, is eagerly awaiting our arrival. Amanda has been living in Italy for a year, in the small resort town of Arona about an hour from Milan. We've just spent four crazy and amazing days wandering around Rome; a city that actually needs four months just to scratch the surface.

Our travel day from New Zealand to Europe was as arduous and uncomfortable as I imagined it would be. We were herded into coach, and endured the narrow seats and lack of legroom throughout the twenty-eight-hour travel day.

Our plane from Auckland left over forty-five minutes late for our seven-hour flight of just over 9000 kilometres to Kuala Lumpur. We had a three-hour layover that happened around 3:00 a.m. internal clock time. We'd been in the KL airport a couple of months earlier on our way to Australia. There are two giant terminals connected by a train line. When we arrived, it said our next flight was departing from the other terminal, so we jumped on the train and headed in that direction. We bought some new books and grabbed a meal and then went to our gate. There we discovered the departure gate had been changed to the previous terminal. So we hiked back through the airport, jumped on the train and got all the way down to the far end where we camped out waiting for our flight.

Forty-five minutes later a Malaysian guy came running up to tell everyone that the gate had been changed again and we needed to get back to the other terminal. For the third time, we jumped on the train and hiked through the terminal. None of us had slept on the plane and Zara and I were both eager to find a bench where we could stretch our bodies straight and maybe catch a few minutes of sleep. But a wonderfully overtired Zion kept a loud comedic monologue running the entire time. I distinctly remember one tangent where he wanted to lie on the bench directly across from Zara that was occupied by his younger sister.

"Just lie here on the other side facing me," I offered. "Mom is ten inches away from you, so you can still talk to her," I said, trying to steer him down the path of least resistance.

"Mom, can you hear me? I want to talk to your face. Mom! I want to lie over there, I want to talk to your face," he repeated over and over for the ENTIRE layover.

So ... no sleep was possible in the Kuala Lumpur departure lounge thanks to Zi.

"I feel like I'm a thousand years old and my body is on automatic," Zara sighed as we finally boarded our last plane. 10,000 kilometres and eight hours later we landed in Rome, twenty-eight hours all told by the old internal clock.

Heading to Europe, we were able to rely on family and friends in many situations. We had arranged to stay with Paulo and Gillian in Rome. Gillian was an incredibly close cousin and friend of Zara's mum growing up, and is Zara's godmother. Our artistic demeanour and attire allowed Paulo to pick us out of the crowd instantly and we made our way to their flat where we had tea and Italian sweet bread called panettone.

We slept three to four hours and got up and had a little lunch. The kids were completely knackered and couldn't be woken up for love or money. We let them sleep and went out to explore Rome with Paulo and Gillian.

We drove down to the Colosseum and walked to the Palantine. Paulo is an amazing guide and provided a running commentary that transported us through time. He took us to the outdoor arena where the chariot races in *Ben Hur* were filmed, a movie he played a few extra parts in. We returned to the flat four hours later to find the kids still completely zonked out. We couldn't wake Riel at all. Zion managed to get up and eat something and then went right back to sleep.

For reasons that were never explained, my dad used to jokingly call us kids Luigi. He'd do this really awful impersonation of the Italian singsong lilt. I almost burst out laughing with childlike glee as we were leaving the apartment on our first morning when Gillian held the door open for her elderly neighbour and greeted him with an energetic, "Buongiorno, Luigi!"

I whispered to Zara, "You just know it's going to be a fantastic day when a Luigi is involved!"

Paulo and Gillian took us to Piazza Borghese, a six kilometre long park in the heart of the city. When we got down to the piazza, Zara and I ordered a couple of cappuccinos, just because it seemed the right and Rome-antic thing to do. Paulo and Gillian helped us map out our day of exploration and left us as we headed down to the Spanish steps. From there we made our way to Trevi Fountain where we sat and devoured the most incredible pizza ever.

At eighty-five feet high and sixty-five feet wide, Trevi is the biggest fountain in the entire city. There is a legend that says that if you throw a coin with your right hand over your left shoulder into the Trevi, it will ensure a return to Rome. We sat there for twenty minutes eating our pizza watching endless tourists line up to chuck money into the fountain. I heard about some newer variations of the legend that say the first coin means you'll return to Rome, a second coin will ensure new romance and a third coin will lead to marriage.

Let me hear all the Capitalist Con-Artists in the crowd say, cha-ching! From the Trevi we wandered over to the Vittoriano, jokingly referred to as the Wedding Cake. The building really is a gaudy, white elephant located smack-dab in the centre of Rome. We passed it many, many times, as we tried valiantly, but ultimately in vain, to navigate our way from the Colosseum to the Palatine to the Pantheon. By the time we caught a bus back to the apartment we were exhausted.

The next day Paulo dropped us at St. Peter's. It was insane to want to explore the centre of the Roman Catholic universe in the days leading up to Easter. Zara and Riel joined the queue that stretched all the way around the courtyard while Zion and I went to get cappuccinos. Eventually we made it through the metal detectors and split up as we walked through the building.

People were shoulder to shoulder inside the church with enough camera flashes going off that we were all at risk of epileptic seizures. It was an incredible walk through this massive monument that was built when most of the world was still sleeping on dirt floors in mud huts. It was beautiful, but in a way that felt like it was created to intimidate and overwhelm, you know ... keep the little guy in his place.

Speaking of little guys, I kept looking down at Riel. She seemed so small walking through the cathedral, but her eyes seemed really bright, like they were taking in more than I could imagine. It is the recurring theme of our journey, to be in the moment and see what is right in front of you, and Riel was immersed.

When touring the world with a couple of pint-sized travelers, you really must make the effort to visit any church or crypt that has a pint-sized grim reaper. So the next day, we got Paulo to drop us off at the Capuchin Crypt. This weird-ass creepfest lies beneath the Capuchin Church of Immaculate Conception. The crypt is filled with the bones of over 4,000 individual monks. Bones are nailed to the wall in a variety of patterns to form flowers, arches, and crosses. There was a chandelier dangling from the ceiling made out of vertebrae.

The official Catholic story says that the crypt isn't supposed to be interpreted as macabre, but as a reminder of the swift passage of life on Earth. But seriously ... it's frigging macabre. There are monks laid out in little vestibules surrounded by stacks of bones, there are skeletons nailed to the ceiling and hanging in their robes from the wall.

Of all the places we went in Rome, this crypt was the one place that forbade taking pictures, which also seemed totally macabre, and a perfect opportunity for our little Flip camera to once again prove its worth. With the tiny little thing cupped in the palm of my hand, I managed to film the Godly ghoulishness on parade.

From the crypt, we headed up to the Galleria Borghese where we were blown away by the Bernini sculptures. After dragging the kids around the gallery for a couple of hours we let them drag us into the park where we rented them little red pedal cars.

Zion was into it until he started passing rickshaws full of kids his own age, and suddenly became a bit self-conscious. Being a caring father, I jumped in Zion's car so Riel wouldn't have to play alone. I managed to flip my car over and crack my head and my butt on the pavement in the first ten seconds, probably fitting punishment for not growing up.

We'd debated the best way to get from Rome to Milan and eventually decided to go by high-speed train. Most of the trip we'd been able to avoid actually having to carry everything at one time, but the Rome train station was one of those times we couldn't avoid it.

Each of us had a main backpack and then we all had a daypack. I also had my Baby Taylor guitar and the kids and Zara had blankets and then the odd water bottle or stuffie or bag of Lego. So yeah, even though we were traveling light, it was still a crap load of stuff.

We got out of Paulo's car, piled on all the bags and Quasimodoed our way through the terminal like a convoy of pack mules. We made a pile near our platform as trains came and went in rapid-fire deployment amidst the incomprehensible chatter of pushy pedestrians and espresso-fueled announcers.

I overheard Zion trying to convince Riel to hand him one of her stuffies, assuring her he'd be careful and considerate.

"Don't worry Riel, I'll be genital," he said, before dissolving into prepubescent giggling. I'm not sure if my Dad ever had moments when I said or did something and he just knew that I was his son. And if he did, it makes me wonder what those moments would have been? Did I ever swing a hammer with dexterity, or talk knowledgeably about a 4-barrel carburetor? I really don't know. But when Zion amuses himself with 'sexual-in-your-end-Os' and wild hip-thrusting dance moves during idyllic family walks through pristine forests … I know he is my son, and I deserve him.

A Glorious Array of Magnificent Fermentation

It was a beautiful day in Rome when we left and pouring rain like a motherflipper in Milan. Zara and I started visually scanning the terminal as Riel and Zion manned the cell phone. Amid a flurry of texts, Amanda managed to pinpoint our location and before we even saw her, we heard a squeal of excitement and turned to see this blonde bombshell pelting through the station toward us.

Describing the reunion in his journal Zion wrote "we were greeted by a full-on Auntie Amanda who almost took down Riel!"

Amanda swept us all up into her arms and enthusiasm as we headed out to the borrowed van, which was double-parked in a No Stopping zone outside the door. Nothing could have proved more that Amanda had fully assimilated the local culture than her flagrant disregard for parking rules. If there were any doubts left in anyone's mind, they were quickly dispelled as she blasted her way, horn-first, through the crowded streets laughing, muttering, exclaiming, and gesticulating wildly with both hands simultaneously.

The dreary overcast day cast a post-apocalyptic pallor over Milan as we sped through soggy streets past grey dilapidated buildings that seemed to sag under decades of wear and tear.

We swapped stories and caught up on the drive, stopping at a store in Arona so we could stock up on groceries before continuing on to the house where we were staying.

The fact that it was Good Friday and we were in an overwhelmingly Catholic country meant it was a mad house. There wasn't a hint of English anywhere, so I couldn't decipher any possible meaning from the Italian labels.

I found myself in the dairy section trying to find coffee cream, milk, and sour cream by shaking containers and looking at pictures. I ended up filling my basket with one of everything and started walking around the store looking for Amanda, Zara, and Riel. When I finally found them, I was informed that I didn't have anything in my basket that we wanted, so back to the fridge I went.

On my way, I got waylaid in the wine aisle. What a glorious array of magnificent fermentation. As I floated dreamily through the selection I discovered most bottles were – 24 Euros. So I ran to the front of the store and exchanged my basket for a cart because this shopping spree had suddenly become deadly serious.

No sooner had I come to the end of the aisle than I saw Courvoisier for 11 Euros; I was speechless. Initially I wasn't going to get it. I was feeling self-conscious that I'd been in the grocery store for almost an hour and had nothing in my cart but wine. I was daydreaming along when Zion came running up with an armful of chips and crackers.

"I know you're not going to understand what cognac is," I told him, "but I just saw a bottle of Courvoisier for 11 Euros. Back home it would cost at least 50 dollars"

Zion loves money; he loves making money, touching it, holding it, playing with it. He especially loves spending my money, so his enthusiasm was not about the cognac as much as it was about buying something over here that would cost a lot over there.

He started searching through the bottles of wine in the cart trying to find the cognac bottle. "Where is it?" he asked excitedly.

"Well, I didn't get it," I said.

"What! Why not? Show me, show me where it is," he said, bustling me back the way I'd come.

There have been moments on the trip when our relationships morph, and we fill the role of being each other's friends. I sing grubby limericks with Zion about farting and penises, and he gets excited about Cognac. It's an exchange.

When we got to the display he used his Lego voice, which meant a lot to me, because I knew he was being sincere. "Oh, Dad, that looks amazing, you've got to get it!"

I happily grabbed a bottle and added it to my growing collection of alcohol. "The real thing, Zi, is how I'm going to pitch the necessity of buying a bottle of Courvoisier for no good reason to Zara."

When we arrived at the till Zion took the lead on the sales pitch, "Mom, you'll never guess what. Dad found a bottle of Courvoisier for 11 Euros, back home it would cost 50 dollars!"

Without missing a beat Zara turned on her heel and headed down the aisle calling back over her shoulder, "Then I'm getting the bottle of Baileys I saw for nine!"

We love Italy, though at this rate we may not remember a lot of it.

We still had one more stop to make at a local toy store, so Zion and Riel could pore over the Lego shelves to decide which set they wanted for Easter. They were insistent that we do an Easter morning treasure hunt like in previous years, so the pressure was on me to deliver a good old-fashioned Winnipeg treasure hunt.

I caught a glimpse of myself in the storefront reflection, my hair standing out in all directions, a smattering of unrelated rumpled clothes pieced together from the bottom of a backpack.

"Wow! I'm really rocking the homeless look," I comment out loud. "Makes sense … as we're HOMELESS!" Zion giggles.

With groceries, wine, and Lego piled to the roof we were finally ready to head to the house. We were chattering about people and places from back home as we cruised through this tiny village when we come around a corner and, WHAM, we found ourselves face to face with Sancarlone, the gigantic statue of Saint Charles Borromeo.

It suddenly felt like we were hobbits on the River Anduin trying to slip past the Pillars of the Kings at the Gates of Argonath. Borromeo actually looked like Isildur and Anárion with his outstretched arm either blessing or barring entry, depending on the condition of your soul.

At 35.10 metres tall, Sancarlone was second only to the Statue of Liberty when it was commissioned. I don't know who in the world builds something so grand in a place so humble.

Arona is situated along Lago Maggiore; it felt quaint, rural and idyllically Italian. We were house-sitting for 10 days. The owners were friends of Amanda and had gone to Denmark for Easter. Lake Maggiore stretched in both directions as the valley fanned out below us. Grey windy roads ran like veins through the landscape dotted with red terracotta roofs. Angera Castle sat high on a promontory on the other side of the lake and the Swiss Alps rose in the distance.

Zion and Riel were the first up in the morning and went outside. They were excited to find the crisp air froze the insides of their noses; they said it smelled like Winnipeg. The narrow roads and ancient rock walls and architecture were exactly what I expected Italy to be like. I made an espresso and took it with me as I went for a walk to explore the area. Walking along the main road winding its way up the hill past the house seemed ill-advised. Italy is a country filled with Mario Andretti knock-offs. Even the panel vans and construction trucks scream by at break-neck speeds.

So I chose the first road that led off to the left. It wound up into another little village with an old monastery and church from the 1600s perched high on the promenade. It was very beautiful and historic. I was sipping an Italian espresso, losing myself in the wonder of it all when I heard some dogs barking. They sounded like big, slavering dogs with Darth Vader vocal chords that I just knew were connected to large bone crushing jaws filled with pointy mandibles and incisors. I stopped and looked around, and there in the orchard just off to the side of the road stood two big German Shepherds. I mean steroid-popping, growth-hormone-injecting big. Both had dark, matted fur that seemed to be bristling, and, of course, both were staring right at me. I couldn't see any leashes or chains and wasn't the slightest bit comforted by the presence of an old dilapidated wooden fence that was probably built by peasants before Columbus crashed into America.

A quick visual survey produced no structures or trees to climb, no other pedestrians or agrarian folk digging in flowerbeds or tending their fruit trees. And even if there were, no one speaks English. All of a sudden it dawned on me, I don't know the house number or the street address where we're staying. I don't know the people's names or the phone number at the house.

"How in the name of all that is pure and holy, does an idyllic stroll through a beautiful Italian village while sipping an espresso turn into a life or death decision," I query heaven.

I swear I can hear celestial giggling.

The memory of the dogs in Malaysia may never leave me, and certainly all the terrifying emotions returned in crashing waves. I looked up and down the road and determined that passing the orchard was the only way back to the house. The dogs were still staring at me intently, not moving an inch. Then I heard the distant sound of a vehicle coming up the hill and started to move toward it. I hoped a local would stop to help me and decided to stay in the middle of the road so they wouldn't have a choice. The moment I started moving so did the dogs, running straight for the road.

Their speed, size, and frenzied barking were God-awful. They stopped at the edge of their property with nothing between us but one horizontal board drooping lazily from two equally decrepit posts.

I didn't look at the dogs as I walked past; they were at most twenty feet away and going beserk, barking and jumping and growling. I had my quick feet on, moving as fast as I could. As the car sped past me, I made my way around the curve as the road swung back down toward the main street. I had just started to take a deep breath, figuring the whole incident was behind me when the two canine dick-heads popped out from a building. The farmland was leveled off and a large retaining wall ran along the edge of the property. As the road I was on swung down and around toward the highway, it was like going down a flight of stairs. At the point where the dogs emerged, their paws were level with my head and near enough for me to count their molars.

They barked a couple of years off my life expectancy and made me ruin a perfectly good pair of underwear. I made my jittery way back to the house, and once I was safely tucked away behind lock and key, poured myself three generous fingers of Courvoisier.

Tour De Franco

Amanda initially moved to Arona to work as an au pair for a corporate executive. The woman turned out to be a manically unstable corporate exec, and one night in a fit of crazy histronics, kicked Amanda out on the street.

Through her trials and tribulations, Amanda was essentially adopted by Franco and Kathrin, an incredible couple she now lovingly refers to as her Italian mom and dad. Bright and early Monday morning, we experienced the Tour de Franco.

Amanda was working, so Franco volunteered to pick us up and show us around. We started with a tour of San Salvatore, an ancient monastery located at the highest point of a long windy road overlooking Lago Maggiore. After sipping espressos and nibbling on pastries, we made our way to the Parco della Villa Pallavincino, Italy's incredibly cool version of a petting zoo. Forgo any preconceived notions of a couple of lame pigs and a cross-eyed duck slumming in a farmer's backyard freebasing table scraps. When Italy rolls out a petting zoo, it includes a nineteenth century neoclassical villa, immaculately sculpted grounds tastefully adorned with azaleas and rhododendrons and A-list animals like silver pheasants, a deergoat, llamas, zebras, and kangaroos.

For lunch, Franco took us to Battipalo, a restaurant run by his friend. We didn't even have to order, as the owner brought out one exquisite course after another. After lunch, we took a ferry across the lake to the village of Laveno where we rode up the mountain in a bucket lift. Riel found the whole concept rather terrifying and repeated incredulously that she was going up a mountain in a bucket. At the top, we were treated to a gorgeous view that encompassed Lago Maggiore, the Alps, the Alpine foot hills and the plains of Lombardy.

That night Franco and Kathrin took us to Ristorante Caverna del Leon d'Oro, for the most authentic and delicious pizza we've ever had. The only payment asked for the entire day was for me to pull my guitar out at the table and play a couple of songs, the very thing I was happy to do.

We started the next day at the Arona street market, where we bought a few essentials in short supply, like socks, and a wicked skull hat for Riel. Part of the deal for house sitting involved looking after Flick, the resident puppy. Riel immediately took point on the task as her personal responsibility. As she was proudly walking Flick through the town square he stopped and laid out a fatty the size of an exhaust pipe.

We were caught unprepared with nary a plastic bag to be found. I've always thought of myself as an animal person, but with all the barking and chasing and public pooping ... I'm starting to think dogs are actually kind of dickish.

From the market, we stopped off at the kids' newest favourite gelato shop before walking over to Amanda's work. As soon as her shift was over, we hit the road and drove down to Rapallo where we dropped our stuff off at our hotel and walked around Portofino.

We packed a picnic supper and went off to discover the hiking paths that lead up to Castello Brown overlooking the harbour. The information we had informed us this was a medium level hike, with lots of stairs and climbing that paid off with stunning views of the Italian Riviera. It was late afternoon as we started up the path and were startled to discover a sign that said the gates barring entrance to the grounds and the path would be locked at 5:00 p.m. Not knowing how long the medium level hike would take, we set a blistering pace, lest we dawdle too much and find ourselves locked in the botanic garden for the night. We rounded a couple of corners, climbed a stairway and were suddenly surrounded by manicured hedges and rock walls that felt like an exquisite maze.

Just then Franco called Amanda looking for an update. Franco is the consummate guide and host and wants to do anything and everything to make sure everyone enjoys his country as much as he does. Amanda told him where we were and what we were doing at that exact moment. Franco Googled the address where we were and told us the residence was on the market for a cool 50 million Euros.

When Amanda hung up we realized the little path and staircase was in fact the entire hike. "I keep forgetting," she said, "that a hike for most Italians is something you do in your Versace or Dolce & Gabbana."

We picked a giant rock in the harbour for our dinner table, and broke out the olives, wine, and cheese. Amanda was curious to find out how we've done living out of a backpack and sharing space with each other for ten months.

It is the kind of activity most people associate with being in their 20s as opposed to a young family. It was a moment for us to reflect and answer that question as four unique individuals.

As the sun set low on the water we laughed and talked about the mutual respect, love, grace, and humour that's needed to do what we're doing, and how most families we've met probably shouldn't do what we're doing. This year isn't just Zara and me doing what we want and dragging Zion and Riel along behind like Sherpas. This year is about the four of us building and living a dream together. It was a magical parental moment, hearing the kids talking about an experience they recognized was changing them forever.

We've been teaching the kids to recognize that they are visible, that they deserve to be seen and heard and that their opinions and ideas are valuable. We don't always have to think or feel the same way or like the same things. Respecting our differences is the key to understanding the unique contributions our gifts and abilities allow us to make.

Every time we said that we were going to Italy people would tell us we had to go to Cinque Terre. Known as the five villages, Monterosso al Mare, Vernazza, Corniglia, Manarola and Riomaggiore are each built along the cliffs of the Italian Riviera accessible only by train and linked by a hiking trail that runs along the Mediterranean.

The next morning we checked out of our hotel early, packed our stuff into the car and hit an oceanside café on our way to the train station. We rode the train from Rapallo to the far end of the trail starting in Monterosso.

In early April, spring seemed to be the perfect time of year. It was warm, but not hot as we strolled along the breathtaking vistas. The path between Monterosso and Vernazza is level, wide and smooth. As we started down the trail, I was thinking it was going to be more of a saunter than a hike, with gusts up to a stroll. As the day progressed so did the difficulty of the trail, winding up and down the cliffs. It would have been fun to do part of the hike and stay overnight in one of the villages, but we were racing around Italy on Amanda's two days off, packing in as many adventures as we could.

We stopped for gelatos and espressos in every village as well as savouring the exquisite cuisine on a patio in Manarola before tackling the last, and most strenuous leg of the hike. Zion and Riel were amazing, scampering and clambering with the best of them, engaging in animated conversations and laughter. As we headed into the last leg of the long hike, Riel passed me as I filmed the trail, pumping her arm in a rallying gesture usually associated with team sports in overtime.

"I love you, little dude," I yelled after her.

She flashed the devil's horns with both hands as she disappeared around the corner.

After a rocking hike that did me in, we still needed to take the train back to Rapallo, grab the car and drive back to Arona. And still the kids never complained.

Happy with apples and snacks they started playing scribble in the backseat where I made a bed for them. They laughed and tickled each other until Zion eventually fell asleep and Riel played games on the iPod. We arrived at the house after 1:00 a.m. and were back up and on the road by 5:30 a.m. heading to Venice. *Zion & Riel - Italy*

 *The video of Italy celebrates the incredible history the family experienced, and incorporates a poem Rik wrote and had translated by Zara's sister Amanda, who was living in Arona. Rik recorded Amanda's vocal track as they sat around the table sipping espressos.*

Italian Stallions at a Caffeine Rodeo

It's at least a four-hour drive each way from Arona to Venice. Amanda's driving and Zara is up front in the passenger seat, so I'm in the back with the kids.

It is a whole other world in the backseat.

I'm tired, and want a coffee and don't have enough legroom. I could go on for a long time crabbing and complaining, and the only thing that keeps me from whining is that my kids never complain once. I have not appreciated what savvy, self-sufficient world travelers they've become. They play scribble games and make nests for themselves, where they roll around giggling, sleeping, or playing on the iPod. Zion made a stick-gum man out of chewing gum and a toothpick. They played with the stupid thing for an hour.

Then they started dreaming up rude names for creatures that Zion would have to draw. Puke-as the Bagsack, Pube-as Buttsag, Buck-as Bumgum, Haggis Snufflechuff and my personal favourite, the a-BUM-able Snowman.

Auto Grill is synonymous with Italian truck stops and rest areas, and there seems to be one every 10 miles. The culture that surrounds the consumption of coffee is very different in Italy. North American coffee culture is about sitting down, hanging out with friends, maybe conducting some business over a fifteen-syllable beverage.

In Italy, it's all about fuel, fuel for loud discussions that sound like everyone is pissed off or getting there. Fuel to drive like maniacs and fuel for the wild arm-waving and gestures that accompany the aforementioned.

At the Auto Grill coffee bars, swarms of swarthy men in leather jackets and sunglasses line up in row upon row. It feels like a rugby match meets a mosh pit.

The barista is the rock star doling out espresso shots like a Vegas dealer. Sitting down while you drink your coffee is such a pussy thing to do in Italy that they actually charge you more. In some cases the price of sitting at a table is twice as much as the coffee, so most just chug it.

The shots are coming hot and fast and the crowd is slamming them back as fast as they get them, like Italian Stallions at a caffeine rodeo. I started singing *Bullet in a Blue Sky* calling out "One Hundred! Two Hundred!" as the guys in front of me threw their heads back.

As much as I am all for experiencing and embracing other cultures, sometimes I just want to be comforted by something familiar like sipping a frigging coffee in the car on a road trip with my friends. I don't want to slam it, cram it, freebase it, or inject it directly into my adrenal gland. I want to sip and savour at my leisure, thank you very much. Is that so wrong; is that too much to ask?

The simple answer is yes. Ordering coffee to go is as bad as ordering it to sit down. I am given a little see-through plastic cup I've only been given by a doctor to pee in. It warps and shrivels like Styrofoam in fire as soon as the coffee is poured into it, becoming malleable putty in my hands. Hands, by the way, that start burning one fingertip at a time as I try to juggle the molten hot lava from left to right.

"What's that," Riel asks as I walk back to the car. I circle my face with my finger, "This is the face of disappointment."

The whole experience was so unsatisfying that before I even got in the car I ended up slamming it back and yelling "Gratzi!" at the top of my lungs. Which is when I realized I wasn't the only one having a disconcerting experience at the Auto Grill.

Zion has been transported from the family bubble into a fish bowl, a fish bowl created by a group of fourteen-year-old Italian girls quite taken with this exotic Canadian specimen. Some "hellos" were thrown his way amidst a flock of batted eyelashes and eager smiles. He left the Auto Grill in a hurry with a curious little sister in tow as she rarely gets to see her older brother fleeing for his life. The Italian girls followed and suddenly Zion found himself stuck outside the car waiting for Amanda with the keys. The girls started to call over to Zion, who tried steadfastly to maintain an oblivious posture.

Finally, his facade broke and he looked at me with incredulous panic, "This would never happen in Canada!"

Sensing that they were getting past his defenses, the girls redoubled their flirtatious efforts and all subterfuge was abandoned as Zion fled to the other side of the car, where he crouched down by the door in abject horror. When Amanda FINALLY came out, he scrambled inside, retreating once more into the bubble.

We got to Venice mid-morning, parked the car, crossed the footbridge into the city and promptly lost Riel. Venice really captured Riel's imagination and she was so excited to see the canals and the gondolas that she'd just blasted on ahead of us. I found her gazing in rapt amazement at the busy waterway.

"It's real, it's really real!" she announced as I walked up.

With one day to experience the city we really just wandered aimlessly, savouring snacks, sipping beverages, wandering in and out of artisan studios. Venice is one of those tourist zones, like Banff, Canada, or Queenstown, New Zealand, where everything feels like a giant souvenir shop and theme park ride.

I wanted to buy a Venetian mask in Venice, though I had no idea how we'd carry it in a backpack, but after passing shop after shop loaded to the gills with the same five designs, the idea seemed more Unitarian than unique.

The quaint gondola drivers in the striped shirts, neck scarves, and flat-rimmed hats loitering in alleyways, hustled crowds of tourists, pawning off overpriced clichés. For your right arm or firstborn child, the gondola drivers happily add an accordion player to serenade your overpriced experience. In spite of the trappings we had a magical day. We were in Venice, and there is nowhere else like it in the world.

Sometimes it feels like we are laying train tracks in a Looney Tunes cartoon, trying to keep our carefree experience rolling.

Sleep is elusive and I spend the wee hours of the morning booking hotels in Nice and Marseille, faxing tax forms back to Canada, and confirming our Europcar rental. I felt like I'd already put in a full day's work as the sun bloomed in a bouquet of pink and dusty rose, illuminating the Alps. The lights from Arona cluster together in the distance. This is our last morning at the villa, tonight we'll crash at Franco and Kathrin's and tomorrow Franco will drive us to Nice.

When we arrived for supper, we discovered Franco and Kathrin had prepared an incredible fondue. As we sat down to eat, I said to Zion, "Oh, you're going to love this, you've never had fondue before, have you?"

"Yes, I have," he replied. I assumed it was another one of those experiences your kids have when they're off at someone else's house, until forty-five seconds later when Kathrin dished out some slices of thin, raw meat on everyone's plate and I saw Zion start to tuck into his with knife and fork.

"What are you doing?" I covertly exclaimed. "You put it on these long forks and put them in this boiling broth in front of you until they're cooked. Then you eat it with some of these dips in the dishes in front of you.

"Oh. yeah … well that makes a lot more sense than what I was about to do," he said nonplussed. Zara was watching our exchange from across the table, marveling at our son's staggering confidence.

We drank lots of wine, scotch, and grappa. Franco kept reminding me that I didn't need to drive, as if that was the only logical reason to avoid getting completely pie-eyed. I liked Franco, and the more grappa I drank the more sense he made.

Franco was quite struck by Riel. He apparently told his daughter that she should get pregnant so he could have a little granddaughter like Riel around. Kathrin said that the daughter's boyfriend was more old fashioned, and wanted them to move in together first and then maybe talk about getting pregnant. Franco supposedly said, no, no, no, just go get pregnant and then come back and live here.

We had such a great time it was hard to believe we had only met them a few days before.

Early Sunday morning we piled our backpacks in Franco's van and took off at 160 kilometres an hour for Nice. We arrived too early to check into our room, so we dropped our bags in the laundry room and walked down to the sea to have some lunch.

When we finally got into our room and the kids settled into their various activities, Zara and I decided to head out to the grocery store and get some food for supper. But on a Sunday afternoon at 4:00 p.m., the city of Nice is apparently closed. We wandered up and down the deserted streets, eventually finding a couple of little open stalls in a fruit market where we were able to cobble together an assortment of olives, cheese, wine, and a baguette. On our way back, it started raining, so I grabbed a bright pink plastic bag and slipped it over the exposed tip of the baguette sticking out of Zara's backpack. As I followed her through the city, it looked like a brightly coloured novelty condom on a giant pro-truding penis. As I giggled to myself, I realized I've been spending too much time with Zion.

The next morning I grabbed a map, got some directions at the front desk and hit the streets of Nice. I needed to get to the Europcar counter at the airport to pick up our rental car. We'd discovered an amazing deal by renting a car in France.

As part of a tourism incentive, taxes and insurance were included, and for the time we planned to be in continental Europe we had our transportation covered. I walked the streets of Nice, periodically finding someone who spoke enough English to point me in the right direction. I managed to catch the right bus, which dropped me off at an airport shuttle stop, where I got on another bus. I didn't actually know which terminal I wanted and just kept guessing. After a circuitous stroll through the concrete jungle I found the counter, filled out the papers, got the keys, and walked across the parking lot to where I discovered an amazing little car.

We'd asked for a diesel, and they'd given us a Leon, which we can't buy in North America, at least at the time of writing. It was brand new with less than a hundred kilometres on it. I raced back to the hotel where the family was waiting with all our bags in the lobby. We planned to explore Nice while we were there, but Nice was not at all accommodating. Interminable construction rendered our GPS useless. Each turn lead us into more construction and more detours lead us further and further away from downtown. Ultimately, we gave up and were happy to see the city fading from view in our rearview mirror.

We stopped at Cannes for lunch. There was a red carpet affair going on for a big international TV conference which we crashed. As we strolled along the red carpet, I kept the camera rolling, walking protectively in front of Zion and Riel proclaiming we just wanted to pass straight through to the van, no video and no photos.

I was not the weirdest person we saw. Finely-coiffed bouffants and beehives remained rigidly in place as comb-overs and mullets flowed freely in the ocean breeze. Many ample bottoms were squeezed mercilessly into skinny jeans as flocks of fashionistas loitered purposefully in front of international camera crews.

By the time I got to Marseille, I was desperate for a haircut of my own. As we were exploring the city, I discovered a salon. No one spoke a word of English, so there were lots of snipping motions with fingers, pointing to the picture on my international driver's license, and back to myself with a thumbs up sign. The whole shop was involved, the front desk staff, all the stylists, and a few customers. They brought out one customer from under a hair dryer because she could speak English, "a leetle", as she put it. We confirmed the plan, bobbed our heads up and down enthusiastically and I crossed my fingers and hoped I hadn't communicated that my head was a giant penis that needed to be circumcised.

After the shearing, we made our way to the harbour where we saw water taxis ferrying people out to Chateau D'If, the prison made famous by Edmond Dante in the *Count of Monte Cristo*. Just before we'd left Canada we'd watched the 2002 movie starring James Caviezel and Guy Pearce with the kids.

Our goal this year was to be spontaneous and adventurous, so we bought four tickets and headed out to the rock. We toured the cells and scampered over the rocks, reading the stories of prisoners who went insane or died at the prison. It was the last thing I would have anticipated when I got up in the morning; we thoroughly enjoyed the surprise.

It was about a three-hour drive from Marseille to Caunes-Minervois where we'd rented a 300-year-old villa. The kids were reading in the back seat so for quite a while it was quiet in the car. Zion was still working his way through the *Sword of Shannara*, the first fantasy book both Zara and I ever read. Zion suddenly broke the silence, "What do the gnomes look like?"

"They're kind of like the orcs in *Lord of the Rings*," Zara told him.

"OK, that makes more sense than what I was thinking. I was picturing these little guys two feet tall with red hats and white beards and it kept talking about all the destruction they'd caused and I was thinking that was weird because you could destroy them with a single kick."

In the Name of God and the Holy Church

Caunes-Minervois is located in the Languedoc-Roussillon area. Languedoc is a derivative of "Langue d'Oc", or the language of the troubadours. It seemed a perfect place for our merry band to spend a week exploring the south of France. The Mediterranean was an hour's drive to the east, to the south we could see the peaks of the Pyrennees and off to the west Toulouse and the Atlantic.

We faithfully followed our GPS as she led us through the windy backcountry to Caunes-Minervois. When we entered the village we started to feel some trepidation and doubted the wisdom of following modern navigational tools through a medieval village. Soon we were driving on cobblestone sidewalks up steep, twisting narrow streets threading our way between people's homes. Welcome to the old world.

We met Nicole and Hans as we were getting out of our car. They were a young couple who'd spent three years renovating the old three-story building. They said when they first walked in they could see the sky from the ground floor. They'd invested an amazing amount of time, effort, and money to develop this property and we were their first renters. They had fresh flowers on the table and wood set up for a fire. All I had to do was light a match and we had a cozy little kitchen to snuggle around in a 300-year-old French villa. It was absolutely fantastic!

The whole area is steeped in crusade history and we spent the week scrambling over crumbling brick and mortar, digging deep into the stories of sieges and horrors visited upon innocents in the name of God and the Holy Church.

The Cathars were a religious group who showed up in the eleventh century. They believed in a good creator and an evil adversary, like God and Satan, but rejected the idea of a priesthood or church buildings. They also believed men and women were equal and they allowed contraception, euthanasia, and suicide.

The Cathars actually taught non-procreative sex was better than procreative, pitting them against the Catholic Church, who, of course, taught just the opposite. The Languedoc region was famous for its liberal culture and acceptance. It attracted many converts and eventually became the big belief on the block.

So much so that Pope Innocent III eventually called a formal Crusade against the Cathars of Languedoc. For a couple of generations starting around 1208 things got pathologically deranged, as 500,000 Languedoc men, women, and children were massacred. The culture was decimated, reading the Bible became a capital crime and tithing was enforced. The success of this psychopathic purge became the blueprint for the Spanish Inquisition.

Twenty minutes down the road from our little village, we discovered the Castles of Lastours. Four independent structures built into the rocky formation, they were at the heart of Cathar activity, and ground zero for some seriously messed up history.

Like Simon de Montfort, the lynchpin and all-around douchebag who brought prisoners up from the village and had their eyes gouged out and their ears, noses, and lips cut off, parading them before the Castles to force them to surrender.

Perhaps trying to get away from the awful story I was telling, Zion and Riel climbed forty feet to the top of the crumbling walls of medieval brick and mortar turned treacherous through time. I tried to follow them but just managed to scramble to the top when vertigo set in. The world started to spin as I looked over the edge of the castle wall, built straight up from the edge of a cliff.

If any of us fell, a sprained ankle or broken wrist would be the least of our worries. I saw Zion on the farthest castle wall. I tried to coax him back to safety, but the Cathar spirit of resistance runs strong, and he ignored me with the single-minded purpose of a thirteen-year-old's sense of invincibility. I couldn't even see Zara and Riel for all the ruins in the way and decided to skid my way unceremoniously back to the ground, whimpering softly as I went.

For all the fear and trepidation, this was one of my favourite locations. It was another bright, sunny spring day, my chronic back and neck pain were almost non-existent, and even though my family seemed to be tempting fate by purposefully standing on the edge of every castle and cliff, we were all healthy and happy, truly in our own little world.

Last night Riel really needed a friend. Zara and Zion were upstairs watching something on the laptop and Riel was playing with Lego. But as I sat down on the little couch in the adjacent room she curled up beside me, with her eager-to-be-involved attitude.

At nine-years old, Riel is at the age where she wants to indulge in some grown up activities, like watching scary movies. I saw Blood and Chocolate on the hard drive and dragged it onto my laptop. We curled up in her bed under the covers to watch a "scary" movie. As the movie started she launched into a cute little speech, "You know, I've been noticing," she started, "that you and I share a lot of things. We both like eating snacks instead of big meals, our names both start with R, and we're both the youngest people in our families."

It was a perfect night to curl up under the covers in a rambling, drafty French cottage, watching werewolves run rampant through the streets of Bucharest.

We are so off the grid in Caunes-Minervois I literally can't even phone home. Thank God I'm not E.T. We can't understand the radio or read the paper and there is no TV.

I find one bar worth of Wi-Fi signal to check email and discover that three days ago Eyjafjallajokull blew in Iceland, spewing enough ash to ground thousands of planes, stranding millions of travelers. There are worse things than being out of touch.

It is Sunday afternoon and we're cruising through the south of France, singing along to Mika's latest CD. The kids are in fine form entertaining themselves at ear-bleeding levels in the backseat. The louder we crank the music the louder they scream and laugh. I realized Zara must have been paying closer attention than

I am when she thrusts her arm into the backseat and yells over the din, "OK that's it: give me the Ninja throwing star tea bag!"

It takes about an hour and a half to drive from Caunes-Minervois to the castle of Peyrepertuse, overlooking the Roussillon Plains. It is one of the "five sons of Carcassonne" along with Aguilar, Queribus, Puilaurens, and Termes.

Peyrepertuse has been occupied since Roman times and is one of the most jaw-dropping and awe-inspiring castles we visited. It literally clings to a jagged spine of rock on top of a mountain ridge. The path into the castle leads through a forest of boxwood and as we climbed up and over rocks, we tried to imagine the amount of effort it would have taken every day to bring the food and water up this trail.

I started creating an alliterative tongue twister for the kids' amusement.

"Peons and poor peasant schlubs schlepping s#% up slippery slopes for ridiculously rich and rascally masters, bearing burdensome barrels of beer and buckets of buns to fill the fantastical faces, fatty acids and asses that move like molasses. Yes, alas this story is crass and fills me with sadness."

I thought it was a creative way to explain the history of exploitation and inequitable distribution of wealth. After listening to me weave the words together for ten minutes Riel finally blurted, "I have no idea what you're talking about," and after a short pause concluded, "but you said the s and a-words."

In Peyrepertuse Zion was in fine form, armed with a stick that doubled as a gun and crossbow he investigated the arrow slots cut into the battlements. He kept my mouth full of "be carefuls" and "don't falls". No matter how liberally enlightened I may feel I am as a parent, and how obviously ineffective these admonishments are on my children's Teflon coated ears, I just can't help myself.

The two of them scampered over the uneven rock, stopping every now and then to take in the 800 metre drop over the south side as they explored ravines and crevices that were probably used 2000 years ago as toilets. I heard them celebrate that they'd discovered the "sacred woman". As the four of us climbed to the upper edge of the castle I asked Zara what she had done to be awarded such a prestigious honorific.

"Just being my normal amazing self," she replied.

Less than ten minutes later, as we made our way down from the peak Zion was accusing Zara of being a heretic. I mentioned the swiftness of her transformation from sacred to heretical. As Zion impishly sniggered, she responded imperially, "To survive the winds of change you have to change alliances like underwear."

Zion & Riel – France

When I'm filling out our homeschooling records later, I don't know whether this conversation should fall into history, woman's studies, or economics.

From Peyrepertuse we needed to make one final stop, at the infamous and notorious Rennes Le Chateau. If you haven't heard of this quaint village that oozes conspiracy from every pore, let me outline a few of the more salient details.

There was a parish priest from the village during the late 19th century who had been receiving vast sums of money that he used to refurbish the local church and build many structures in the area. The priest died in 1917, leaving the secret of where his cash came from with his housekeeper. She apparently promised to spill the beans on her deathbed, but had a stroke, which left her paralyzed and unable to speak. This set tongues a-wagging, fueling lots of great conspiracies regarding the source of the priest's money. Was it the lost treasure of the Templars? Or perhaps tied to the Cathars in the area, or maybe buried Visigoth gold?

But then, there were the murders … grisly murders. An old reclusive priest was bashed to bits on All Saints' Eve in 1897 with fire tongs and an ax, before being reverently laid on the ground with his hands crossed over his chest. Three bodies were eventually found buried in his garden. Then there was the guy who cared for the housekeeper after her paralyzing stroke. He was killed in a horrific car crash.

Most sinister of all was the rumour that the priest had been blackmailing the Church with some terrible secret. This theory got more traction when it was reported that the priest's confession before his death was so shocking the priest who heard it denied him absolution and last rites.

The basic gist of the conspiracy was that Jesus and Mary Magdalene, legitimate nobility from the Judaic Houses of Benjamin and David, married and sired heirs. Jesus did not die on the cross but went either to England or India.

I know what you're thinking ... someone should write a mystery novel or better yet, make a movie about this; they could call it *The Da Vinci Code*.

This is why we had to make the trip to Rennes Le Chateau. This little village has managed to wrap itself up with Magdalene's heirs, Visigoth families, the sacred Merovingian ruling family, the Knights Templar, the downfall of the Cathars, and the Rosicrucian manifesto. It's entirely possible the weapons of mass destruction no one could find in Iraq are actually hidden somewhere underneath Rennes Le Chateau.

I grew up in a small town; I know how hard it can be to generate renewable revenue streams. So I respect the ingenuity of this little village that has, if nothing else, created a thriving tourist business. Thousands of people a year visit, and every store we passed had cards, books, and maps for sale, all perpetuating various strains of the mystery.

There are only a few subjects that can get Zara talking animatedly for hours; Rennes Le Chateau is one of them. The drive through the countryside flew by the window as Zion, Riel, and I were regaled with names, dates, and grizzly details as Zara rattled off an impressive grasp of the intricacies surrounding this village. With such an auspicious build-up Riel was understandably pissed off to discover we just missed being able to enter the famous little church.

She pounded on the doors with uncharacteristic determination before turning around and saying, "Well that sucks! We travel halfway around the world and miss it by twenty minutes!"

We peered in the windows and snuck around in the gardens. The kids climbed up the rocks and retaining walls around the back of the church. As usual, I had the camera rolling and, catching us up in the conspiratorial vibe of the village, started whispering urgently that they were going to get caught and we needed to run. The end of our France video has the three of us running pellmell down the path from Rennes Le Chateau before realizing that we'd left the sacred woman behind.

In France the family explores the ruins of Cathar castles, walk the red carpet in Cannes, visit Chateau D'If, and run from conspiracy theorists in Rennes-le-Château

The Bee's Knees is Now the Cat's Ass

Today we begin our pilgrimage from Caunes-Minervois, France, to Billund, Denmark, also known as Mecca to Lego lovers around the world, including the two zealots in the backseat. Our GPS says it will take seventeen hours to drive. We are going to take three days to make the journey ... so Zion and Riel can cleanse themselves spiritually. We will spend the first night in Dijon, then onto Offenbach, Germany, and plan to arrive in Billund by 6:00 p.m. on the third day.

After driving for five hours we stop at a gas station at Lyon. I've spent the last several weeks trying to get Zion to get out and stay out of Riel's bizness. Of course, as the oldest child, Zion believes it is his God-given right to provide a running commentary on everything Riel says and does. While I'm filling the tank Riel is cleaning the windshield and Zion is standing there giving a play by play, on how she is doing it wrong.

"Go critique Mom," I suggested, "see what kind of reception you get."

He runs around to the other side of the car and starts screaming in Zara's face.

"You suck, you call that washing!"

"I said critique, not criticize!"

"Oh," he pauses dramatically in mid-rant. "Mom, now can you see the danger of words."

One of the problems we've had with booking hotels in advance is knowing where the hotel is in relation to amenities. We also learned months ago that while a picture may be worth a thousand words, those words can add up to a lot of cock and bull. You'd swear by the photo you're going to be frolicking in powdery sand a stone's throw from a natural hot spring sipping homemade Mai Tai's. Then you show up and discover you're in a wood panel station wagon in a hillbilly's backyard eating boiled wieners.

So of course, the hotel we'd booked in Dijon was right downtown, and of course we'd arrived during rush hour. We were creeping along when suddenly the gigantic tour bus beside us started to pull into our lane. I laid on the horn, hit the brakes and watched as he drifted in and out of the lane in front of us. Moments later, after losing any semblance of giving a s#%, the driver drifted back into the lane sideswiping the car in front of us. This really sucked because now the two sluggish arteries were clogged with screaming Frenchmen, flapping their arms and gums at each other in the middle of the road. A goodly time later, we finally arrived at our destination and tumbled into our room with grateful hearts.

The kids are at Lego Con 5. They know we are only hours away from Legoland and the pressure is mounting. How big will it really be? Will it surpass their incredibly high expectations? Is that even possible? They are building and breaking down their Lego weaponry with zeal.

From Dijon we hit the road and drove to Offenbach, Germany. We were only a few miles across the German border when we saw a sign that said 'Ausfahrt'. As soon as we passed it, I heard Zion giggling in the backseat. "Hey Riel, I just saw a sign that said ass-fart," he said.

As he leaned forward I said, "You just saw the sign, didn't you?" "Yeah," he laughed, "what an awesome sign. I love this country."

Once again, we'd booked in advance, this time at the Hotel Monte Cristo. It not only sounded cool, but we'd just ridden the Edmond Dante water taxi to Chateau D'If in Marseille. It seemed so fitting, so romantic, so serendipitous for us to stay in the Hotel Monte Cristo.

It should have been called Hotel D'If. In the 60s it might have been the bee's knees, but in the new millennium it's more like the cat's ass. As we drove down empty streets lined with cold grey brick buildings and faded weathered signs advertising XXX and Live Girls, my apprehension grew. When we pulled into the hotel parking lot, we were the only car in sight. The door to the lobby was ornately carved, but looked as if it was built to withstand a police battering ram. There was a guy in the lobby whose presence and purpose was never clear, but I don't think he ever left his post.

If you have ever found yourself checking into a room with your wife and two lovely children somewhere on the other side of the world, and have a gnawing suspicion that you may have checked into a mafia safe house, then you' ll know how I was feeling.

I asked the girl at the front desk if there was anywhere she'd recommend for supper and she directed me a couple of blocks up the street to Tony's, a 'great pizza place'.

I walked into Tony's between 6.30 and 7.00 p.m. Even given the later European dinner hour, I was surprised to discover that I was the only customer in the entire place. I turned around and looked at the door to see if I'd missed a closed sign. I walked up to the bar, where there was a young good-looking guy in his early 20s.

"Hi, do you speak English?" I asked. "Ya, a leetle," he replied.

Behind the young guy there was an older dude sitting on a stool, maybe early 40s, thick barrel chest, black leather jacket; "The Muscle" I jokingly thought. The pizzas were only 4 Euros each, which I assumed meant they were personal size, so I ordered four.

I pulled out my visa card to pay and the young guy managed to say they didn't take visa, though there were visa signs on the counter, the till, and the front door, only cash.

My spider-sense started tingling and my hyper-intuitive imagination kicked in. I immediately recognized I was in a real life German version of the *Sopranos*. The kid behind the counter was Chris. Polly, his Capo, was the guy sitting behind him. Tony must be in the back. It all made sense; I was pretty sure we were staying in a mafia-run hotel so why wouldn't I be ordering pizza in a German mafia restaurant. I paid the cash.

Not wanting to do or say any thing that would get a cap popped anywhere near my ass, I walked down to the grocery store, where it dawned on me: we're *in* Germany, where they produce some of the finest white wine in the world, *and*, it is available for 3 Euros a bottle. I bought as many as I could carry.

I staggered back up the street, labouring under the weight of all my Riesling, back to Tony Soprano's place. I'm pretty sure they just ordered a pizza from an actual pizza place, and had it delivered to the back door. Chris handed it to me, as if it just came out of the oven, but there wasn't even a faint aroma of anything cooking in the building. And the pizzas were gigantic.

I returned to the Monte Cristo through the outer perimeter, past the sentry posted in the lobby and back to our room, carrying more pizza and wine than we could ever hope to consume. Zara, Zion, and Riel sat in stunned silence as I came through the door, rendered speechless by the excessive quantity. The pizza was good, the wine was even better and as evening dissolved into a haze, we were a day closer to Denmark.

I woke up in the middle of the night, and as I lay there in the dark thinking about the trip the next day, I heard someone in the hall. Someone coming back late from a party I thought to myself. That is when I heard the doorknob on our room jiggle softly.

I sat up. With no carpet on the floor there was enough space under the door that I could see the shadow moving in the hallway. The doorknob clicked again, like someone was trying to force it, or force something into it.

If you have ever been sitting in a dark room in your underwear, in a hotel most likely run by the German mafia, on a street where the only establishments have two or three Xs in the name, as your beautiful wife and lovely children sleep peacefully beside you, then you can know how I was feeling.

My overactive imagination was on a crash-n-burn trajectory as I lay there freaked out of my mind. What should I do? Should I wake everyone up? Do I confront the person at the door?

The Hotel Monte Cristo doesn't have phones in the rooms, which I never even noticed, but suddenly it seemed like a total set up. Even if they did, there isn't anyone at the front desk during the night *and* it dawned on me, I don't even know how to call the police. Buying pay-as-you-go SIM cards for our cell phone was certainly economical, but the minute we crossed the border into Germany, the France card stopped working.

I went to the window, searching for an escape route. We were on the first floor and could conceivably jump out the window. But what would we do then … run to the car? Do we leave our stuff or take the time to pack? I thought about barricading the door, but other than the two beds, there were only a couple of nightstands and a sideboard for the coffee machine. I tried to prop the one chair in the room up under the doorknob, like they do in movies, but without carpet the chair just kept slipping and sliding. The whole time I was quietly scrambling around in the dark, trying not to wake my family. No need to alarm them with the potential horrors of falling prey to Frankie Four-Fingers and Mickie Stiletto Heels … especially as I was freaking out enough for all four of us. It was a slow terrifying night that I spent jumping at every noise, periodically dozing with my back against the door until morning finally crept down the grey, colourless street and the furtive noises in the hall disappeared.

DENMARK/SWEDEN

Embryonic Building Blocks & Lego Genetics

The little town of Billund, Denmark, lies in Central Jutland, about a three-hour drive from Copenhagen. For the keepers of the holy Lego faith, Billund is Nirvana, the Promised Land; it's Graceland and the heart and soul of the greatest story ever told.

A Dane named Ole Kirk Christiansen and his son Godtfred invented Lego. In Latin, Lego means, "I study" or "I put together". It's a safe bet Ole Kirk was probably just thinking "Leg godt", two Danish words that mean "play well".

The town of Billund exists because of Lego. It is the home of the Lego Group head office, and the factory which manufactures close to 90% of the company's products.

We booked two nights at the Zleep Hotel, a bargain basement chain situated by the airport. For all its monastic austerity, it was what we'd been looking for all year. The rooms had beds and a bathroom; it was clean, quiet and cheap and nothing else mattered.

To hear Zion tell it (and we did, over and over and over again), this was the day he and Riel had been waiting for, the very purpose they'd been created for. Not just from the day they were born, but actually from the moment their mother's egg had broken out of its follicle and commandoed its way through the fallopian tubes enroute from her ovary to the uterus. It was there, that a Lego-shaped sperm fertilized a Lego-shaped egg and became the embryonic Lego building block of his Lego-loving genetic make up.

We got up with the alarm at 8:30 a.m. Zion had been awake for hours, quivering in his bed in anticipation. The continental breakfast wasn't complimentary so I went down to the lobby to check it out. I had no idea how much a Danish Krone was worth, but 240 DKK seemed like a lot for the four of us to each have a piece of bread and marmalade. So I drove down to the grocery store and attempted to navigate more incomprehensible packaging without understanding a word. Shopping this way is kind of like Christmas, you never know what you're going to get until you open the box.

It was cold and overcast as we strolled out of the hotel; the anticipation was electric. For the kids it was the equivalent of Christmas, the end of school, and their birthday rolled into one. Here was an actual amusement park built out of and dedicated to Lego. For Zara and me it was one of those days you hope will live up to the incredibly high expectations of your kids. Thank the Lego-gods it did.

At first, the weather didn't seem to be cooperating. We'd had nothing but sun for most of the year, but by coming to Denmark we'd driven back up to the part of the northern hemisphere where things like snow were once again possible. And on and off during the day there were patches of rain, but basically it just managed to keep the crowds incredibly thin at Legoland. For about $150 we all got in, and once we were in we discovered that all the rides were free.

The kids charged straight for the Pick a Brick section. For the uncircumcised Philistines, Pick a Brick is an area full of huge bins. Each bin is filled with specific Lego bricks and specific colours. If you're a burgeoning Lego designer, Pick a Brick allows you to build your own creations from the ground up brick by brick. For years, Zion has combined his love of Lego with his love of *Halo, Call of Duty*, and *Star Wars*. Pick a Brick offers him a rare opportunity to fully indulge himself. He has books of detailed sketches with line drawings of visions he has in his head, complete with a parts list underneath, painstakingly detailing each piece he'll need.

Riel also loves Pick a Brick, but for different reasons. She often wants boxes of Lego for specific little bits and bobs in the set. Pick a Brick is Riel's opportunity to buy a bag of Lego puppies and horses, loaves of bread, and other assorted gems. It was magic all day long.

There was a Lego city of Copenhagen, and the U.S. State building with three quarters of a million pieces. A Lego safari, with life size elephants, flamingos, zebras, and vultures, each one with the tell-tale blocky ridges. And rides, oh my God, the rides. There was a Lego canoe ride that wound past skunks, raccoons, wolves, bears, and other woodland creatures all made out of Lego.

The rainy overcast day in April meant that Legoland was virtually deserted. We never had to wait for a ride, running around the turnstiles over and over again to get on the roller coaster. After the roller coaster's first huge drop Riel screamed, "I almost fainted!" For lots of rides we were able to just stay on and keep riding again and again.

Then we headed to the Temple of Doom, where a ride winds through the spooky temple as passengers try to shoot glowing targets with laser guns. Zion and I jumped into the same car and immediately started talking some serious trash about kicking each other's a-word. Zion beat me, though not nearly as bad as I thought it would be.

But to our sputtering surprise, and Zion's utter horror, Zara kicked both our keisters. Seems her crazy penchant for reading instructions paid off once again, as she read that the purple lights were worth 1000 points each, while the other lights were worth single digits. It's at times like these that Zara's quiet, calm demeanour can come off as incredibly smug and condescending.

We babbled our way from the Temple to the theatre to take in the 4-D animated feature in the Lego theatre. The 4th D involved spraying the audience with water, which was inopportune on a cold rainy day.

Riel loved the Temple of Doom and the rollercoaster. Zion loved the Lego creations. He's spent many hours building in his room. I think he alone could really appreciate the man-hours and creative energy necessary to build such spectacles. We'd walked by massive life-sized animals, humans, and huge panoramic recreations when suddenly he exclaimed, "Oh, that is so cool! Dad, can I have the Flip?" and proceeded to get a close up of a Lego pop machine with miniature Coke and Pepsi cans.

Then it was time for Riel to get behind the wheel. Kids can get their Lego driving license by entering a half-hour driver-training course. Kids were divided up by language and given a license plate with their country's flag. I guess not enough Canadians visit to warrant having even one Canada license plate on hand, so Riel chose Great Britain.

But as the only English speaking kid, she got no instruction at all. Not shy behind the wheel, Riel drove like a woman possessed. Pedal down with wind in her face, she blew through stop signs and car washes as if she owned the place. I was just waiting for her to flash a one-finger salute as a kid with Swedish plates cut her off.

Still coming down off their Lego high, in spite of eight hours of nonstop walking, the kids strode purposefully into a cold, stiff breeze as the rain came and went. We made it back to the hotel and finished off our Mafia groceries as the kids set up their new Lego sets. The kids' friends watching the videos expressed a great deal of jealousy when we posted *Zion & Riel – Legoland!!!*

After our deeply-moving religious experience in Denmark, it was time to head to Sweden.

Back in 1996, just before Zion was born, I'd had a chance to tour Sweden. I'd met some incredible musicians and, thanks to Facebook, was able to reconnect with them after thirteen years. Peder is a guitar player and Tina is a singer. They live in Landskrona with their three kids, Natalie, Joel, and Amelie, and when they heard we were coming to the area, invited us to come crash at their place.

We had an awesome first night. Joel is sixteen years old but seems like an old soul trapped in a strapping Viking frame. The fact that he was already rocking a goatee made him seem more man than teen.

Sweden had incredibly fast broadband. Joel had *Call of Duty*, and Zion had a one-track mind: basically, hijacking Joel's room, computer, and COD. Peder and Tina's nineteen-year-old daughter Natalie had just gotten a cute little black lab puppy named Alice.

Riel was in H-E-A-V-E-N and played and petted Alice

mercilessly. Amelie was six and had the least amount of English to work with, but she did amazingly. Alice was like a canine version of the United Nations, bridging the gap between the two girls.

The kids often found driving around Europe disorienting. They'd crawl into the back of the car in Italy and get out in France or Germany. To them everything looked the same, but one minute we'd be saying, "gratzi" and the next, "merci" or "danke."

The first morning in Sweden, I had one of those moments. Not only do Swedes love a great cup of coffee, they make it in coffee pots and drink it leisurely from mugs. I no longer had to feel like a dork just because I wanted to savour and not slam my coffee. It felt like home away from home.

Spring had come to Sweden and Peder decided to break out the BBQ for the season. North American BBQs run on propane but across Europe everyone uses charcoal bricks. Every time I commented on the difference, I was told the bricks were more natural and made the meat taste better. After being sold this bill of goods, I watched with amusement as Peder dumped a bag of synthetically manufactured black bricks in the bottom of the BBQ and proceeded to empty a half litre of lighter fluid trying to get them lit.

Landskrona is located down on the southern end of Sweden on the stretch of water that connects the Baltic and the North Sea. You can easily look across the water and see Denmark.

It was a gorgeous spring day; the country was coming alive and the air was filled with the sweet scent of things growing. The ocean was brilliant blue as we hiked along the cliffs to a green meadow where we spread out picnic blankets and had fika. Fika is a Swedish coffee break that involves sweet breads and delicious, dark roast coffee.

We hadn't hung out with another family for months, so it was awesome when Peder took the next day off work so we could head into the Tropikariet, an indoor animal sanctuary located in Helsingborg. It was like walking onto the set of a movie as the structure allowed us to walk right into rooms with the animals as lemurs and monkeys swung around our heads.

That night Peder and I took Zion, Riel, Joel, and Amelie into the aquatic centre in Landskrona. It was a really cool facility with bridges and walkways and a climbing wall on the side of the pool where you could climb to the top and then let go and plunge into the water.

While being painfully aware of my many overblown eccentricities, I try not to be entirely governed by them. I chose this night to face my germophobia head-on and sat in the hot tub with Riel. My skin crawls at the thought of entering public hot tubs. To me they're just cauldrons of roiling bum juice and bellybutton lint. To enter the water at all took a sheer force of will and determination.

I glanced at the two submerged men in the tub as their disembodied heads bobbed in the swirling foam. They didn't seem any more disgusting than any other stranger I'd climb into a tub with. But I had barely sat down when the guy to my left stood up. He was wearing a shag rug on his back and the pile just kept getting thicker and richer the further south it grew. He started playing a syncopated rhythm on his hairy gut with his big meaty palms that smacked like seal flippers, pap, pap a dap, dap, tat, tat.

At that EXACT moment, his friend pulled one of his feet out of the water, held it up in front of his face and started cleaning goo out from between his toes and flicking whatever he found into the water. I threw up a little bit in my mouth as I scrambled for high ground.

I was standing outside the women's change room waiting for Riel when she came out shaking her head dramatically. "That change room was disgusting," she stated emphatically with a grimace. "All those women walked around naked ... and they have all hit puberty!"

I was still laughing when I got to the car, which made Zion want to know what was going on. When I told him he turned to Riel and said, "That's going to happen to you too Riel ... it's going to hit you right in the crotch!"

I marked this conversation down as a homeschooling health class taught by a guest instructor.

Legoland is one of Zion and Riel's favourite memories. It was epic! It was amazing!

The Scandinavian Centipede is Closer Than It Appears

We arrived in Stockholm, capital city of Sweden. Stockholm is built on fourteen islands connected by fifty-seven bridges. It's an incredible archipelago with over 30,000 islands. After all the relatives on Zara's side of the family that we've stayed with, Sweden is the first time my extended family made an appearance.

My grandfather immigrated to Canada from Sweden and my grandmother from Norway, so Scandinavia is the land of my ancestors. Though our surname has always been pronounced Leaf, no one ever got that from the Swedish spelling of Leuf, so my dad legally changed his last name before I was born. Heading up to Stockholm was my first opportunity to visit the Leuf clan as we made our way to Christer and Lena's place in Järfälla. Christer and my Dad are cousins, but I honestly have no idea if that makes me a second cousin or once removed.

We started our first day with a great Swedish breakfast at about 9:00 a.m. It was Scandinavian fare with toast, flat and hard breads, cheese, marmalade, tomatoes, and some ham. I didn't realize Zara and I were raising carnivores, but any time meat is included at a meal they attack it with passion, in this case gobbling up all of the ham set out for everyone at the table. Distinctly absent from the menu were the processed sugar cereals so common back home. I was having one of those delusional moments as a parent, when you believe that your children actually share your values and lifestyle choices, like abstaining from highly refined sugary breakfast cereals. Of course no sooner had I patted myself on the back for being such an amazing father than I was sent to the grocery store to buy some frigging Honey Nut Cheerios. For about a half hour, I was an awesome Dad.

Christer drove us to the station and we hopped on the train into Stockholm. We were heading to the Vasa Museum. I found it fascinating that this Scandinavian culture with its Viking heritage and reputation for sailing all over the world wreaking havoc and mayhem also has one of the most incredible nautical faux pas in naval history.

On August 10, 1628, a sixty-four-gun warship christened the Vasa sank in the Stockholm harbour on its maiden voyage. It didn't even sail 1500 metres before it rolled over and plunged to the bottom. Three hundred and thirty-three years later, they managed to raise the ship from the sea floor, making it the only fully intact 17th century ship that has ever been salvaged. We watched a historic video in the theatre that really set the stage before the official English tour started.

I was just getting my Flip out of my pocket when the tour guide walked by me. She was an imposing woman, easily as tall as I am, with the shoulders of a linebacker. Then she opened her mouth and announced the tour was starting. It was such a deeply resonant manly voice that I immediately thought I was experiencing first-hand some of that world-renowned progressive Swedish culture where museums openly hire cross-dressing tour guides. In the end, she was all woman, except maybe her vocal chords. At one point Christer leaned over to me and said, "I never realized that we actually *can* sound like the Swedish Chef on the Muppets."

From the museum we took the ferry to Gamla Stan, Stockholm's old town, and one of the best-preserved medieval city centres in the world. Gamla Stan was built during the 1300s and we spent hours walking through the buildings and neighbourhoods older than our country. A personal highlight for me was the monument of Saint George and the Dragon. If you're like me, and grew up being dragged to church in North America, you really need to get out and see the awesome stuff in churches around the world.

The Cathedral of Stockholm, called Storkyrkan, was consecrated in 1306. All the royal weddings and coronations take place there, and thousands of people are buried under the church. The 15th century statue of St. George and the Dragon depicts an armoured knight who has run his lance through the dragon and with his raised sword is about to deliver a killing blow. Hanging from a chain around his neck is a box, supposedly containing St. George's bones.

The dragon is lying on its back surrounded by odds and sods of consumed body parts while the dragon's offspring are crawling among the rubble. The dragon is bisexual with male and female naughty bits, symbolizing evil can multiply on its own. The dragon's one foreleg is clutching the broken lance, while the hind leg is pushing on the horse's belly. The fact that this is in a church is just awesome!

It was an idyllic beautiful spring day as we sat and drank cappuccinos in Stortorget, the oldest square in Gamla Stan, while Christer told us the story of the Stockholm massacre that took place in this very square back in 1520.

The kids have begun to realize there are never any stories about a group of citizens that gathered to pet fuzzy bunnies and bake cookies together. It's always massacres and beheadings and famines and the storming of gates with ensuing atrocities. Kind of makes a guy hope that we can live in a time when nothing much happens.

Our second day at Christer and Lena's was Valborgsmässoafton, the holiday with a million dollar name. The Swedish King, Carl XVI Gustaf is turning 60, but the holiday isn't really about him. Valborgsmässoafton is named after a nun named "Valborg" who was made a saint on May 1, 779, and this date carries her name in the Swedish calendar. Viking fertility celebrations took place around April 30 and due to Valborg being declared a saint at that time of year, her name became associated with the celebrations. Valborg was worshipped in the same way that Vikings had celebrated spring and as they spread throughout Europe, the two dates became mixed together.

Across Sweden people gather in the evening on Valborgsmässoafton to light large bonfires, and sing songs of spring. By the time we arrived, the sun had set behind the hills leaving us to walk through the forest illuminated by a bluish, dusky half-light. It was early spring, so the trees were still free of leaves and foliage. As we made our way through the woods, we could hear a chorus of male voices singing. It sounded like a choir of Dwarves from Moria.

Eventually we discovered the clearing where a men's choir was singing traditional spring songs. A huge bonfire had just been lit. The chorus of voices singing and chattering in a sing-songy Swedish lilt, the crisp clear spring air and the smell of wood smoke and crackling branches created a mystical vibe. Riel was enamoured with a little longhaired pocket puppy sporting ribbons and bows in national colours while Zion and I picked out the guys in charge of the fireworks. No matter where you go in the world it's the guys in army jackets with ponytails who like to blow things up.

The next day Christer dropped us off and we caught the train to Central Station and met his brother Pelle. It was May Day, and there were demonstrations going on in different parts of Stockholm as political parties and workers' groups protested. Pelle took us by the Drottningholm Palace, the private residence of the Swedish royal family, before taking us for a drive through the countryside.

Pelle is one of those drivers who is aware that he is driving at his own pace, and feels no compulsion to conform to those around him. As we wound our way along the narrow country road I watched the line of cars in the rearview mirror grow like a Scandinavian centipede. I loved it when Pelle acknowledged the traffic jam by simply saying, "I like my speed."

We eventually made our way back to Järfälla where Christer and Lena organized a family reunion. We had an awesome time meeting distant rellies and partying together as guitars were passed around and we all took turns sharing songs. As the sun began to set and the temperature started to drop, we moved inside and gathered around the piano. I took up a spot at the back of the room with Christer and Lena's daughter Johanna and her partner Jonas, as we joked and commented on the scene before us. Perhaps thinking that the Canadians were being left out because they'd been singing in Swedish someone asked me for a request. I thought ABBA would be the great unifier, which is when the wheels really jumped the tracks and everything fell apart in a heap of unknown chords and lyrics. ABBA wept.

Zion was chowing down on the food but later that night discovered that he's allergic to avocado. Wanting to describe his ordeal in dramatic terms, he mistakenly assumed that because it sounded like diarrhea, it also meant something like diarrhea and pronounced, "That's the last time I eat avocado. I got wicked gonorrhea!"

The next day we headed south, about five hours from Stockholm to Smaland, to the Kingdom of Crystal. Hand blown glass has been made in Sweden since the 1700s. To retain their distinct identity in the changing world market, around a dozen glasswork studios and a handful of municipalities joined together to create a singular brand called Kosta Boda. We reserved a room at a hostel in Langjaso for 520,000 Krs, which at roughly 52 Euros was the cheapest accommodations we'd found in Europe. We arrived to find that renting sheets for the night equaled the price of the room, so we spent the next hour driving around Emmaboda searching for someone who spoke enough English to help us buy sheets. Charades ensued.

In the morning, we headed out to watch the glassblowers at work in Afors, Orrefors, Kosta, and Maleras. This was a magic day, and we wished we'd known more about the Kingdom of Crystal because we would have spent days in the area. The different studios are located just down the road from each other, so once you're there, you can easily jump from studio to studio. We had no idea what artists could do with glass and were just mesmerized. This was the only place on our entire trip we broke the rules and bought something to bring home.

Historically, when the glassblowers went home, workers, hunters and transients (Zion calls them rubbies) would gather in the glassworks for Hyttsill, which means, herring in the foundry. Salted herring would be fried in the pipe where during the day finished glassware had been cooling. You can still experience Hyttsill in Grasriket and enjoy trays of crispy pork, isterband sausage, baked potatoes, lingonberry jam, and Smaland curd cake. Long tables are set out as food is heated up in the large furnace, while musicians sing songs and tell stories. We didn't know any of this before we got there. For our next trip to Sweden, we're packing some sheets and spending a week.

The Rampage of Tintin the Terrible

We arrived in Helsingborg in time for dinner and my second musical reunion. When I toured Sweden in 1996, I stayed with Hakan and Margaretta. After a week of rehearsals and shows, we had a day off and Hakan and Margaretta and Peder and Tina and a few other musicians decided to take the Canadians to the beach for the day.

As soon as we got to the ocean, I was drawn by the sound of the surf pounding on the rocky shore. I took off across a rocky area jumping from boulder to boulder as I made my way down to the shore. Looking out I was totally in awe of the majestic beauty and vastness of creation. I was lost in worshipful revelry when I glanced over to my left, and there not thirty feet away were about a dozen buck-naked Swedish women ... all over the age of 65. (Zion's eyes are not the only ones that have been burned out of their sockets.)

The Swedes were all giggling when I got back.

"Ya Rik, that part of the beach is for women. They don't really like it when men go there," Hakan said as they all laughed.

In the intervening years since I've seen them, Hakan and Margaretta had produced three beautiful kids, Jonatan, Frieda, and Julia. We had a reunion over dinner catching up on the last thirteen years. The next day their kids were in school and Hakan and Margaretta both went to work, so I worked on songs while Zara and Riel watched the *Vampire Diaries* on the laptop.

Hakan's company has season's tickets for the local soccer team who were having a great season. They happened to be playing that night and Hakan invited me to tag along. Like many Swedes, Hakan towers above me at 6'7". We met outside his office where he came striding out in his suit with a bright red sport cap perched on his head. I felt like a little kid again trying to keep up to my dad's impossibly long strides. On the way, Hakan shared some of the dangers of international expansion. When his company opened a branch in Asia they had to change their company name because the literal translation from Swedish meant 'go f#% yourself'.

"If we not change the name, we get no business," he added rather unnecessarily.

It was a fun night, although in all honesty, I thought European soccer fans always got pissed up, sang dirty songs and beat the crap out of each other. While the drunken violence was non-existent the sweet buns and Zoégas they served for fika was delicious.

I managed to get the winning goal on film and used it for the end of *Zion & Riel - Sweden*.

On Saturday we drove up to Hakan and Margaretta's cabin. It was one of the few times we hung out with another family with kids close to Zion and Riel's age. We spent the afternoon bowling and strolling along the harbour before heading back to the cabin for an incredible salmon supper. After an awesome day we drove back to Helsingborg, but when we got back to the house all hell broke loose as Tintin the Terrible, the family's dog, went on a rampage. The kids were all watching a movie when we suddenly heard growling, barking, and a shriek from one of the girls. This was followed immediately by crying and parents running through the house, some incomprehensible yelling in Swedish. It was nail-biting drama all the way. For reasons unknown he had bitten Frieda and I figured his days were numbered when Hakan stopped midstride and stared at me and said, "I cannot have this terrible Tintin in my house anymore!"

Tintin had transformed Hakan into a no-s#% Swede. While their family was preoccupied with tending to the injured, Riel had grabbed a laptop and crawled into her bed to watch the *Vampire Diaries*, an adolescent soap opera that seesaws between kissing and killing in a PG-13 sort of way.

The show was Riel's double-edged sword. The vampires weren't too scary, just scary enough, but it was all the kissing that really grossed her out. At a prudish nine years of age, Riel felt this was disgusting behaviour and would always throw her hands up in front of her face.

While the rest of her family yelled at Tintin and tended to her injured sister, six-year-old Julia scooted into the room and crawled under the covers with Riel, who promptly shut the movie down and closed the laptop, rolled over and pretended to go to sleep until Julia left. After she was gone, Riel looked up and said, "I turned it off, because it was totally inappropriate for her!" She paused before adding, "I'm nine and it's inappropriate for me ... but I still like it."

From Sweden, we planned to make our way to Switzerland for a second family wedding. It was going to be a reunion of sorts as many of the rellies at Matthew and Kelly's wedding in Malaysia would be at this wedding.

We decided not to book a hotel in advance and figure it out along the way. So we just started driving, until we hit Hannover where we hit the mother of all traffic jams. My under-the-breath exasperated muttering was suddenly shattered by a teeth-rattling belch from the backseat. "Don't worry, everyone," Zion announced, "it will smell like strawberries, chocolate and fruit punch, and maybe beef jerky and dill pickle chips."

"A winning combination," Zara responded as she searched for an opening in traffic, "where's the food network when you need them."

So we took the first off-ramp and made our way down a random road to some little hamlet with a huge hotel where the guy in charge spoke just enough English to tell me that they weren't open. He pointed down the road where we found another hotel where the woman in charge spoke even less English; in fact, she didn't speak any at all. It felt like a reward challenge on Survivor with accommodations on the line.

I threw myself into the performance of a lifetime, creating rich visual textures through expansive hand gestures and animated facial contortions. I believe I was able to communicate volumes about myself as a person and my journey of discovery as a human being. I think the diorama I made out of toothpicks and creamers sealed the deal.

The bartender managed to communicate that the room I'd just rented wasn't actually attached to the pub. I also knew as I walked out of the pub that my family was going to sit in the car mocking me as I walked in circles trying to figure out where the room was. So I insisted Zara get out and help me.

If you happen to have an attractive six-foot blonde at your disposal, you have one of the most powerful resources on the planet when it comes to enlisting the aid of male bystanders. Before we knew it, a group of guys were directing us to where we needed to go.

We finally found the guesthouse and a small, cramped, little cubbyhole of a room with two single beds that smelled like dirty socks and armpits. It was our Hannover home for the night. I enlisted Zion and Riel as my co-conspirators and we broke into a linen cupboard in the lobby and borrowed a bunch of sheets, towels and blankets, and made nests for the kids on the floor. It was one of those hilarious nights when overcoming some adverse circumstances bonded us together. We laughed and joked until we cried, blowing off steam with a voracious wrestling/tickling match.

In the morning I woke up with my face about a foot from Zion's. As I lay there, he opened his eyes, looked at me for about ten seconds and said, "From now on I only want to be referred to as Fuzzle." We lay in bed giggling until we eventually woke up Zara and Riel who told us we sucked for being so loud.

When we finally got organized and continued on our way to Rothenburg, Switzerland, traffic on the autobahn was heavy. We thought we'd fly through Germany at the speed of sound and wondered why all the drivers weren't at work. At a gas station, we discovered it was Ascension Day, the holiday that celebrates the 40th day since Easter and the day Jesus ascended to heaven. Which means it's been 40 days since we explored the glorious array of magnificent fermentation in Arona, Italy.

We thought we'd fly through Germany at the speed of sound and wondered why all the drivers weren't at work. At a gas station, we discovered it was Ascension Day, the holiday that celebrates the 40th day since Easter and the day Jesus ascended to heaven.

In Sweden the family travels from Landskrona to Stockholm to the Kingdom of Crystal, where internationally renowned glassblowers blow their minds.

SWITZERLAND/
GERMANY

One Man's Coffee Break is Another Woman's Vagina

We arrived in the tiny little village of Rothenburg for another wedding. Back in Malaysia, we'd partied with Zara's Aunt Jojo at Matthew and Kelly's wedding.

Jojo has more energy for adventure than almost anyone I've ever met, and we were excited to meet up with her again. Celebrating her daughter's wedding was as good a reason as any as far as we were concerned. We were staying at the Chaernsmatt Hotel, which seemed part hostel, part hotel, possibly run by a taxidermist. I don't know what else could explain the large display case filled with stuffed woodland creatures.

Rothenburg is a little hamlet. The hotel shut down at 7:00 p.m. and the staff went home. There was no one at the front desk, the restaurant was closed, and our room key was the only thing that would get us back into the building. Because it was a holiday weekend pretty much everything else in the village was shut as well. God help you if you arrived without a car and wanted supper, and that is exactly what was happening to numerous wedding guests. But eventually we were reunited with Amanda who arrived from Italy, Chris and Katherine came from England, and Peter and Christine from Australia.

The next morning we walked into Rothenburg with Amanda to buy some clothes for the wedding and pick up some food. Riel bought some funky Gothchic sandals. Admiring herself in the mirror she said, "I like them; they're my style … with a hint of elegantness."

We found a great little Swiss bakery. Still coming down off

my Swedish sweet bread, cross cultural experience, I suggested it would be a great time for a little fika.

"What did you just say?" Amanda exclaimed, blushing ever so slightly. "Fika," I replied excitedly, "cause I love fika, can't get enough, fika, fika, fika, ummmm, yummy and delicious fika."

I remember smacking my lips and lolling my tongue dramatically in my profession of undying devotion to fika.

Amanda looked around uncomfortably. "Yeah ... um, in Italian, fica is a dirty word for ah," she paused, looking at Zion and Riel, trying to figure out how best to proceed, "a woman's ... you know, hoo-ha, her pookie, her secret grotto."

She took our stunned silence for lack of comprehension and inexplicably continued.

"It's another word for a woman's punani, her jiggly puff, pooh bear, you know, her little lady, come on you guys, a Va Jay Jay, you know, clunge, minge, for God's sake, her fanny!"

Up to this point, the kids thought Amanda was listing off cartoon characters, but their British roots had familiarized them with the 'F' word.

Zion coughed juice out of his nose and Riel scrunched her face up and said, "Eww, gross."

My first thought was that it is no wonder there's been so much war and conflict in human history. For all we know the Vikings started out as a bunch of adventuresome guys who liked sailing and coffee breaks with sweet bread. Maybe one day they ran into a group of Italians and in the process of inviting them for a coffee break ended up saying something inappropriate about some guy's girlfriend.

One man's coffee break is another woman's vagina.

The next day a mixer was planned for all the wedding guests. We filed into what seemed like a turret from an ancient stone castle, passing under a number of stuffed witches on brooms hanging from giant wooden beams. We climbed a staircase to the second floor where long tables were set out around the perimeter of the room. The wedding is in Switzerland, the groom's side is German and the bride's English. I can't help feeling like the mixer is actually some ambitious geopolitical statement. Guests are encouraged to mingle and get to know each other, but after my performance art piece trying to get a hotel room in Hannover, I know just how flexible a person needs to be to cross the language barrier.

I'm listening to the chatter around me when Riel pulls on my sleeve. I look down as she whispers, "I don't want this," pointing to her plate.

I almost let out a startled yelp when I see what looks like a grey phallic sausage with yellow spit-up sauce on her plate.

"Where the frig did you get that?" I asked, slightly nauseous.

"Someone gave it to me when I was looking for juice," she said. We managed to pawn it off on one of the other cousins when he wasn't looking.

The next day was the wedding. It was a cold, overcast spring day as we filed into the old brick church. There was a guy who kind of played the bagpipes warming up. The combination of the incredibly resonant brick building and the tendency of the piper to hit the odd note sharp and flat started to make my right eye twitch. To distract myself I tried to take in the décor. That is when I actually noticed the giant statues of the Mother Mary with swords plunged into her chest. The largest statue that hung on the wall right above us depicted seven swords all plunged deep into her chest.

I've said it before but seriously you just never know what you're going to see in a European church. On our way back to the hotel the day before, Riel and I were walking along when she noticed a crucifix. She'd noticed that sometimes the cross has a guy on it, and sometimes it doesn't, and she wanted to know why. I told her it was because we kept popping back and forth from Catholic to Protestant countries. Of course that led to the dreaded question, "What is the difference between Catholics and Protestants?"

For the first time in my life, I wished my kids just wanted to talk about where babies come from. We were just starting to get into it as we entered our hotel room, catching Zion and Zara up into our conversation.

"Well, they both believe in the same God, they use the same Bible, and basically believe about 98% of the same stuff," I said.

"But the 2% they disagree on has been enough to want to kill each other for 2000 years," Zara concluded.

In an attempt to make this historic enmity comprehensible on a personal scale, I told them that at one point Zara with her Catholic upbringing and me with my Protestant roots would have made our getting married a scandalous outrage. Without missing a beat, Zion combined an amalgam of medieval folklore and horror genre mythology to sum up his religious conclusion, "So basically … you're a lycan and mom is a vampire."

As he buried his head back in the Lego bin, I thought it was the most productive conversation about religion our family has ever had.

I marked it down in the homeschooling journal as religious studies.

At the wedding reception Riel took off to play with a new little friend, abandoning Zion who was incredulous he'd been seated at the kids table. Auntie Amanda to the rescue. Seeing his plight Amanda waved Zion over to the twenty-something's table. As the reception plodded on, Zion kept his table thoroughly entertained as he transformed the desserts and decor into a Gummy Bear Massacre. Some Gummy Bears were strangling, while others were drowning in cups. Some had their heads burned in candles while forks stabbed others and a giant spoon crushed one unfortunate little duffer.

The longer the reception went on the worse I started to feel. Knowing I was coming down with something, we enlisted Zara's cousin Shaun to ferry us back to the hotel. By the time I got back to the room, I was feeling positively awful. Zara and the kids were already there and were in the process of trying to figure out where some really loud creepy music was coming from. It sounded like big band music and it was resonating through the hotel. We finally determined that it was coming from the room above us. I slogged my way up the stairs where I realized most of the third floor of the hotel was actually one gigantic suite.

I knocked on the door politely at first. Then more insistent, finally I progressed to full-on bastard knocking. But no one came to the door no matter how much of a bastard I was. I slunk back to my room in a sick and surly mood and crawled back into bed. I was just about to drift off to sleep when Zara mused aloud that it was actually kind of disturbing.

"I hope someone's not being killed or assaulted up there."

It took a couple of milliseconds for that seed to take root in my imaginative subconscious and bloom into a full-blown psychotic conviction. It was actually so obvious I couldn't believe I'd missed it. The closed doors, the absence of staff, the display case filled with stuffed dead animals. Floor three probably had its own grisly display case of international people groups and nationalities.

So back up the stairs I went, starting this time in full-on bastard mode and moving quickly into incensed, self-righteous rage. I fell into a syncopated rhythm, BOOM, BOOM, BOOM, "Oh come on!" BOOM, BOOM, "This is asinine!"

It was kind of meditative and after a few repetitive minutes I sort of zoned out, so I'm not exactly sure how long I pounded. Eventually I gave up and went to bed. Fifteen minutes later the music suddenly stopped. Lying there in the throes of sickness steeped in the eerie quiet, our room illuminated by the flickering bluish silver light from Zara's laptop, I fell asleep watching the ceiling, waiting for blood to start pooling in the stipple.

A Callous Cad & a Brood of Dirty-Faced Street Urchins

Last night we arrived at castle Rohrsdorf outside Dresden, Germany. It was a seven-hour drive from Rothenburg, Switzerland. Both Zion and I are sick for the first time since leaving home. I think the rain, feeling like crap and too many WWII movies tainted my mind and projected an oppressive pallor over Deutschland.

I admitted to Zion and Riel I really didn't know what we were going to find. I'd made this contact through a friend of a friend before we left home. Telling the kids it was a castle didn't conjure any romantic notions of medieval times; it just made them think of the 200-year old scary asylum barn I tried to get them to sleep in when we were in New Zealand.

"If it's sick and gross we're going to go stay at a hotel though, right?" Zion asked, in a way that said, I'm not asking, I'm telling you.

I stood outside in the rain ringing the doorbell of a dark forbidding-looking old hotel while the family stayed in the car watching. I rang a few times and was just starting to give up hope that this day was going to have a happy ending when a woman's voice came over the little speaker, "Guten Tag."

Uh oh. What if they don't speak English? I inexplicably started uttering partial sentences in broken English in a confused attempt to be more easily understood. Thankfully, the woman on the other end cut me off.

"Is this Rik Leaf ? OK, yah. We'll be right down."

I gave the old thumbs up signal to the family, who climbed out of the car so we could make a united front.

Arno and Dani live in the old hotel in Rohrsdorf with their two kids, Lena and Levi, and a small community of artists. The place was deserted; it was like the Overlook Hotel in *The Shining*, without Jack Nicholson trying to kill us. A wealthy Christian from North America had bought the hotel a few years earlier. I have no idea why, or to what end, nor did I give two hoots, as we were ushered into a fabulously deserted old hotel.

Arno gave us a tour, starting with the massive commercial kitchen where he told us to use anything we'd like. The dining room area, the bar, the meeting rooms across the lobby, everything was vacant and empty. We walked up the long, wide stone stairs, covered in blood red carpet. We followed Arno down a hallway of empty rooms, where he had one for Zara and me and one for Zion and Riel.

In spite of the spacious accommodations, we ended up all crawling into the big queen bed and watching *The Olympians* together on the laptop.

For the next three days, it rained and we hardly went anywhere. At this point in our trip, we were collectively exhausted. When you go on a vacation for a week, you can keep up a manic pace of activity. But if you're living a nomadic life, there are times you just need to veg and not go anywhere or do anything, like you would at home, if you had one.

We basically stayed in bed, read books, and watched movies. The kids, of course, turned their room into a Lego repository. Doing nothing felt like heaven; no pressure to go anywhere, do anything or see anyone. At night, the kids would freak themselves out by exploring the abandoned hotel. They would venture out into the pitch-black hallway that was equipped with motion-sensitive lights that would come on just in front of them as they walked. We'd hear them whispering in the hall, then a squeal and a shriek followed by running footsteps ending with a slamming door and muffled laughter. It was eerie enough without Jack, and if we weren't so committed to doing nothing, we would have filmed another horror movie.

My cousin Rob lives in Heidelberg. He grew up in Japan but spent most of his adult life living in Germany. It had been at least fifteen years since I'd seen him. But when he knew we were in Germany, he said he had to make the trip to hook up with us. Arno was in the process of giving me a tour of the facility and the recording studio when someone came in to tell me I had a visitor. I walked out into the courtyard where a vaguely familiar face split into a huge grin and started talking a hundred miles an hour.

"Hey cuz, what's up! Holy shiza, I've been driving in circles for the last couple of hours. I couldn't find this place and I was like, WTF, you know! But now I'm here so it's all good ... man, it's been a long time!"

We decided to visit Prague the next day. We weren't allowed to take our Europcar rental into the Czech Republic, so we jumped into Rob's car and were already inside the Czech Republic before we even knew it.

With only one day to explore and no contacts we had no choice, we had to be tourists in Prague. We walked along the famous bridge that crosses the River Vltava. Started in 1357 by King Charles IV, the bridge was finished in the early 1400s. The bridge really captured Zion's imagination and he bought a painting of the Charles Bridge from a local artist.

From there we wandered over to the Old Town Bridge Tower, a beautiful Gothic tower guarding one end of Charles Bridge. The ancient gate was completed in 1380 and was originally built to protect the Old Town against northern invaders. The gate was partially destroyed by a failed attempt of marauding Swedes in 1648. (Probably just invited the wrong guy for fika.) Advertised as the largest gastronomic event in the country, the Czech Beer Festival kicked off the day we were in Prague. In an attempt to embrace the cross-cultural culinary experience, I lined up and bought some gigantic BBQ sausages and large pints of beer, which assured our guts were gurgling participants in the gastronomic event.

When we got back to Dresden, Arno and Dani had scored us tickets to a concert at the Dresden Frauenkirche, where a member of their community of artists was performing. For over 200 years, the church's distinctive dome had filled the city's skyline, but during the Allied bombing at the end of WWII, it was destroyed. For almost fifty years, the church lay in a pile of rubble in the middle of the city, but the residents weren't about to let the sanctuary slip quietly into history. The bricks from the rubble were catalogued and used to rebuild the structure with new bricks added where necessary. I kept sliding down in my seat so I could stare up at the bell-shaped interior as music resonated from every fibre of that magnificent building.

The next morning we were eating breakfast in the empty dining room when Arno walked in and started peppering us with stories of living in Germany at the end of the cold war. When I asked him what actually happened to finally bring down the Berlin Wall, he smiled and said, "It was a mistake."

On November 9, 1989 the East German government decided to introduce new travel regulations that would let East Berliners travel to the West. The original press release included a condition that travel would depend on citizens being granted official permission by the GDR. Günter Schabowski, the bureau member in charge of delivering the press release, apparently decided at the last minute to remove the word "permission" from the press release. People knew how easily permission could be denied and Schabowski was worried the public would freak out. At the press conference, a journalist asked when the new policy would become effective. Schabowski mistakenly declared it was effective immediately. Within hours, tens of thousands of Berliners flooded checkpoints demanding to be let through. The border guards didn't know anything about Schabowski's press conference and no one wanted to take responsibility for a possible blood bath, so eventually the guards opened the gate and stood back and let history fade into the future. Politicians never seem more productive than when they're unprepared.

Arno had us on the edge our seats as he described moving to Dresden at the end of the cold war. The people in charge were gone and for a period of time no one really replaced them. It was the Wild West.

Arno set up a shop selling radios and TVs and other electronic things out of an apartment he shared with a bunch of people. One day a biker named Olli came in, looked around and asked Arno if he had any electronics that didn't work. Arno pointed to a stack in the corner. Olli promptly picked up the lot and disappeared. A few days later he returned with the merchandise repaired and announced they were going into a partnership. Eventually they opened a shop, but one day when they came to work everything was gone. They'd been cleaned out in the night. Like the storyline for a TV show, Olli put his feelers out on the street and a couple of days later had located their merchandise. When they broke in to steal their stuff back, they discovered a virtual armoury and a basement full of automatic weapons. This obviously meant really bad people had stolen from them and by stealing their stuff back, they were really opening a can of whoop-ass. Sure enough, a few days later a guy came in the store waving a gun around wanting to know how they'd gotten everything back. Olli burst in kicking ass and taking names.

The morning flew by on the wings of Arno's stories, and made me wish I could make a documentary about his life.

It was Zara's birthday and the crew at castle Rohrsdorf whipped up a kicking party. The immense kitchen was buzzing with activity. When I asked Arno if there was anything I could do, he steered me toward the BBQ. I was given so much beef I could barely fit it all on the grill. He came around the corner moments later and exclaimed happily, "Oh, what a beautiful sight. That must be half a cow's ass!"

Ronald and Girt are another couple in the community. We'd spent a few minutes talking with Ronald earlier in the week, hearing his stories of growing up in East Germany and where he was when the wall came down. He told Zara he had a birthday gift for her as he dug down into his army pants and pulled out a piece of the Berlin Wall that he'd smashed off as an eighteen year old. It even had some graffiti on it. Just before we left I managed to post *Zion & Riel – Prague & Germany.*

The next day we bade our new friends "Auf Wiedersehen", and drove nine-and-a-half hours to the "City of Light". We've spent months learning to travel in a way that's best for us and decided we'd give ourselves one day to see and do as much as we could in Paris. Armed with a pocket-size tourist map and our GPS, we headed into the centre of the city.

We wandered in the pouring rain in the general direction of Notre Dame, picking up French pastries and chatting about Quasi Motto, Esmeralda, Captain Phoebus, and Frollo on the way.

After Notre Dame, we walked the five kilometres to the Eiffel Tower, guided through the mist by our trusty GPS. On the soggy walk along the river, I distracted the kids with the gory details from the movie *American Werewolf in Paris*.

At the beginning of the film, three American adrenalin junkies sneak up the Eiffel Tower in the middle of the night so one of them can bungee jump from the top. At the top, they see a young French woman climb onto the rail preparing to jump to her death. Just as the young hero reaches to pull her down, she jumps and he jumps after her. He manages to grab her ankle on the way down and the bungee stretches to within a few feet of the grass where he lets go, gently depositing her safe and sound. At that point, everyone pretty much turns into a werewolf or a snack.

When we got to the base of the tower we were literally besieged by manic street hustlers trying to pawn off some of the cheapest tourist tack we'd seen. One lady followed me relentlessly across the entire length of the square pleading, "Please, please. PLEASE!," getting louder and louder with each step. She managed to inject a heartbroken quiver into her voice that made it sound as if she was on the verge of an emotional breakdown. Which made me feel like the callous cad who was walking out and leaving her to raise our brood of dirty-faced street urchins on her own. She was tugging on my jacket and screaming so loudly that I was tempted to play my part with all my heart and soul and yell, "Leave me, be woman. I'm a wild Stallion and need to run free!"

By the time I had extricated myself from the rabid thespian, I discovered Riel looking up at the tower with a look of abject horror. She turned and said, "I am way too afraid of heights to go up there."

Suddenly I was the one pleading, "Please, please. PLEASE!"

I tried to bribe her with pastries, chocolate, ponies, and puppies. In the end, generous heapings of helpful praise and encouragement were needed to coax our frightened foal onto the elevator. Riel also knows how to play a role, and kept in her shell-shocked character for the entire time we were at the top lest I forget her due rewards.

We'd badgered Zion all year to bring his camera and use it. The Eiffel Tower was one of the few times I remember him using it. I came up beside him as he was taking pictures when he turned, "This is one of the highlights of the entire trip for me," he said excitedly. "I never thought I'd ever be standing on top of the Eiffel Tower."

The next day we were scheduled to fly from Charles de Gaulle to the Luton airport north of London. I used Skype to call Europcar to see if we could change our drop off location from the downtown address to the airport. The other three sat on the beds in the hotel room snickering into their pillows as they listened to my comedic conversation with the French attendant.

"Bonjour, Europcar," a woman said.

"Hello, my name is Rik and I am scheduled to return my car today," I said. "Non!"the attendant replied forcefully.

"Excuse me?" I said, unsure what exactly she was disagreeing with. "Yes. OK," she continued.

"I'm scheduled to return my rental to the downtown location and wondered if I could return it to the Charles de Gaulle airport?" I asked.

"Non!" she shouted. "You are not scheduled to return the car to the airport." "Yeah, I know. That's why I'm calling. I just wondered if I could change it because it would just be so much more convenient," I explained.

"Non!" she shouted again. Before I could ask if there was any way she could reconsider, she concluded adamantly, "Oui, yes. OK, no problem."

I had no idea if this was a French thing, a French female thing, or a Europcar France thing.

We spent our last day in continental Europe kicking around the Charles de Gaulle airport waiting for our flight to the U.K. It felt like we'd spent two amazing months climbing around in history books. I sometimes find myself staring off into space thinking about Bernini's sculptures in Rome or the glassblowers in Sweden and the fact that we have a chunk of the Berlin Wall in the bottom of a backpack. Zion and Riel still get jittery when they talk about Legoland in Denmark.

England is our last stop. Flying into Luton was a great idea. It's small and easy to navigate. We grabbed our shuttle bus, picked up our little Peugeot and drove through the beautiful windy road to the Bell Inn & Pub. After two months of traveling in Italy, France, Denmark, Sweden, Switzerland, and Germany, it was awesome to be in a country where we spoke the language, even if we were back to driving on the left side of the road.

Prague & Germany is another homage to the wealth of history and cross-cultural exploration.

ENGLAND

Carpet Bombing Brighton's Downtown

Back in 1998, Tribe of One headlined a festival in Toronto, Canada, with a band from England. Paul was the lead singer of that band, and we hit it off like a couple of brothers from other mothers. Through Facebook, Paul and I had reconnected. When he found out we were coming to the UK, he invited us to come stay at their place in Shoreham-by-Sea. We happened to arrive on a weekend when Paul's family had made plans to be away, but he invited us to stay at their place anyway.

In 2000, when Zion was three-and-a-half years old and Zara was pregnant with Riel, we spent six weeks touring in the U.K. On that tour we made a day trip to the Brighton Pier. The Pier was developed back in 1899 as an entertainment attraction and is a whirlwind of colour and sound with games, and rides, cafes and restaurants attracting large crowds.

On that bright summer day back in 2000, something happened to Zion. After spending a bit of time wandering around the pier we started to leave, which is when our happy, content little toddler flipped his proverbial lid. He was screaming, and crying and freaking out and absolutely nothing would console him. This went on for at least forty-five minutes as we walked around downtown, until driven to distraction, I placed my hand on his head and asked God to quiet his spirit.

It was like something out of a deliverance movie. Not only did he immediately quiet down, he promptly fell asleep in his stroller and woke up an hour later back to his normal, happy contented little self. (And no, I didn't have a Chloroform soaked rag in my hand!)

Our family has joked ever since about Zion being possessed by the evil carnival spirits that haunt the Brighton Pier. As we walked onto the pier, Riel was afraid that the spirits of rage and anger would possess her too.

We were on our way back to the car at the end of the day when some jerk s#% all over us … literally. Some random seagull, who had probably pigged out all day on fatty, deep fried foods, discharged a load of mucousy diarrhea, mostly on Riel, who took it personally. Looking at her jacket she exclaimed with uncharacteristic venom, "Wow. Seagulls are dinks!"

All of us were hit in one way or another in the carpet-bombing of Brighton's downtown and headed back to Paul and Sarah's to do a load of laundry.

From Shoreham-by-Sea we headed to Folkestone, enroute to the White Cliffs of Dover. We checked into the Windsor, a crazy old hotel that looked and felt like drunken carpenters with inner ear problems had constructed it.

Over the course of the year, finding accommodations has often felt as if we were playing the lottery. Tickets cost anywhere from $70 to $150 and you really have no way of knowing if you've won or lost until you open the door to your room.

These hallways were narrow, uneven warrens filled with random steps that made it feel like an obstacle course. The steep, creaky, uneven staircase seemed like the safest option compared to the ancient elevator. Only after we were totally underwhelmed by the quality did I search for customer reviews online. As I read out loud we all started to laugh:

"We didn't expect it to be quite so bad. Never again!"

"We all felt unsafe, no smoke alarms, broken floors, windows don't open and no hot running water. It smelt disgusting and rooms were dirty. We left after 30 mins."

"When we reached the hotel, it was so small that we were finding it difficult to even take our luggage to our rooms via the only old century lift in the hotel. The whole atmosphere was suffocating. It was like living in an unsafe place which could catch fire anytime."

Super early in the morning, I'm wakened by the sound of someone rustling around in our room. It takes me a minute to wake up enough to realize that Zara is still sleeping beside me and the kids are both still zonked out in the bed next to us. I try not to move or give any indication I'm awake. As I lie there, my mind races as I try to figure out what I should do. I open my eyes imperceptibly in an effort to see if there is anything I can use as a weapon. I can't see anything and just decide to leap out of bed and confront the intruder. I tense my muscles and jump, landing both feet shoulder width apart on the balls of my feet, arms extended at a 45-degree angle ready to grapple with my adversary. The room appears empty, but I locate the rustling sound behind the curtain. I creep forward ready to bellow like the devil and scare the holy bejezus out of whoever is there. Through the crack, I can see movement. Whoever it is sure isn't trying to be quiet. I yank the curtain and come face to face with the dregs of seagull society; the stupid douche was sitting on the ledge of the open window mowing his way through our groceries.

"Oh, sick! You frigging dink," I whisper under my breath.

I quickly pull the curtains closed and try to push his thieving ass off the ledge, but he keeps hopping from side to side evading my not so subtle suggestion. The confrontation escalates, as I start throwing rabbit punches through the curtains, trying to land combination left and right jabs.

"It's not even five in the morning," I puff hoarsely, trying to evict the intruder without waking up my family.

I finally resort to some awkward ninja kicks and eventually he flies off, leaving our groceries in a disgusting heap. I look up and meet the eyes of an old woman standing on the sidewalk staring at me. I'm wearing my boxers, breathing heavily as I mutter to myself. I shrug my shoulders and wave as she gives a little disgusted shake of her head and keeps walking.

When everyone gets up, I relay the events of the early morning fiasco. The kids beg for a reenactment of the ninja kicks, which they find hilarious. However, the fact that the seagull has eaten their breakfast ham is no laughing matter. As Riel looks out the window, I hear her mutter, "What a dink!"

We're in Folkestone to see the famous White Cliffs of Dover. Julius Caesar mentions them in his account of the Roman invasion in 55 BC. Shakespeare wrote about them in *King Lear*. Robin of Loxley returned to England via these shores in Kevin Costner's *Robin Hood, Prince of Thieves*. For many Brits the White Cliffs are the last thing they see as they leave or the first thing they see on their return to the country.

The chalky white cliffs are over 350 feet high and line the shore at the narrowest part of the English Channel. On a clear day, they can easily be seen from France. Zara's grandfather was a pilot in the RAF and fought in the Battle of Britain, much of which took place over the area. It was a gorgeous spring day, perfect for commandoing to the edge and peering hundreds of feet down to the water. It was one of the first really hot, summery days in England, so we passed many chalky-white Brits as well, pulling off their shirts for the first time all season.

On our way back to the hotel, we discovered a Battle of Britain memorial. Winston Churchill's famous quote greets visitors: "Never was so much owed by so many to so few". As we wandered through the memorial, Zara discovered her Grandfather's name listed among the victorious few.

Known as the "City of Dreaming Spires", Oxford has been a centre of learning for almost a thousand years. The architecture of Oxford's universities includes virtually every English period since the Saxons.

It comes off as a regal city, some might even go so far as to say highfalutin, with all the fancy domes, cobblestones, and colonnades. People from all over the world tour Oxford for its rich intellectual heritage and cultural magnificence.

But that is not the Oxford tour we're going on: our tour is delving deep into the dark corridors of Oxford's seedy underbelly. It is a tour filled with racy stories of spinal injuries, pissed-up young Brits, and crumbling masonry.

We made our way from Dover to spend a few days with Bob, Claire, Annie, and Eddie. We hadn't seen them since the wedding in Malaysia six months ago. We arrived on Sunday afternoon and immediately found ourselves playing cricket in the garden. Zion was back at the wicket bashing balls into the forest just so he could watch the adults chase them. Riel picked up with Annie where they had left off, and the girls disappeared within minutes.

After dinner, Bob took Zara and me into Oxford for a tour. Bob is not only a distinguished British surgeon and accomplished sailor, he is one hell of a tour guide. He kept up an awesome running monologue, though not the kind that would be broadcast on any of the tour buses we passed.

As we crossed the Thames and passed the marker commemorating Roger Bannister's four-minute mile, Bob described the May Day celebration in Oxford. Pubs stay open twenty-four hours and at 6:00 a.m. on Sunday morning, the Magdalen College choir gathers to sing the Hymnus Eucharisticus from the top of Magdalen tower in a 500-year-old tradition. Historically, thousands of people gather on the bridge to listen to the beatific serenade of angelic voices rise toward heaven in rapturous praise. However, over the years, an alarming number of inebriated students jumping off the bridge has marred the performance. The lucky ones hit the middle of the river, but very often revellers miscalculate, and land too close to shore, creating too many spinal injuries too many years in a row. Now they close the bridge. Bob painted a vivid mental picture of the angelic voices drowning in the retching of a thousand pissed-up Brits.

We passed the exam school where many students take their finals. Traditionally, friends wait outside to cover them in eggs and flour when they finish. Apparently, chucking celebratory shite on your friends to honour scholastic achievement is an international rite of passage. Bob told us of one young guy who climbed up on the roof to pour eggs on his girlfriend. Only just as she came out, he slipped and fell, plummeting three stories to the cobblestones where he lay bleeding until a section of masonry broke free, killing him instantly.

Bob wove these twisted tales of woe as we sauntered through manicured lawns and gardens that exuded a palpable superiority.

We were on a liquid tour of Oxford that started at the Bear Pub, included Turf Tavern, and ended up at the Eagle and Child, made famous by the Inklings. We sat at the table under the plaque that reads, "C.S. Lewis, Tolkien, Charles Williams and others met regularly on this spot. The conversations that have taken place here have profoundly influenced the development of 20th century English literature."

Maybe it's something they put in the beer in Oxford, but I started feeling smarter and more literate the more I drank. By the end of the tour, I was sure I was profoundly influencing 21st century literature and tried to convince some Swedish tourists we should jump off the bridge into the Thames to prove it.

On Wednesday, Riel went to school with Annie as a special Canadian guest. She came back wired as if she'd been slamming espresso shots with chocolate chip chasers. Private school in England was unlike anything Riel had ever experienced before, as she excitedly described baking bread bowls and blueberry muffins, scampering over elaborate jungle gyms and obstacle courses, and kids riding horses at recess.

The Richest People In the World

From Oxford, we rolled on to Winchester, arriving in the middle of a torrential downpour. Winchester felt like an anciently cool place with history stretching back farther than Prince Charles' hairline. We were killing time downtown in a funky little toy store when I doled out a couple of five-pound notes and told the kids they should buy something. It was a classic parenting moment when I tried to exceed my children's expectations with an exciting outing, or in this case, an unlooked for act of generosity, and it all just went sideways. For two minutes, they were happy, but then Zion wanted to know if I would cover any extra amount necessary for a purchase he might want to make that would exceed five pounds. I told him that I would not.

"Well, what about covering the taxes?" he asked.

"You've got five pounds to do whatever you want, but that's all you've got," I repeated over and over. The whole thing turned into a gong show as Zion started pulling hypothetical scenarios out of his formidable imagination and blasting away at my rigid financial exterior, searching for cracks in the facade.

"Do acquisitions fall into a different category than experiences?" "No, you just have five pounds."

"What if it's a gift for someone else?"

He created a vast array of scenarios, exchanging different people in the equations to see if the rules were different for him than for Riel.

Somehow in the process of assuring him that Riel was no better and no worse off than he was, Riel felt slighted, and became convinced she was getting the short end of the five-pound note. On and on it went, and every time I pronounced an end to the conversation Zion managed to squirm in one more question. He was a one-man press corp. digging relentlessly for the truth.

We were squawking like a brood of hens as we milled around in the drizzle and mist. We finally ended up in a different toy store and wouldn't you know, Riel found an awesome knitting/crocheting kit that was 6.99. When we agreed to help her buy it we might as well have hoofed Zion in the nards.

"What a crock!" he exclaimed in his outside voice, spinning on the spot as he started to look for anything priced just marginally over 6.99 with a ferocity that said, "I pity the fool that tries to say no to me now!"

Eventually we rolled up to Christopher and Katherine's place. We'd partied together for three weeks in Malaysia, and saw them again briefly at the wedding in Switzerland, but it had been half a year since we'd seen their boys.

Alex struck me as the quintessential English lad. In first grade, he had impeccable British pronunciation and a truly astounding passion for the World Cup. His younger brothers Ben and Oscar spent their days with their nanny and their nights filling the house with the kind of full-bodied robustness Starbucks has been trying to get into their coffee for years. The boys might have forgotten Zara and me, but no little boys from the family wedding in Malaysia could forget Zion. It was exciting and terrifying for the boys and I imagined Alex whispering, "Bloody hell, Benny, I'm right gobsmacked I am!"

We spent the next day trolling the sights and sounds of Winchester, including the massive Cathedral, one of the largest Gothic cathedrals in Europe. Jane Austen is buried there, though no one seems to know why, as she was relatively unknown at the time of her death. There is a statue of Joan of Arc that is pointedly arranged so that she looks away from the chapel of Cardinal Beaufort who attended her trial and condemned her to death. Why their statues were placed in the same church is beyond me.

My favourite item was the 12th century font that had elaborate scenes carved into the sides. The carvings told stories about how Saint Nicholas (aka Santa Claus) became the patron saint of children. One panel shows Saint Nicholas with a child standing beside him. To his left is a butcher with an axe and behind the butcher is his wife. To their right are three dead boys in a barrel. As legend tells it, the three lost boys sought shelter for the night. The butcher welcomed them into his house. When they fell asleep, he cut off their heads and stuffed their bodies in a brine barrel to use as meat in his sausages.

I mean seriously, the crazy stuff we keep finding in churches in Europe makes me think I might actually be a parishioner if I lived there.

Anyway, Saint Nicholas came along and also needed a place to stay. Playing like the script of a one-hour TV show, the butcher's conscience is seared and he confesses everything to Saint Nicolas, who in turn brings the boys back to life, forever becoming the guardian of boys and girls everywhere.

So, sort of *CSI* meets *X-Files* the and broadcast on the Faith Network. Most memorable of all, was the story behind the statue of a bugger named Bill. In the early 1900s, the eastern end of the cathedral was in danger of collapsing. A deep-sea diver named William Walker spent six years working alone, under water, in complete blackness, shoring up the foundations of the cathedral.

The king eventually declared that William had "saved the cathedral with his own two hands" and requisitioned a statue to honour William. But when it was unveiled the statue was actually of the engineer, Sir Francis Fox. A photo had been given as a guide and the sculptor had picked the wrong man! One of the relatives reportedly bellowed, "That bugger's not Bill!"

The World Cup is on in South Africa and England is ramping up to play the U.S.A. Everywhere we go English fans are flying the flag of St. George's Cross. Having sufficiently recovered from my liquid tour of Oxford, I felt I needed to watch at least one soccer game in an English pub.

I'll admit it; I thought all English pubs would be like the ones in *Lock, Stock and Two Smoking Barrels and Snatch*. I envisioned blokes and busty barmaids smoking fags and pounding pints of bitter, singing raucous choruses about fannies and arses. Chris agreed to take me on my field trip to the pub down the street. I tried to mask my incredulity upon entering the tastefully decorated establishment filled with polite Englishmen and women. The rowdiest highlight was a middle-aged woman who broke her wine glass and muttered, "Bollocks!" A couple days later we hit the road and were barely a half hour outside Winchester, cruising along the A303 when lo and behold if we don't pop over a rise and see Stonehenge ... frigging Stonehenge sitting *right there* beside the highway!

My first thought was that you don't just blast past Stonehenge and snap a picture out the driver's window. You hit the brakes, swerve across two lanes of traffic amid screeching tires and blaring horns, wave apologetically to the motorists hitting the ditch while yelling out the window in your best fake Aussie accent, "No worries mate!"

We pulled into the parking lot and donned the radio headgear and walked around Stonehenge listening to the narrator describe the scene, the history, and all that is unknown about this fascinating mystery. I was stunned that something like Stonehenge is just sitting beside the highway. The year has been full of surprises, but this one is a favourite of mine.

An hour or so later we all piled back in our car and continued on our way to Cornwall and the village of Port Isaac.

Brits love Cornwall. I mean, they're not the only ones, but seriously, they *love* Cornwall. It is essentially the farthest tip of the southwestern peninsula of the country. To the north and west, it is surrounded by the Atlantic Ocean and to the south is the English Channel. We were heading to Cornwall to visit Rob and Nikki and their girls Toots and Eliza. We had not seen them since the night in Australia when I ran my face into a metal pole.

Once again, our GPS led us through the centre of a village, down what truly seemed to be a narrow cobblestone sidewalk. As pedestrians clamoured into doorways and arches to avoid taking a side mirror to the plums, I kept waiting for someone to ask what in the world we thought we were doing. Within hours, I'd be riding back along the same street with Rob who would scream up the hill in his van in reverse!

Rob and Nikki have a shop in the village and a house they built on the side of the cliff overlooking the bay. Toots stood out on the road to wave us down as we arrived at their amazing home. A series of fortunate events allowed the family to build a home customized to accommodate Eliza's wheelchair. Everything from the height of light switches and width of hallways, to the elevator to the girls' room on the second floor. It was perfect. It was exciting to meet with them again and swap five months' worth of stories and adventures.

On our first day in Cornwall, we headed to Tintagel Castle, just a hop, skip and a jump from Port Isaac. The ruins are scattered along the rugged coast that juts out into the Atlantic. Rob and Nikki told us to explore the ruins and Arthurian legends and then walk along the coast to the village of Trebarwith Strand where they would meet us.

We hiked around the crumbling walls, ate snacks, and filmed video segments for our next YouTube video. Then we struck off down a little path that meandered along the edge of the coast. Somewhere along the way, Zion found a ratty-ass ball about the size of a grapefruit. He named it George, and started to guide it along the path with a stick.

Out of respect for the World Cup, he wasn't allowed to touch George with his hands. For the entire hour and a half he talked constantly to George, introduced George to Auntie Riel and G'pa and G'ma. He would encouragingly coax George over obstacles and up hills, and call after him as he rolled down, "George, you be careful! George, it's not a race! OK, honey, wait for Dad; I'm right behind you."

It's fascinating and humiliating to hear yourself through the lips of your children.

At the last descent from the cliff to the shore, George tumbled and bumbled his way a vast distance without any help from Zion. Before I even caught up to him, I could hear Zion's exuberant praise squealing in the voice new parents reserve for their babies, "Who's a good ball, that's right, George, you are! Yes you are, yes you are. Whooz-a-gud-widdle-piddlingkins?"

Rob and Nikki showed up and we all got some pasties and sat on the beach warming ourselves in the sun and gazing out over the crystal blue water. That was about the time we really started to understand why Brits love Cornwall so much.

In the evening, we packed up a bunch of food and all jumped in the van and wound our way down to the bay for supper on the beach. Rob had this brilliant little two-gallon metal pail. We gathered up a bunch of twigs and sticks and started a fire in the bottom of the pail. Once it got going he added a few coals, popped a little wire grill in the top and voilà, we were barbequing on the beach. Playing guitar on a little patch of grass as the sun set over the ocean, eating roasted goodies off a little BBQ pail with friends we'd met by chance at a hostel on the other side of the globe ... we were the richest people in the world.

Teeth, Talons & Cuddly Balls of Fluff

The next day we headed down to the Eden Eco Project, an old clay mine that had been transformed into a Rainforest Biome. The Guinness Book of Records describes the Biomes as the biggest conservatories in the world. We spent hours trekking through the Rainforest and Mediterranean biomes. David Attenborough was on location filming that day, but a highly trained special ops production assistant thwarted our efforts to crash the set. When we told Zion and Riel that David was the narrator from *Planet Earth* DVDs, they seriously wanted to confront the man. When we got the series, we thought the kids would love them, but they always resisted watching. Finally, they admitted that they hated them because every story started with a soft, cute, cuddly baby-ball of fluff, and after they'd fallen in love with it, they would have to watch as some combination of claws, teeth, and talons would rip the cute, cuddly ball of fluff to bits.

We had one organic confrontation as we rounded some lemon trees and encountered a long, grey-haired fellow in a tie-dyed hippie shirt, singing songs that sounded as if they'd been smoked more than written. He turned out to be a children's performer, which is what they call singer/songwriters who don't know how to sing or write songs.

That night Rob and Nikki took us down to the River Camel across from Padstow, where we met with some friends of theirs, including Barry – The Cornish Hunter/Gatherer. The tide was just starting to come back in as Zion, Riel, and I followed Barry to a point along the estuary where he started casting a circular net out into the water. The net was maybe eight feet in diameter and had about the same length of leash. Barry threw the net and dragged it back in, half a dozen times, and on the last drag brought in two mullet.

It was all very exciting for us prairie folk. The kids were dutifully impressed and I felt like an incredible documentary film-maker capturing such a visceral moment. Then Barry grabbed the fish and proceeded to rip their chins up over their heads. The kids were stunned into silence. For all the death, destruction, and may-hem Zion has experienced through first person shooter games, he still has the heart of a pacifist, and after this gritty experience, is possibly a vegetarian as well.

Our happy bantering died as quickly as the fish and Zion and Riel didn't turn their backs on Barry for the rest of the night. As soon as we got back to the fire Zion proceeded to give Zara the blow by blow narrative, peppered with phrases like, "ripped their faces off " and "blood came gushing out of their necks". Like a dark family secret, we never spoke of Padstow and the mullet again (probably because we all found them so delicious).

The next day we drove to Wadebridge where we rented bikes and rode five miles along the Camel Trail up to Padstow. The trail is an easy ride built on a disused railway line that runs beside the river. This doesn't mean that two Canadian kids can't still com-plain about the strenuous nature of the escapade.

It was a gorgeous mid-June day. School was still in ses-sion, most people were working, and once again, it felt as if we had a little corner of paradise to ourselves. We strolled through Wadebridge, popping in and out of shops. We grabbed fish and chips and sat on the pier with our legs dangling over the water. Riel had obviously worked through her Seagulls-are-Dinks issues from Brighton, and we spent most of our time trying to keep her from throwing chips to the seagulls who were dive-bombing us like kamikaze Luftwaffe.

Then it was time to ride the five miles back to Wadebridge. I was admittedly not looking forward to listening to Riel whine about the ride, so before she could even think about it, I started doing a play-by-play. Our bikes all had rental numbers attached to the handlebars, so as she started to pass me I started braying like a race commentator.

"We've got 3 on the outside, 3 is holding strong, but here comes 56! 56 is making her move, 56 leaves 3 behind like a bad smell, but here comes 71! It's 56 and 71, neck and neck with 71 creeping ahead on the outside, but don't forget about 3, 3 isn't done yet!"

I kept thinking at any moment the kids would get tired of the game and quit, but the race lasted the entire five miles and ended in a photo finish with 71 narrowly edging a victory by the slightest of margins. Zion turned to me; his face flushed with excitement and exercise and said, "That was probably the most fun I've had on a bike, ever!"

For our last day in Port Isaac, Nikki and Eliza took us into the village for a little tour. The collection of 18th and 19th century cottages were neatly arranged along narrow cobblestone streets that line the hillsides like a painting. Eliza and her amazing wheelchair blasted ahead of us, and I got the distinct impression she took great pleasure in zipping to the top of a hill, and then feigning impatience with our plodding pace, calling out, "Come on, slow pokes; I haven't got all day," as we wheezed our way up the slope behind her.

In the afternoon Rob and Toots took us to Polzeath where we scrambled around on the beach searching for shells. Then we went for a swim in very nippley water. Actually, everybody else swam while I went for a gentlemanly stroll through the shallows. The cold water made my bones ache and my vocal chords tighten. If the involuntary shrieks emitting from my lips were any indication of my vocal potential, I think a high C is absolutely doable.

After the swim we were all "top-modeling it" on the beach. That's what we called it any time we needed to change out of wet swimmers in a public place with nothing but towels wrapped around us for privacy.

I was absent-mindedly watching Zara change; just in case a revealing moment presented itself, I didn't want to miss the show. When I looked up, Riel was standing four feet away with a disapproving look on her face, her lips pursed in a thin line and her hands on her hips, tapping her foot in judgment. I couldn't help feeling as if I was back in high school, wilting under the withering gaze of a mother who'd caught me deep in lustful intentions.

That night we headed down to the Oyster Festival, an event organized by some local businesses. You know you're partying with locals when you drive through a guy's barnyard and park in his pasture.

Zion and Riel gorged themselves on large helpings of fresh strawberries and thick English cream, while I ventured precariously into sampling a locally brewed, bitter cider/beer hybrid that tasted like high-test moonshine. It simultaneously cleared out the cobwebs while rolling in a boozy fog.

A sickeningly sweet, bright pink concoction was foisted upon Zara, who managed a thimble-full before quietly commenting, "That's the drink stretch-panted women buy."

As darkness descended on Porthilly Point, the crowd packed into a giant tent to experience *The Destroyers*, a 15 piece mêlée of instrumentalists, vocalists, and composers who play furiously-paced gypsy folk music. We danced the night away as the massive band laid down infectious grooves and a demonic little white-haired man in a black fedora slammed poetic verses about Methuselah Mouse and the end of the world.

We bade Rob, Nikki, Toots, and Eliza farewell with the hope that one day they will come stay with us, and headed to Maidstone to see Zara's aunt and uncle's place. Richard and Lorna live in a wonderful place called the Old Vicarage where a beautiful grand piano sits in a large sitting room overlooking a stately garden. I recorded a schlocky version of Lionel Richie's song, *Hello*. Zion and Riel lent their angelic voices to the project, each singing a verse and harmonizing on the chorus. Using the lyrics as a template, they filmed a new YouTube video called *Stuffie Love*. While they laughed and thundered around next to me, I edited our footage from Port Isaac and uploaded our latest film, *Zion & Riel – Medieval Myths & Musical Mayhem*.

That night Richard and Lorna served us a truly authentic English meal with lamb and mint pudding and a banana/toffee desert called Banoffee, as the guys talked excitedly about the quail-hunting club they'd just joined.

We are nearing the end. The kids want to bump up our return date, but we still want to explore London. We were going to stay with an old roommate of mine named Ryan.

In the decade since we'd seen each other, Ryan had gotten married to a girl from Poland. Anna has a very highfalutin title, something to do with the Vice Director of the Polish Institute. There was also a First Secretary bit in there, along with Cultural something or other. Attaché may have been involved. Whoever she is and whatever she does, I think it all goes down at the Polish Embassy. I made notes in my Day-Timer and then promptly spilled red wine on the page smudging everything into an indecipherable mess.

Ryan and Anna live in downtown London so we spent the morning weighing our options. We have our rental car booked until the day before we fly home. But parking in London for three days could cost half the month's rental. But if we return it early, we'll be left schlepping our backpacks around tubes and trains in London, not an attractive mental image. We decided to return the car to Gatwick early and put our big backpacks in storage at the airport and keep day bags for the last three days. We got to the airport, dropped off the car and started to navigate the endless corridors looking for some sign that would indicate which terminal we would be flying from when we return. We discovered we were in the wrong terminal, so we hopped on a shuttle bus with all our packs. At the next terminal, we rode escalators and elevators trying to find the baggage storage place. The three-pound-a-day price advertised online was a clever ruse and we discovered that it is actually eight pounds per day per bag, so 32 pounds a day, which translates to over $60.00 a day for the privilege of stuffing our bags in someone's closet. The employee making minimum wage behind the counter shrugs his shoulders at my pissed-off incredulity and mutters, "What can I say, man, monopolies suck and this company has the entire airport sewed up."

"Yes, good sir, monopolies do suck," I replied, as I sucked it up and forked over our packs and my Visa card.

We had no sooner left the baggage counter than we discovered we're actually going to be flying out of the terminal we were originally in. We went back to the counter less than ten minutes later and told the guy we had made a mistake and wanted to know if we could transfer our bags from this terminal to the other one.

Nope. Monopoly is not a game ... it is a humiliating kick in the crotch. Wishing desperately for a manager to magically appear so I could appropriately direct the pointy end of my observation in the right direction, I swallowed my shame and self-righteous rage and left the bottom-rung employee unscathed.

We headed out, back through the concourse, onto another shuttle bus, back to the first terminal, through another winding concourse where we eventually found the booth where we could purchase our tickets and board the train into London.

"No airport has ever owned us like that one," Zion wearily exclaimed as we collapsed in our seats.

Through a series of text messages Ryan guided us across London one terminal at a time until we finally saw him walking down the sidewalk toward us. We followed him back to his apartment building and climbed a creaking uneven staircase. Just before he entered the apartment he turned. "You are now entering the sovereign territory of Poland."

I have to say it was the easiest border crossing ever. We were even allowed to keep our fingernail clippers and water bottles.

Ryan had mentioned that his son Rohan had a great Lego collection. Zion and Riel discovered a kindred spirit in Rohan and soon we heard the sounds of little fingers and hands digging furiously in giant bins of plastic bits coming from down the hall.

The next day we headed to Hamleys, the greatest toy store in London.

We ate sushi in the park and wandered through Camden Town and then over to Buckingham Palace. As we stood before the bastion of British sophistication, Ryan launched into a diatribe on an obscure law that legally permits a pregnant woman to relieve herself in a policeman's hat. That sparked an informed discussion that included other gems, including the law that states that it's illegal to die in the House of Lords or to eat a mince pie on

Christmas Day. Also, no Welshman may enter Shrewsbury on the Sabbath and if they do, you are apparently allowed to kill them with a crossbow made from catgut. That was the best homeschooling history class ever.

Arthurian legends, a liquid tour of Oxford, wandering through Winchester, stumbling upon Stonehenge, traipsing around Cornwall and dancing madly to crazy gypsy music.

Dark Clouds & Silver Linings

I woke up and printed our flight itinerary. Which is when I discovered that the change the airline had made, the change that I'd accepted, hadn't just moved the flight back an hour and a half, it had also moved the flight up a day. Which meant our flight was leaving in forty-five minutes. I will never forget the sinking feeling and ensuing panic. The last flight in a trip around the world and we missed it, because I had misread the email. I spent the next five hours slogging through the phone call from hell.

I called the airline. Air Transat had no more flights scheduled for later that day, the next day or the next day or the day after that. They also said they couldn't help me because I'd booked the tickets through CheapOAir. I called CheapOAir and realized many things, including what a violent person I could be if I could crawl through a telephone line.

It was a black comedy of errors as I sat on hold for twenty minutes until I finally got someone on the line who eventually transferred me, and in the transfer, the call was dropped. I called back, waited another fifteen minutes and had to go through it all again, at which point I'd used up all the minutes on my cell phone and the line went dead.

I called again, waited another twenty minutes at which point I was given the direct number for Air Transat at Gatwick. Once I finally got through, I discovered I'd been given the number to United Emirates at LaGuardia Airport in NYC. I kept the door to the bedroom shut as I paced the floor. Zara and the kids tried to keep their spirits up in the next room as my torrent of profanity floated through the air ducts.

Eventually I had to suck it up, call Air Canada, and drop

four thousand dollars to buy us new tickets. As we left Ryan and Anna's place my stomach was a cesspool of toxic nerves and acid. Our last day was supposed to be idyllic, lazing about on a houseboat while we floated down the Thames. We'd blown the entire day and arrived at suppertime.

Johnny and Juliet and their kids had all been at the wedding in Malaysia half a year earlier. They were all waiting on the houseboat and eager to empathize and nurse us back to bright spirits, one bottle of wine at a time.

If there was a silver lining to the dark cloud, it was discovering we'd actually learned something this year. Out of the four of us, I think it was a discovery I needed the most. We'd learned how to embrace the moment we were in, and how to let others go. We were able to let the anxiety and stress of our hell-day go, so we could embrace the chilled white wine, hors d'oeuvres and aperitifs mixed with love and laughter as London slid by on either side. I climbed up on top of the houseboat with my guitar and started playing and singing. Even after the terrible day I couldn't help myself, I just let it go. I realized that the events of the day belonged to the day, but the sun was setting, and this was evening. And evening doesn't have to give a s#% about the s#% of the day.

The night was every bit as amazing as the morning was awful. The Thames isn't very wide, and as Johnny navigated toward the bank to pass another boat I was within twenty-five feet of a bunch of people running and walking along the path. Everyone in earshot became the audience as I sang and bantered into an invisible mic as Londoners laughed and clapped along: best concert I've ever played in London. We sailed on as Zion and Riel took turns at the helm piloting the boat down the river. It was super fun to spend our last night in London on a houseboat.

When we were in Malaysia, Johnny and Juliet would do more before breakfast than our family would do all day. We'd stumble down to the pool, blurry eyed and baggy tailed and hear stories of the mountains they'd just climbed and fruit farms they'd toured.

The only real religious feelings I still have are guilt and shame. The thought that I might sleep in jerked me awake every hour through the night in a cold sweat. I pictured our hosts rising early and baking scones to go with clotted cream and freshly picked berries that they had gathered from the banks of the Thames and brewing espressos on an open fire of English hardwoods while their artistic guests lounged indolently in bed.

I was literally terrified when I woke up to the sounds of lines being cast and the creaking of the boat against a dock as instructions were whispered on deck.

"Crap! We must have slept in!" I exhaled with the resignation of the damned as I scurried to find my clothes. Neither Zara nor I had a watch, or a clock, so we didn't actually know what time it was as we clambered on deck.

Now admittedly, I'm not a morning person, but this was a morning worth waking up for.

Johnny had sailed us down the river so that we could wake up a stone's throw from Hampton Court. Hampton Court was built by Cardinal Thomas Wolsey in the 1500s. If you weren't a fan of the *Tudors* TV series you may not know that Wolsey was also a good mate of King Henry VIII. In the late 1520s, Henry was desperate to divorce his first wife Katherine. When the Pope wouldn't grant the divorce, good mate Wolsey took a social tumble as Henry kicked his can to the curb and stole his crib. Henry then spent massive sums of money transforming Hampton Court even further.

So there we were sipping an exquisite cup of coffee on the river Thames. Not a wave or a ripple disturbed the crystal reflection of lush green trees and grass. As the sun broke over the palace, golden arrows pierced bell towers and turrets, streaming through branches and leaves hanging like a veil over the river.

It was like Van Gogh, Peter Jackson, and David Attenborough created the perfect morning. A mother duck paddled by, trailed by a fleet of downy balls of fluff. Two German Shepherds frolicked on a grassy knoll, their giant pink tongues lolling out of their grinning mouths like fruit roll ups. A gorgeous athletic blonde with bronzed skin and lean, sinewy arms rowed by. I watched her seamless stroke propel her like poetry as she passed under a stone bridge as pedestrians strolled by unawares.

It was so beautiful I almost burst out laughing and crying at the same time. I'd spent the year learning to open my heart and soul to embrace the moment.

This was one I didn't want to let go and tried to capture in our next video, *Zion & Riel - From Thames to Three Hills*.

And then it was time; time to head for home, or at least back to Canada where we will have to find a home. There were just a few teensy-weensy little hurdles we still needed to navigate, like Greater London.

We hiked up to Surbiton Station and caught our first train in a chain of many to arrive at Gatwick. Once there, we took a shuttle over to the second terminal to get our backpacks out of hock. To add insult to injury, we couldn't get a flight out of Gatwick. So we had to take the train up to Gatwick to get all our bags and then make our way to Heathrow. The thought of schlepping all our bags through the underground was unthinkable. So I'd booked an inter airport shuttle taxi, essentially paying through the nose for a humiliating experience.

When we arrived in Heathrow for our final flight, it was exciting to see the familiar red Maple Leaf symbol over the Air Canada ticket counter. I tried to convince myself it was poetic to be carried home on the wings of our national airline. But we didn't even make it to our seats before poetry became a casualty.

God bless Air Canada and all its bloated, unionized glory, because I sure can't. I'm not sure if the blame lies with the downturn in the economy or the outrageous salaries for the fat cats and head honchos, or maybe it's just plain old middling mismanagement, but it was immediately apparent that anyone without at least four decades of servitude in the union had been laid off.

Any hint of youthful optimism and vivacious vigour had been scoured from the cabin. Our flight crew resembled the cast of the Golden Girls and we immediately gave them names like Snow White's dwarves: Grumpy, Surly, Crabby, and Bitchy.

Riel and I were standing in the aisle as an elderly passenger tried to stuff her carry-on bag into the overhead bin. People kept trying to squeeze by her, which wasn't helping anything, especially her. As the last person darted past her, I just stood waiting patiently for her. Bitchy was on the other side of this woman and looked over her head and said, "Can everyone just HOLD ON, while this lady gets settled!"

I couldn't have agreed more, and was in the middle of doing just that. Apparently Bitchy wasn't happy with me quietly accommodating this instruction and continued. "Sir, can you just HOLD ON for a minute," she demanded.

As I was standing motionless at least five feet from the elderly woman who was still struggling with her stuff, I figured I was clearly HOLDING ON.

I just smiled encouragingly in the direction of the old woman in case she turned and looked at me. I wanted to express my support.

Bitchy, who this entire time, God bless her, hadn't actually lifted a finger to help the lady, practically hollered at me, "Do you speak English?"

"What do you want me to say?" I said, looking deep into her soulless eyes. Eyes she rolled in theatrical fashion and harrumphed loudly as Riel and I passed her.

Booking the day before, we weren't able to get four seats together, so Riel and I were in the centre aisle a few rows behind Zara and Zion.

"Well, let's hope Bitchy isn't our flight attendant," I said to Riel as we settled in. But as always, God listens to my prayers so he can thwart me and teach me valuable lessons of humility. Bitchy and Crabby were our flight attendants for the next eight hours.

But by this point, we were seasoned world travelers at the top of our game, and a couple of surly stewardesses were no match for our spirit of adventure and irreverent sense of humour. Riel and I spent hours drawing satirical stick figure comics of the cabin crew, giggling like a couple of nine year-old schoolgirls. After Riel assembled her Lego, which by this point was an in-flight ritual as familiar as security confiscating nail clippers, we used the little plastic people to further mock and deride Bitchy and Crabby with Lego dioramas. Good times. Good times.

The seat beside Riel was vacant which meant that after all

our immature shenanigans, she was able to lie down and sleep through the remaining, eye-rolling service.

Eight hours after take-off we landed in Canada, eight months to the day since we'd flown to Hawaii.

Waking on a houseboat on the River Thames outside Hampton Court the last morning abroad, the family begins the epic trip back to Canada.

CANADA

Digging Deep, Down the Homeless Stretch

We are back in "The Peg" where our story began in all its nose-plowing glory. Winnipeg is situated at the geographic centre of North America, and it has certainly been at the centre of our story as a family for a decade.

This is where Zion said his first words, which incidentally were not Mama, or Dada, but an impishly insolent "See ya", as he waved goodbye to his doting parents.

It was here, on a dark and stormy night, as the wind made leaves spin on limbs of giant elm trees bent low into the pose of downward facing dog, that Riel was born on a shower curtain spread out on our living room floor.

Winnipeg is where Zara painted her first painting and became a tattoo artist, where I started Tribe of One, wrote most of my songs and recorded all my CDs.

In spite of all these great memories and magic moments, we feel like it is time to move on. Out of all the possible places we could go, we have decided to move to Vancouver Island, and try our luck at being "Sea People".

But first, we want to say goodbye to Winnipeg, "Leaf Style". We drop Riel off at Kayla's place where they fall into the energetic activities of nine-year-old best friends. After leaving Riel, we drive around the corner and don't even come to a full stop before Zion has bounded out the van and is through his best friend's front door. The little bugger didn't even bother to say "See ya." It is a week of lasts. The last time we pack snacks and walk to our favourite park, the last blast on bike trails winding along the Red River.

The last time I dance my ass off in Old Market Square as *Moses Mayes*, local maestros of danceable funk fusion, slap groove-heavy beats off cobblestone streets and turn the Exchange District into a giant house party.

Things we have done thousands of times before suddenly feel like a rite of passage, bringing a sense of closure to the circle of life.

After a week of goodbyes, the day finally comes to load up the van for one last drive.

By the time we get to Vancouver, it's the long weekend, and the ferries to the Island are typically full, so we have reserved a spot on the last sailing of the day. We check in early and spend an hour wandering along the shops and piers in Horseshoe Bay. In one last accident-prone clustermug, I manage to fall headlong into an angry mob of rose bushes with razor-sharp thorns that pierce my flesh and my pride.

My inadvertent tumbling routine deposits me unceremoniously on the pavement in front of my family. As I stand up Zara sighs, unsurprised as ever, "Oh, my God, babe, you're bleeding."

The Pacific was as black as the night and the clouds kept the stars hidden from view. The four of us gathered at the front of the ferry as we sailed through the darkness, waiting to see some glimpse of lights from the Island, where we hope to find a light to call our own.

For our little family this has been the *Year of the Snail*, as we have Quasimodoed our way around the globe like four homeless millionaires, investing in dreams and memories that will last a lifetime.

Along the way we became badass Carpe Diem Connoisseurs, embracing the palette of possibilities and perfecting the art of making *nowhere* special. We became masterful at creating and consuming the finest moments every day, and in the process, discovered how to live deep and travel light. We sold everything we had and spent our life savings on the adventure of a lifetime. No regrets.

Once we get off the ferry we start following the directions we were given to lead us to our new home. As we pass through

Duncan Zion starts giggling in the backseat, "Hey Riel, I just saw a sign that said Dinkwater."

"Eww ... why would someone call a street, D-word water?" she responds. "It was Drinkwater," Zara clarifies from the front seat.

"Are we almost there," Zion responds a couple of seconds later, "because I've got to let loose some dinkwater."

I can tell this catchphrase is going to be around for a while.

"Just up ahead you're going to be turning left on Koksilah Road," Zara says. "Are you serious? I'm going to be living off a road called Cock-Zilla?" I exclaim as Zion giggles in the backseat.

"Yeah, but no pressure," she replies.

"They're really into penises around here, aren't they?" Zion laughs.

"Gross," Riel replies reflexively.

As we drive down the long driveway to our new house, new roommates and new chapter, the clock hits midnight, August 1. I put the van in park and turn the motor off. No one opens a door, and for a long moment it is dead quiet.

"Well guys ... I guess we better go see what our new life looks like."

Thirteen- and fourteen-year-old Mack and Logan are noisily jumping on the trampoline in the pitch black, exchanging flying ninja kicks. In a New York minute, Zion is exchanging welcoming blows with his peeps.

Through the open window on the second floor we can hear an acoustic guitar as seventeen-year-old Jared plays through U2's. As we come in the front door, we see sixteen-year-old Keziah curled up on the couch with Quigley, the resident Pug, who immediately jumps up and races to the door to noisily greet us. Riel and Quigley quickly fall into a firm embrace.

We wander through the house, now home to six teens and four adults. It is strange to find our old stuff piled up in the corners of our new life. Paul and Corey open a bottle of wine they'd bought for the moment called "Glimmer of Hope".

We raise our glasses in a toast to a world of infinite possibilities as I read the label:

"The ship sank; her answer was a firm 'no.'

Your financial advisor skipped town with everything, including 'her.' Whether it be rough seas, infernal heartache, or an unbearable streak of miserable luck, what eventually, dependably, and yet inexplicably gets us through the roughest of life's rough spots is a glimmer of hope."

Hours later, we headed downstairs where the kids were asleep on a mattress in the front room. They'd dragged their travel pillows and blankets in from the van and made a nest for themselves in the midst of the chaos, just like they'd done all year.

Zara and I stood for a moment, taking in the peaceful serenity of their sleeping faces amid the clutter and confusion that comes from a creative life. We looked at each other and at the same time started laughing.

"Well, this is going to be an adventure!"